T0319516

Luminos is the Open Access monograph publishing program from UC Press. Luminos provides a framework for preserving and reinvigorating monograph publishing for the future and increases the reach and visibility of important scholarly work. Titles published in the UC Press Luminos model are published with the same high standards for selection, peer review, production, and marketing as those in our traditional program. www.luminosoa.org

Unjust Conditions

Unjust Conditions

*Women's Work and the Hidden Cost of
Cash Transfer Programs*

———

Tara Patricia Cookson

UNIVERSITY OF CALIFORNIA PRESS

University of California Press, one of the most distinguished university presses in the United States, enriches lives around the world by advancing scholarship in the humanities, social sciences, and natural sciences. Its activities are supported by the UC Press Foundation and by philanthropic contributions from individuals and institutions. For more information, visit www.ucpress.edu.

University of California Press
Oakland, California

Suggested citation: Cookson, T. P. *Unjust Conditions: Women's Work and the Hidden Cost of Cash Transfer Programs.* Oakland: University of California Press, 2018. DOI: https://doi.org/10.1525/luminos.49

Cataloging-in-Publication data is on file at the Library of Congress.

ISBN 978-0-520-29699-2 (paperback edition)
ISBN 978-0-520-96952-0 (e-edition)

To Anita, Carmelina, Elvia, Maritza, Noemi, Rocio, and Victoria.
And to Cecilia, whose vision for development is based on what women
know is already there, instead of what others think is lacking.

The world will look different if we move care from its current peripheral location to a place near the centre of human life.

JOAN TRONTO, *MORAL BOUNDARIES*, 1993

CONTENTS

ILLUSTRATIONS

MAPS

FIGURES

PREFACE

I have chosen to write this book in a way that is informed by critical theories of development and feminist scholarship, but that places lived experience front and center. My professional engagements with international development and global health have taught me many things. One of these has to do with the contemporary fanaticism around "data-driven development." While undoubtedly well intentioned, the obsession with data comes with a number of risks. For instance, nongovernmental organizations and other development actors reliant on external funding are increasingly pressured to produce measurements of the problems they intend to solve and the impacts they are (and are not) having. While not inherently problematic (interventions of any sort ought to be justified), this research is often time-crunched and underfunded. As a result, it may not be rigorous and/ or it may be so tightly oriented toward practical usage that it may lack a critical analysis altogether.

On the other hand, universities produce a great deal of rigorous research from a critical perspective. The research is often "slow," having taken place over extended periods of time and having been subjected to peer review. University researchers are more likely to discover and make use of a diverse range of qualitative and quantitative research methods. These are benefits of academic research, but there is also a downside. Unlike gray literature studies, much academic research is inaccessible postpublication. It lands behind restricted-access paywalls that make it off-limits to nonacademic policy makers, social entrepreneurs, funders, development practitioners, and interested members of the public. During a portion of the time I spent writing this book, I was working as an independent research consultant and did not have a university affiliation. As a result of this I had to borrow my romantic partner's university login information to access articles that I myself had authored! A great deal of English-language academic research is also inaccessible to academics who reside in underfunded institutions, often in the very countries in which most development studies are carried out. One consequence of all this is that the important insights generated by slow research too seldom influence policy debates in the ways that they could.

This circumstance, in which development interventions are increasingly data-driven but the data is not diverse, has shaped my approach to the book at hand. This book is based on well-funded, "slow" research, and it is published in an open-access format. My hope is that the research will enrich classroom discussions and scholarly argument, and that its influence also will extend beyond the silos of the academy to find pragmatic utility in the boardrooms of international development institutions, meeting spaces of nonprofit organizations, and dinner conversations of hopeful social entrepreneurs and tireless human rights activists.

ACKNOWLEDGMENTS

This book, and the research that informs it, was made possible by the generous and caring support of people and institutions across three continents, for which I am profoundly thankful.

First and foremost, I would like acknowledge my research participants, who remain anonymous here, but to whom I am enduringly grateful for allowing me into their homes and their places of employment, and for sharing the details and their interpretations of their everyday lives.

In Peru, I found support in many corners. Thank you to Lewis Taylor, for inviting me to a fiesta in his home, where, in his words, I conducted "the first two months of my research" in a little under three hours. I am indebted to Cecilia, my closest ally during field research, whose energy, sharp critique of development, and love of her country, colors every page of this book. I am thankful for my many friends in Cajamarca, including Rosi, Pepe, and Xochi, for their hospitality and conversation; Mirtha, whose critique of the "perverse" forms that development can take provoked deeper analytical work; Patrick, Heidi, and Tessa, whose Van Gogh Café was a home away from home; and Kyra, for countless conversations on dilapidated spinning bikes and, four years later, over *humitas* and pickled onions in Salas. I am grateful for Mark Yeung's company during the trying course of fieldwork; his professional encounters with Peru's elites also offered nuance and context that I would otherwise not have had.

The intellectual contributions to this book were extensive. Words hardly capture my gratitude for the enduring guidance and generous readings provided by Sarah Radcliffe, whose commitment to the women with whom she works and to producing scholarship of integrity, is a source of inspiration. Thank you to

Christine Oppong for mentorship during fieldwork's foggy moments, for readings of chapters, and for many, many discussions about care. During my dissertation viva, Maxine Molyneux and Liz Watson provoked my thinking about power, and that discussion has informed the analysis I present in the pages that follow. The next day, Maxine encouraged me to write this book. I have benefited from feedback and conversations at conferences, workshops, reading groups, and seminars, with Penelope Anthias, Jelke Boesten, Lorena Fuentes, Jasmine Gideon, Laura Loyola-Hernandez, Hayley Jones, Lena Lavinas, Stephanie Rousseau, Sofia Zaragocin, Vicky Lawson, Sarah Elwood, and the Relational Poverty Network. I am grateful to Emily Rosser, who during a patchy Toronto-Cajamarca Skype call suggested that I read Dorothy Smith's *Institutional Ethnography*, which changed the course of this research for the better. Megan Rivers-Moore offered support in preparing the book proposal, and Lizzie Richardson provided comments on a draft of my *Antipode* paper that continue to inform how I think and write about inclusion. Anna Cant, Brianne Kent, Constanza Tabbush, Miranda Bryant, and my anonymous reviewers enriched this manuscript through thorough and helpful readings of many draft chapters. Thank you to Alissa Trotz, for introducing me to critical feminist theories of care, and for encouraging me to apply to the University of Cambridge and the Gates Cambridge Scholarship so that I might pursue the studies that led to this book.

My family and friends provided endless support throughout the course of research and writing. Thank you to my parents: my father, whose support comes in all forms, including the cost of a conference call from the Mexico City Marriot Hotel in order to interview for the Gates Cambridge Scholarship; and my mother, whose reassurance emboldened me through altitude and home sickness alike. My sister Shauna's unwavering support through many long-distance phone calls helped me through the lonelier moments that come with field research and long stretches of writing. My papa sent me to Cambridge with my beloved late nana's dictionary, and I like to think that her love of words helped me tell a more evocative story, just as his Sunday-night phone calls grounded my weeks. Ethnographic work requires a sense of adventure and openness; I am grateful to Michele for fostering within me an appreciation of life experiences distinct from my own. Thank you to Morgan Del Vento, Andrew Gruen, Katie Hammond, Ria Kitsch, Toby Norman, Kylie Prokopetz, Victor Roy, Lesley Tarasoff, Anna Tobert, and Halliki Voolma for phone calls and visits in all four countries in which the work of this book took place.

Generous financial support for the research, presentation, and writing of this book was provided by the Social Sciences and Humanities Research Council of Canada, the Gates Cambridge Trust, Wolfson College, the Tim and Wendy Whitmore Fund, the William Vaughan Lewis Fund, the Peter Lake Fund, the Simon Bolivar Fund, the Latin American Studies Association, and the Emerging Scholar Award from *Gender Place and Culture: A Journal of Feminist Geography*.

Other institutions provided me with additional support. In Lima, the Instituto de Estudios Peruanos generously provided me with work space, a library, and exchanges with its excellent team of researchers, especially Johanna Yancari Cueva. The Department of Geography and its staff at the University of Cambridge provided me a home in which to begin this project, and the Department of Geography at the University of British Columbia a home in which to complete it. And finally, thank you to University of California Press, including the faculty editorial board reviewer for offering generative feedback on this book's conclusion, Bonita Hurd for her careful edits, and the thoughtful editorial advice of Naomi Schneider and Benjy Malings.

And finally, not a day goes by that I am not grateful for Isaac Holeman, whose intellectual partnership, loving encouragement, careful readings of countless drafts, and inspiring commitment to a more just world amounted to a contribution much larger than what I can capture with numbers or with words.

Knowing that a book and the ideas upon which it stands are fruits of the labors of more people than is possible to measure, I have likely missed contributors here. But perhaps most importantly, I hope that I have done justice to the everyday lives and experiences so generously shared with me by the mothers who participate in this program of conditional aid.

MAP 1. Peru. Created by Bill Nelson.

Introduction

Making Aid Conditional

"This is probably the root of intergenerational poverty," said [World Bank President Jim] Kim. "Stunted women who are malnourished become pregnant. Just because they were stunted and malnourished doesn't mean that their children have to be, but they probably end up not having sufficient nutrition when they are pregnant and they give birth and their children are stunted and it just goes on."

FROM AN EXCLUSIVE PUBLISHED IN *THE GUARDIAN*.

In July of 2013, I huddled closely with Yesenia, a mother of two and a respected community leader. We sat on a low wooden bench in the quiet green courtyard behind her home, high in the brown mountains of Andean Peru. I met Yesenia while doing research on the gendered impacts of Peru's conditional cash transfer program, Juntos. Like most of the other women in the village, Yesenia received a small cash payment every two months from Juntos, so long as she met a number of conditions related to her children's use of health and education services. I had called Yesenia earlier that morning, hoping for one last visit before I left Peru for the United Kingdom, where I would write up my research findings. Yesenia was unusually upset when she answered the phone, so I immediately caught a rumbling *combi* (minibus) to the village near her home. Along the way I met Yesenia's young neighbor Judit, who was my research assistant, and we ascended the hill to Yesenia's earthen home on foot. We found Yesenia alone under her Andean eggplant tree, folded over in despair. Yesenia confided that she had been diagnosed with breast cancer. Sobbing, she clutched my hand to her breast, asking if I could feel the noxious lump.

Yesenia was a reserved, strong woman. Once trained by a nonprofit organization as a community health worker, she now ran the state day-care program out of a room with a packed-earth floor in her two-story house, work that was unpaid but which allowed her an opportunity for self-development. Her kind husband migrated to the far-away coast for work, which meant that she was the primary caregiver for her two children. As we sat in her garden, Yesenia explained to me that the nearest cancer treatment center was in Trujillo, a ten-hour journey by bus from her village. Going to Trujillo would mean leaving her two children behind—but who, she wept, would care for them? There was also the issue of finances—Yesenia's Juntos payment would not cover the cost of living in the city while she accessed treatment.

Later, Judit and I descended the hill from Yesenia's house. At seventeen, quiet Judit was perceptive. When she did get talking, she was often frank. Breaking the silence we held on our walk, Judit remarked that for rural women in such circumstances as Yesenia, "the only option is to die or hope that God saves you."

Grounded in the stories of women like Yesenia, this book provides an alternative view of one of the fastest-growing new measures in global health and development: making aid conditional. From Mexico and Brazil to Indonesia and New York, relief from the most acute impacts of poverty is often made conditional upon the capacity of the poor to demonstrate their willingness to lift themselves out of poverty. Conditional cash transfer (CCT) programs, which *The Economist* magazine crowned in 2010 as "the world's favorite new anti-poverty device," provide poor households with cash incentives to adopt the health- and education-seeking behaviors that development experts see as imperative to improving their lives.

THE EVIDENCE FOR CCTS

At the 2017 World Economic Forum, World Bank president Jim Kim praised the Peruvian CCT program Juntos for its impacts on malnutrition and economic growth: "We're going to say to every country in the world that has a problem with stunting, we're ready to bring you the Peru formula. We're willing to provide financing for these conditional cash transfers. CCTs are great anyway. They help poor people. They stimulate the economy, they are a great thing to do." Over the past decade and a half, CCTs have been lauded by some of the world's most powerful development actors. In 2004, the president of the Centre for Global Development proclaimed that CCTs were "as close as you can come to a magic bullet in development." By 2017, sixty-seven countries had implemented at least one conditional cash transfer program, a figure that is up from two countries in 1997 and which has doubled since 2008 (World Bank 2017). In Latin America alone CCTs reach over 135 million people (Stampini and Tornarolli 2012).

Enthusiasm for a conditional approach to poverty relief is grounded in an extensive and compelling research literature documenting the immediate impacts of CCTs on children's interactions with health and education services. Jim Kim's recent statements reflect Peru's applause-worthy reduction in stunting, from 30 percent in 2007 to 17.5 percent in 2013, as well as a reduction in neonatal and under-five mortality (Huicho et al. 2016). This decline coincides with the introduction of Peru's CCT program, Juntos, a World Bank–supported program intended to tackle the acute impacts of poverty.

CCTs originated in Latin America, and today they are among the most evaluated social programs on the planet. The majority of evidence on CCT impacts comes from the Mexican program now called Progresa, which is one of the earliest, and now largest, CCTs. Regular evaluations were built into the program administration at the outset, and this set a significant precedent. Today, we have a robust body of evidence that policy makers draw on to maintain and expand existing programs and to support implementation of new initiatives. Most of the available evidence derives from quantitative research, especially experimental methods such as randomized control trials and quasi-experimental methods (e.g., regression discontinuity, propensity score matching, instrumental variable, and difference-in-differences; Lagarde et al. 2007; Leroy et al. 2009; Kabeer and Waddington 2015). This literature is largely concerned with measuring primary program objectives related to household consumption and the uptake of health and education services. While acknowledging some variation related to program design, the existing quantitative evidence tells us that CCTs are, overall, effective and efficient mechanisms for altering the health- and education-seeking behavior of poor households.

For instance, regarding health and nutrition, we know that CCTs are *effective* at increasing utilization of health services (Gertler 2000; Attanasio et al. 2005; Levy and Ohls 2007; Galasso 2011) and increasing household food consumption (Hoddinott and Skoufias 2004; Angelucci and Attanasio 2009; Resende and Oliveira 2008; Handa et al. 2009). Where CCT programs have been implemented with the goal of reducing maternal mortality, they have effectively increased pregnant women's use of health services, including antenatal care and in-facility births (Lim et al. 2010; Glassman et al. 2013). CCTs have been linked to a reduction in neonatal, infant, and child mortality and, in particular, deaths attributable to poverty-related causes such as malnutrition and diarrhea (Barham 2011; Rasella et al. 2013). CCTs have been shown to produce better growth outcomes in children (i.e., reduction in stunting; Gertler 2004; Fernald et al. 2010; Andersen et al. 2015; Kandpal et al. 2016) and improvement in children's motor skills and cognitive development (Fernald et al. 2008). Both outcomes are likely related to uptake of health services and increased household consumption. CCTs have also been successfully deployed to increase vaccination rates for such diseases as tuberculosis, measles, diphtheria, pertussis, tetanus, and polio (Morris et al. 2004; Barham 2005; Barham and Maluccio 2009).

Regarding the aim of building human capital through education, studies show that CCTs are effective at increasing school enrollment (Schultz 2004; Sadoulet et al. 2004; Behrman et al. 2005; Cardoso and Souza 2003; Dammert 2009; Attanasio et al. 2010). As is the case with health service usage, there is some variability related to gender, age, ethnicity, and location, but overall the evidence indicates a positive uptake. A study in Mexico found that CCTs effectively reduced both the gender gap and the ethnicity gap in school attendance (Bando et al. 2005). Relatedly, in a number of cases CCTs have helped reduce child labor, while not eliminating it entirely (Schultz 2004). CCTs show a particular propensity for reducing boys' participation in paid labor (Sadoulet et al. 2004; Behrman et al. 2005) and girls' unpaid domestic labor (Skoufias et al. 2001). Of course, the size of the incentive influences the reduction in labor participation—if it is not large enough to replace lost wages, children continue to work (Cardoso and Souza 2003).

CCTs have also been linked to some significant "spillover" impacts. While they are not designed as traditional safety net programs, which help beneficiaries weather shocks or crises such as illness, loss of employment, or natural disasters, CCTs can serve as a sort of "insurance" in such times. For example, modest cash transfers have the effect of smoothing consumption patterns in some households. Practically speaking, this means that even in relatively harder times, more people can find enough food to eat without relying on coping mechanisms with negative long-term impacts, such as selling assets or removing children from school (Maluccio and Flores 2005).

In summary, whether we look at consumption, health appointments, or school attendance, we know that CCTs are often highly effective at achieving the program's primary aims, at least in the short-term. Drawing on this data, CCT proponents suggest that cash incentives are an *efficient* mechanism for interrupting the intergenerational cycle of poverty. The sum of money that these programs transfer to poor households is relatively modest for the sizable increase in service utilization that they are able to generate. As a result it is understandable that Jim Kim and many others sing the praises of CCTs and advocate making aid conditional as a vital new measure in attempts to solve the problems of poverty.

Yet proponents have a number of concerns, and some quantitative researchers are beginning to turn their attention toward these questions. For instance, the jury is out with respect to whether we should attribute efficacy to all or just some common elements of program design (Leroy et al. 2009; de Brauw and Hoddinott 2011). While some research stresses the role of conditionality, other studies point to the increase in household income, or the health and nutrition trainings tacked on as complementary program elements. Generalized claims about the positive economic impacts of CCTs have been questioned on the basis that most evidence to this effect comes from the Mexican program and may not hold for other countries (Kabeer and Waddington 2015).

Some researchers have also begun to draw a question mark over long-term outcomes. The evidence that we do have on sustained impact is at best mixed and remains largely inconclusive. Increasingly, this literature concedes that in addition to quantitative increases in health and education service usage (i.e., more people attending school and health appointments), the *quality* of those services also influences the substance and durability of positive outcomes (Cecchini and

Soares 2015). For instance, even in cases where CCTs have had significant positive impacts on use of antenatal care services and in-facility births, researchers emphasize the need for women who attend health facilities to receive at least minimum-quality obstetric care (Lim et al. 2010).

Yet as mature and rigorous as the quantitative literature may be, comparative statistics cannot grasp all that we may learn from the experiences of women like Yesenia. Quantitative research has taught us little about the side effects or unintended consequences of making aid conditional. Most program evaluations focus on outcomes for children, and so we know very little about efficiencies with respect to household budgets or impacts on gender relations. Conspicuously absent from much of the quantitative evidence base and related policy literature is a substantive grappling with the fact that CCT programs rely on women's unpaid labor. Mothers are typically expected to do the work of meeting program conditions, while fathers are typically entirely absent from program design. Can we say confidently that CCTs are efficient when viewed from the perspective of the mothers who must meet program conditions? Probably not, if we rely only on quantitative findings. While comprising a much smaller body of literature, qualitative social science research has drawn attention to a number of gaps not tackled by the more dominant quantitative approach.

The available qualitative research draws a critical question mark over the capacity of CCTs to have "transformative" effects on the systems and structures that produce poverty in the first place (Molyneux et al. 2016; Hickey and King 2016). The research does not deny positive impacts outright; rather it draws out nuances that are more difficult to capture in bigger and more rigid data sets. For instance, ethnographic research reveals that CCT recipient communities use the programs to improve the conditions of their lives in ways that the government never intended. In northeastern Brazil, savvy recipients capitalize on the increase in local bureaucratic infrastructure to advocate developing a community development agenda that meets their needs (Garmany 2017). Yet this positive microscale impact has less to do with conditionality itself and is likely better attributed to an increase in decentralized state intervention.

While qualitative research from a critical feminist perspective has acknowledged some improvements to individual women's economic empowerment, it is much more skeptical of the capacity of CCTs to transform the root causes of women's poverty and subordinate social status. A set of qualitative studies focused on these questions reveals how CCT programs often place blame for poverty on poor mothers and generate an undue burden on women's time (Best 2013; Bradshaw and Víquez 2008; Cookson 2016; Corboz 2013; Gammage 2011; Hossain 2010; Molyneux 2006; Molyneux and Thomson 2011; Nagels 2014; Tabbush 2011).

The available feminist research raises important questions requiring further quantitative *and* qualitative inquiry. These include, but certainly are not limited to, women's time use, household budgets, gender relations within households, power dynamics within communities, interactions between women and state institutions, impacts on ethnic and racial relations, and the gendered implications of rural program implementation. Unfortunately, the concerns raised in this body of evidence have yet to exert substantial influence on program design, raising questions about knowledge translation and why some forms of knowledge are considered so much more authoritative than others.

It is reasonable to suggest that the dominant quantitative mode of evaluating CCT impacts has created what we might refer to as *systematic blind spots* (a term I borrow from Salmaan Keshavjee 2014), particularly as they relate to the experiences of the mothers responsible for meeting program conditions. As I argue throughout this book, attending to these blind spots will force us to reframe our understanding of the effects of conditionality, as well as the sense in which conditionality is "efficient." To begin the project of addressing these blind spots, we need to first trace the reasons why conditions were adopted in international development and social policy.

CONTEXT: MAKING AID CONDITIONAL

Despite the force of capital and conviction behind a global project of "development" over the past half century, poverty persists.
GILBERT RIST, "DEVELOPMENT AS BUZZWORD," 2010

I arrived in Peru's capital city, Lima, in the thick of a heavy, seasonal sea-mist fog that locals fondly refer to as *la garúa*.[1] It was September 2012, and I was there to study the country's largest social intervention, a conditional cash transfer program called Juntos, which in English means "Together." Visible through the dense gray were brightly colored billboards and banners advertising new investments in social programs. A little over a year earlier, Peruvian voters had elected a center-left president named Ollanta Humala, who had campaigned on a platform of "social inclusion." The thrust of his inclusive agenda was a promise to provide the historically poor and marginalized majority with a bigger stake in the country's recent and rapid economic growth. In Humala's election, Peru joined the ranks of other Latin American countries, like Bolivia, Ecuador, Nicaragua, and Argentina, in swinging to the left, ushering into power candidates cozy with the Chavista-style governance of pro-poor Venezuela.

One of Humala's first acts as president was to create the Ministry of Development and Social Inclusion (MIDIS), which was to oversee a number of social programs that would help deliver on his campaign promises. The largest program to come under MIDIS's purview was Juntos, which at the time was six years old. Policy makers told me that the social programs that had come before Juntos were more akin to handouts and were prone to corruption. In contrast, Juntos helped the poor to help themselves. At the time, Peru was one of the more recent countries to jump on board a trend sweeping through the region: providing poor mothers with cash payments on the condition that they invest in the health and education of their children.

In some respects CCTs were the practical expression of a wider contextual shift in international development thinking. During the 1980s, the development paradigm in Latin America was driven by the Washington Consensus, which encompassed a set of neoliberal structural adjustment policies imposed by the World Bank and International Monetary Fund. Among other things, structural adjustment policies devolved responsibility for welfare to communities and households by stripping away public supports and making services such as health care and education privately provided—and in many cases, prohibitively expensive (Bakker and Gill 2008). Women bore the brunt of this policy shift as they assumed responsibility for an increased burden of care work (Elson 1995; Benería 1999). As time passed, social indicators, including progress toward the UN Millennium Goals, showed deterioration in the livelihood conditions of women and children, rural populations, and ethnic minorities (UNDP 2003). By the 1990s, rates of poverty and inequality had risen starkly in Latin America and globally, leading some to term it a "decade of despair" (UNDP 2003).

The period that followed is often referred to as the "post-Washington Consensus" (Stiglitz 1998). Authoritative development institutions, the World Bank foremost among them, shifted focus to redressing the devastating impacts of austerity and privatization through a raft of social policies (Barrientos et al. 2008; Molyneux 2007; Ruckert 2010). Social policy encompasses the political organization of all that is necessary to produce and maintain a healthy, productive population, including social assistance and insurance, health care and education (see Mahon and Robinson 2011; Ruckert 2010). On one hand, the World Bank continued to emphasize the privatization of services related to health and education (Pearce 2006, as cited in Ruckert 2010). On the other hand, it promoted and financed "social inclusion" programs that were intended to ensure health and education coverage for "excluded" groups that could not afford or access market-based services (Roy 2010; Ruckert 2010).[2] The logic driving this response understood poverty and exclusion as resulting from an individual incapacity to participate in the labor market because of a lack of human capital—the skills, experience, and good health gained through education and access to preventative care. Governments throughout Latin America adopted variations of an "inclusive development" framework combining market-driven macroeconomic policy with social policies targeting rural populations, indigenous groups, and other poor people (Grugel and Riggirozzi 2009; Macdonald and Ruckert 2009; Andolina et al. 2009; Yates and K. Bakker 2014).

Within this "inclusive" shift, conditional cash transfers surfaced as the policy tool of choice (Ruckert 2010; Cecchini and Madariaga 2011). The first CCT programs emerged in Mexico (Prospera, subsequently renamed Oportunidades and later Progresa) and Brazil (Bolsa Familia) in the mid-1990s. These programs responded to criticism from funders and the public that social programs were often poorly targeted, were inefficient with regard to administrative expenditures, and did little to interrupt the intergenerational transmission of poverty (Rawlings and Rubio 2005). From the outset, CCTs used census data to target only those households identified as poor. With some variations, CCTs involve the payment of a small sum of money—an incentive—to poor families on a monthly or bimonthly basis. The cash is contingent upon the fulfillment of certain programmatic conditions intended to build children's human capital, such as school attendance and use of health services, and pregnant women's attendance at prenatal appointments.

Most CCTs enlist mothers as the cash recipients, because women tend to be the children's primary caregivers and are considered more likely than men to invest the cash in the household. The programs claimed to overcome previous inefficiencies in social welfare by requiring beneficiaries to be active participants in the achievement of program goals (Molyneux 2007). This does not mean that CCTs are an example of a participatory development or "active citizenship" approach that attempts to grant community members agency and voice in projects intended to improve their well-being (see Hickey 2010). Rather, CCT program goals and the conditions intended to achieve them are set by experts and implemented by teams of program staff, who do not consult the mothers responsible for ensuring they and their children attend services in a timely manner. Research among women CCT recipients in Uruguay, Nicaragua, Mexico, and Peru has shown that women participate under intense social pressure to be "responsible" mothers and good community members, even when meeting program conditions places unreasonable demands on their time and resources (Molyneux 2006; Bradshaw and Víquez 2008; Corboz 2013). Nevertheless, the nature and breadth of the action required—of women—is not often questioned in public conversations, which tend overwhelmingly to laud the merits of conditional aid.

The early Mexican and Brazilian programs have undergone a number of transformations related to targeting and administration. They have also grown exponentially. In Brazil in 2016, nearly 55 million people—one-quarter of the population—lived in households enrolled in Bolsa Familia. In Mexico, that figure was 29 million, also nearly a quarter of the population (ECLAC 2018). The rapidity with which CCTs have spread globally has led economic geographers Jamie Peck and Nik Theodore to characterize them as "fast policy" (Peck and Theodore 2015a). Building on the momentum of the Mexican and Brazilian experiments, regional experts travel to Africa, South and Southeast Asia, and even New York to share technical knowledge and assist in the implementation of new programs. Today, with the technical and financial support of the World Bank and other international development agencies, variants of CCT programs reach more than half a billion people.

THE THEORETICAL UNDERPINNINGS OF CCTS

CCTs draw on conventional economic theory, which posits that people make rational decisions based on a cost-benefit analysis using the information they have available to them (Medlin and de Walque 2008). As a "demand-side" intervention, CCTs are recognized as a mechanism for helping people overcome financial barriers that may affect their decision to access education and, even more so, health services (Ranganathan and Lagarde 2012). For instance, cash transfers may help families pay for education, health care, or medications when these goods are not free. They may also defray the indirect costs of using health services, for example those associated with transportation. Writing about global health programs more generally, medical anthropologist Paul Farmer has discussed such practical and unavoidable expenses as the donkey transfer fee (Farmer 2003, 149). If a family cannot well afford the trip to and from the health clinic, they may choose to forgo care even when it is "free" upon reaching the clinic, especially if that care is preventative rather than curative.

Finally, according to mainstream economics, cash transfers may help mitigate opportunity costs—the potential income forgone through spending time accessing services rather than on revenue-generating activities. All of these cost-mitigating benefits can easily be attributed to households having more cash on hand. In many places in the world, cash transfer programs that do not impose specific behavioral conditions do exist on a considerable scale. Why, then, impose conditions?

There are a few reasons. Evidence suggests that conditional cash transfers can correct "misguided beliefs" held by the poor that serve as barriers to their good health and education (Fiszbein et al. 2009; Gaarder et al. 2010). Another theory upon which CCTs are based comes from the field of behavioral economics: that most people are not very good at making upfront investments in order to obtain modest future benefits.[3] Sometimes this is because of deep-seated cultural beliefs. For instance, skepticism in response to vaccination, and a preference for educating boys instead of girls (because the latter are more likely to work in the home), are driven at least in part by culture but end up affecting public health and gendered rates of poverty. Behavioral economists suggest that the use of a "nudge" can correct for irrational beliefs and shortsighted decision making (Thaler and Sunstein 2008). CCTs are a great example of a nudge at work. Using the case of vaccinations and girls' education, a moderate cash incentive can help nudge individual households to seek preventative health care and educate all children through to graduation.

Another reason for imposing conditions is that they represent a form of "social contract" between providers and recipients of social assistance. CCTs are guided by the notion of "coresponsibility," or a shared responsibility between household and state for overcoming poverty (the Peruvian CCT is called "Together" for just this reason). Some types of social support, such as welfare payments, charitable handouts and food stamps, do not typically include a specific element of account-ability on the part of recipients. In contrast, CCTs require households to demon-strate a certain set of behavioral changes deemed necessary for improving their circumstances. They must actively demonstrate a willingness to improve their own lives by meeting specific conditions. In Peru and many other countries, these con-ditions are referred to as "coresponsibilities."

RESPONSIBLE MOTHERHOOD

The gendered policy preference for mothers, instead of fathers, to receive the cash transfer has social implications. Women are held responsible for meeting the pro-gram conditions, or coresponsibilities, and so must organize their time and labor around ensuring that these are met. In communities where Juntos is implemented, mothers often commented upon the responsible or irresponsible behaviors of their female neighbors and fellow Juntos recipients, mostly in relation to how they cared for their children. Researchers interested in the gendered impacts of CCTs in countries other than Peru have questioned the ethics of interventions that devolve responsibility for overcoming poverty to poor mothers and, in the process, pro-duce sticky social norms related to "responsible motherhood" (Molyneux 2006; see also Bradshaw 2008).

These critiques merit attention. Should a mother's poverty really be taken as evidence that she acts irresponsibly? At a moment when her own health was in question, Yesenia's most urgent concerns revolved around who would care for her children if she were unable. Cases such as hers challenge the prevailing assumption in contemporary development and social policy that poor women need incentives to properly mother their offspring. Even before Juntos, Yesenia did everything within her means to ensure the survival of her children, whom she raised largely on her own. She took advantage of opportunities for training and microentrepre-neurship, volunteered her labor to provide community services, and now faith-fully met the conditions that Juntos required. By all accounts, she already was the sort of responsible mother that development experts hope to achieve through use of behavioral incentives.

Responsible motherhood in rural Peru manifested itself in a number of unin-tended ways. When witty, twenty-six-year-old Josepa was pregnant with the sec-ond of two children, she was abandoned by her husband for a younger woman. Faced with few options, pregnant Josepa left her philandering husband and moved back in with her parents in a village some three hours away. Like other families in the village, Josepa's parents were subsistence farmers, and on their property was a great *granadilla* tree that produced a sour-sweet fruit that her children devoured. One afternoon as we sat in the yard, Josepa explained to me that she had been receiving the Juntos payments for nearly eight months. When she moved back to the village, her sister had been enrolled in the program, and Josepa had hoped for the day that the census takers would come by and register her details. Sure enough, one day they arrived, and in due course she was summoned to a community meeting and asked to provide the required documentation so that she could enroll in the program.

Given that there was no other paid work available, Josepa was grateful for the "little bit of help" that the cash payment provided. In order to receive Juntos's monthly payment of one hundred soles (thirty-five US dollars), mothers like Josepa were required to meet a standard set of seemingly reasonable conditions. These included attendance at prenatal exams, children's regular growth-and-nutrition checkups until the age of five, and school attendance with fewer than three absences per month until eighteen years of age or graduation. Program implementation and compliance with conditions was monitored by frontline program staff called local managers.[4] Given that one of Josepa's children was under five, and the other just over, she was required to meet both the health- and education-related conditions. The local managers would record Josepa's compliance, and if she did as required, she would join the majority of her neighbors, who received monthly cash payments.[5]

Over the course of my ethnographic fieldwork with women in the Andes, I discovered that the practice of providing and earning a cash incentive did not play out exactly as policy makers intended. Juntos recipients like Josepa were made to believe that their coresponsibilities extended far beyond the reasonable set of conditions laid out in official policy documents. In the villages where I conducted research, responsible motherhood involved much more than the use of basic health and education services on behalf of one's children. It also required participation in a whole host of activities deriving from more powerful people's ideas about what it takes for rural families to overcome their poverty—or in more sinister cases, activities that helped authorities maintain and acquire more power. When I asked Josepa what she had to do to receive the "little bit of help" that Juntos provided, she responded, "Whatever the local manager tells me to." Josepa, like all of the other Juntos mothers I spoke with, did not have a clear picture of what was officially required of her, because she was not provided one by the authorities entrusted with implementing the antipoverty program. In fact, the system of imposing conditions in the rural countryside was so distorted by program staff and other local authorities that none of the Juntos mothers I met knew what the program conditions "officially" entailed.

In addition to the requirement that children attend school and health appointments, women in my interviews cited a variable combination of activities. I call these *shadow conditions*. These activities included having hospital births rather than home births; growing a garden; keeping hygiene instruments (toothbrush, soap) organized; cooking for the school lunch program; having a latrine; leaving babies at the state day-care center; participating in parades; painting the Juntos flag on the outside of one's house; marching to demonstrate support for a politician's reelection campaign; contributing toward the medical costs incurred when a neighbor breaks a leg; having a *cocina mejorada* (smokeless stove); contributing funds for school parties; participating in a regional cooking fair; and attending literacy workshops. None of these were official policy requirements, and at first I thought that these women were simply wrong. However, after months of these conversations I began to see that this was a systematic tendency; in all of the interviews I conducted, women named at least two of these tasks; typically they named four or five.

In practice, Juntos mothers often found these other tasks indistinguishable from official conditions. This was through no fault of their own, as shadow conditions were often organized by local program managers, teachers, health clinic staff, and local government authorities, who used threats of expulsion from the program in order to get women to participate. As I elaborate in chapter 6, Juntos, like other CCT programs, was institutionally organized in a way that granted local managers the discretion to enforce shadow conditions. While women's participation in "extra," "voluntary," or "community" tasks has previously been documented in a small number of CCT evaluations, it has rarely been treated as a matter of significant social concern. This book breaks with tradition by demonstrating that shadow conditions are a manifestation of the coercive power of incentives in a context of deep social and economic inequality. As one employee of a grassroots NGO that worked with rural communities commented to me, this was Juntos at its most "perverse."

How can we understand the experiences of women like Yesenia and Josepa? How can the everyday lives of poor mothers reorient our interpretation of all the data that tells us CCT programs are "a great thing to do"? In the following section, I argue that quantitative surveys and experiments should be interpreted in light of a deep grounding in local historical context and slow, nuanced, ethnographic fieldwork.

AN INSTITUTIONAL ETHNOGRAPHY IN PERU

I arrived in Peru in 2012, right around the time that tech mogul turned philanthropist Bill Gates told the Spanish newspaper *El Pais* that Latin American countries should no longer receive international aid. Gates used Peru as an example, referring to it as a "middle-income country" with a wealth of mineral resources to exploit. There was no reason, he claimed, that Peru should not be "as rich as a European country" (Aguirre et al. 2012). While perhaps true in theory, this kind of statement renders invisible key drivers of poverty and inequality like colonialism, global capital, and the power and greed of richer countries. It also sidelines the very real issue of inequality within countries. Like many Latin American nations, Peru is unevenly developed.[6] While the country possesses, as Gates says, a wealth of natural resources and has the gross domestic product of a middle-income nation, its riches are not evenly enjoyed. Peru's landscapes reflect stark inequities in investment and, as a result, quality of life. The coastal region of Peru—where Lima is located—has a much lower overall incidence of poverty than the central mountainous region and the humid tropical forest region referred to as the selva. The Peruvian government took these geographical inequities into account when deciding to implement Juntos in the rural sierra and selva but not the more urban coastal region.

Analyses of cash-based aid frequently overlook the geographical particularities of the communities and broader regions in which CCT programs are implemented. As a result, we risk developing blind spots that conceal the ways that geography and policy collide to produce unintended consequences—positive and negative alike. The spaces and livelihoods across which Juntos is designed and implemented are exceptionally diverse not only in terms of climate, geography, and demographics but also in terms of infrastructure, industry, and employment. In the section that follows, I introduce the research sites, situating these in relation to the much larger, unevenly developed national landscape.

Peru, an Unevenly Developed Country

This study was conducted in two regions of the country: metropolitan Lima, where Juntos was designed and is administered, and the department of Cajamarca, one of the rural areas where Juntos is implemented. Cajamarca is situated high in the northern Andean mountain range. Research there was conducted in two districts, which I have renamed to preserve their anonymity: Labaconas and Santa Ana, both of which are located over two thousand meters above sea level.[7] Within these, I conducted observations and interviews in the district capitals and a handful of villages of varied size. This region of the country, known as the sierra, has a geography, economy, and social landscape that differ from those of the coastal and Amazon regions.

Historically, Cajamarca was a key site of the Spanish conquest. It was in Cajamarca city in 1532 that the last Inca king, Atahualpa, was killed by Spaniard Francisco Pizarro in a brutal massacre of Inca peoples. This battle led to three hundred years of Spanish colonial rule and a sweeping transformation of precolonial culture. By the late nineteenth century, the majority of Cajamarcan residents were Spanish speaking and identified as mestizo rather than indigenous.[8] Livelihood patterns were also dramatically transformed. By 1940, approximately 28 percent of the rural population lived on haciendas (agricultural estates), a rate significantly higher than in any other Peruvian region (Deere 1990). Wealth was concentrated among a small number of hacienda landowners, who in turn controlled rural labor power. The hacienda class traced its origins back to Spanish rule and tended to follow familial inheritance practices, while its poorly remunerated labor was sourced from peasant families of indigenous or mestizo decent (Deere 1990). Under this arrangement, the region became a leading producer of grains, beef, and dairy; the latter in particular remains an important regional export commodity today.

FIGURE 1. Grimalda and her husband guide her prized bull home after grazing. Photo by the author.

In the 1960s and 1970s, agrarian reforms implemented under the Fernando Belaúnde and Juan Velasco governments changed the socioeconomic structure of the region. Landowners were forced to sell off their holdings or have them expropriated by the state, at which point the land was redistributed in small parcels to individual families who had previously been employed as laborers (Mayer 2009). This colonial legacy is evident today in the stratification between a largely mestizo, urban professional population, and a rural smallholder agriculturalist population. While large parts of the Andean and Amazonian regions are characterized as "indigenous," in the districts where I conducted fieldwork and across Cajamarca, the majority of indigenous descendants self-define as campesinos/campesinas, a term that indicates smallholders or peasant farmers and agriculturalists (figure 1). As descendants of Inca and other pre-Spaniard cultures, campesinos are an indigenous group recognized in national legislation and by the International Labour Organization's Convention 169. However, their historical relationship to land, their agricultural practices, and their engagement with market economies distinguish them from a number of other Peruvian indigenous groups (Ruiz Muller 2006).

The Andean sierra also bears the inequitable markings of global capital. For decades, foreign investment in the extractive industries has created landscapes of social stratification. The world's second-largest gold mine, Yanacocha, is a massive "open pit" situated at four thousand meters above sea level within one of the

FIGURE 2. Public services do not reach all Andean households. Photo by the author.

poorest regions in the country. While Cajamarca city has benefited from a new private health clinic and international school, these perks are largely accessible only to the families of mine employees and those in the city who have in some way profited off the mine's existence. I attended the health clinic as a patient once, but none of the Juntos mothers who participated in my study were able to, owing to their low incomes and lack of health insurance.

In the highlands of the Peruvian Andes, CCT recipients are low-income, rural campesinas who have historically experienced exclusion based on their gender, class, and ethnicity and the geographical location of their homes.[9] In 2013, the poverty rate in rural Peru was 48 percent, compared to 16.1 percent in urban Peru (INEI 2014b). Cajamarca was (and remains) the poorest department in the country: in 2013, 52.9 percent of households were poor and 27 percent of households were extremely poor (INEI 2014b). Geographical disparities exist within the department itself. Wealth is concentrated in urban centers, and the poorest people live in the most isolated areas of the department (figure 2). Stark geographical inequities also exist in access to health care and education (INEI 2014b). In contrast to urban areas, health and education services in rural Peru are historically limited and of low quality. The symptoms of systematic underinvestment in vital services are dire. For instance, more than 50 percent of maternal deaths in the country are concentrated in eight of the twenty-four departments. All of these eight are rural, and Cajamarca department is one of them (UNICEF 2014).[10]

Such statistics ought to be unsurprising, given that rural women face significant barriers to health. In 2013, a national statistical survey found that 65.3 percent of rural women reported distance to the clinic as a barrier to obtaining health care, compared with 33.6 percent of urban women (INEI 2014a). After having overcome geographical hurdles such as lack of transportation, rural women also face the possibility that treatment may be unavailable. Absenteeism and understaffing in rural health clinics is a persistent problem in rural Peru, and 91.4 percent of women reported believing that there might not be anyone to attend them when they seek medical attention for an illness (INEI 2014a). While national health insurance is technically available to low-income Peruvians, it does not cover all medical costs. Nearly three-quarters of rural women reported that finding the money to pay for care when they were in need of medical attention was a problem (INEI 2014a).

Rural landscapes marked by poor infrastructure are a salient feature of this book. In rural Peru, only 56.6 percent of households have access to potable water, and only 46 percent have access to sanitary services (INEI 2014b). Inadequate infrastructure also affected how Juntos was implemented and what poor women were forced to do in order to earn their cash incentive. Transportation routes in rural Peru vary in availability, and fatal road accidents are common. In the districts of this study, some villages were at least partly connected to the district capital by a dirt road (figure 3). Women from those villages were able to use some form of communal transport on the days of the week in which this was available. Even so, access depended on the weather. As in much of the rest of the Peruvian sierra, during the rainy season—from October to April—these roads often became impassable. Other villages were not accessible by road and were connected to the district capital only by footpath. High rates of poverty in rural Peru drove the decision taken by policy makers to focus the implementation of Juntos in rural areas. Yet the research presented in this book shows how cash incentives do not necessarily eliminate geographical inequities and, in many cases, can actively exacerbate them.

Programa Juntos

Peru's CCT program is the Programa Nacional de Apoyo Directo a los Más Pobres, or "Juntos" (National Programme for Direct Help to the Poorest, "Together"). The program was created April 7, 2005, during the presidency of Alejandro Toledo. The Toledo administration found inspiration in the Mexican and Brazilian CCTs and proclaimed that Juntos would serve as a step toward tackling the country's serious inequality issue. Toledo garnered public and political support for the program by pointing to the international success of CCTs and the growing body of evidence indicating that CCTs were effective and efficient means of addressing poverty (Jones et al. 2008, 256).

The Juntos program vision is "to restore the basic rights of households whose members have regular access to quality basic services in education, health and

FIGURE 3. Villages where Juntos recipients lived were often connected to the services in larger populated centers by a single road or by footpaths. Photo by the author.

nutrition, corresponding to full exercise of their citizenship, and to improve their quality of life and human capital development, thereby reducing the intergenerational transfer of poverty" (Juntos 2015a). Juntos is meant to achieve this vision through two central functions. The first is through the direct transfer of monetary incentives to poor households in rural areas. The second is through use of conditions related to accessing health and education services (MIDIS 2012c). The policy-making and centralized administrative functions of Juntos take place in Lima, either at program headquarters or within the Ministry of Development and Social Inclusion, where Juntos has been housed since 2012.

Juntos determined household eligibility using data derived from the national census (Sistema de Focalización de Hogares).[11] In order to qualify for Juntos, households had to meet a standard set of criteria: they had to have resided in the geographical area of intervention for at least six months; fall within the two poorest quintiles (poor and extremely poor); and have at least one person classified as an "objective member," which included pregnant women, and children or youth under nineteen years of age or not yet graduated from secondary school. Once a household had been determined to be eligible, all objective members were enrolled and a household representative, generally the mother, became a "Juntos user." By

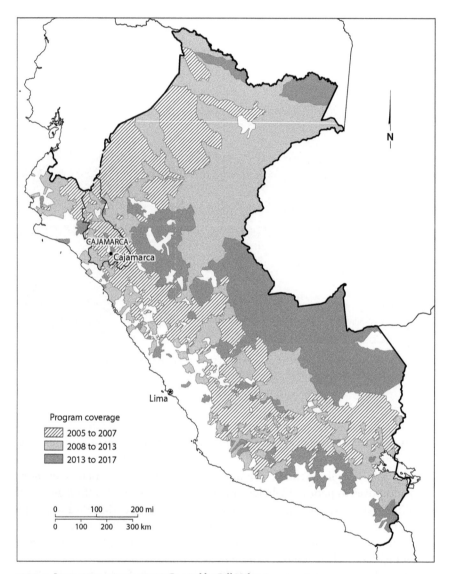

MAP 2. Juntos program coverage. Created by Bill Nelson.

the close of 2013, Juntos was the largest social program in the country, counting 718,275 affiliated households and reaching 1,553,772 children and 17,170 expectant women (Juntos 2015b). At the time, the program intervened in fourteen regions, 140 out of a total of 196 provinces, 1,097 districts, and 39,645 populated centers. Cajamarca had the highest number of CCT-affiliated households, so when I left Lima, that is where I went.

Once a mother was enrolled in Juntos, she became responsible for meeting the program conditions, or "coresponsibilities." Juntos defined *coresponsibility* as "the responsibility shared between the household, whose members must use health and education services in an opportune manner according to stage in the lifecycle, and the state institutions which provide said services" (MIDIS 2013b). At the time of my research, health services included monthly prenatal exams for pregnant women; monthly checkups for children aged 0–11 months; checkups every two months for children aged 12–23 months; and checkups every three months for children aged 24–36 months. It was expected that, at health appointments, children would receive nutritional monitoring, physical evaluation, immunization, and vitamin A and iron supplementation.

In the event that households had access to a certified early-childhood education center, children from 36 months to six years of age were required to attend, with no more than three absences per month. If the area of Juntos intervention did not have an early-childhood education center, households were still required to continue with regular health checkups. Mothers with children aged six to nineteen years old were required to ensure that the children attended classes; if a child was absent more than three times for no reason, mothers lost the next month's payout.[12] Mothers were required to meet all of the conditions for each and every one of their children, with no exceptions. If a youth dropped out of school against his or her parents' wishes, which was not uncommon, the entire family was suspended from the program.

Whether or not conditions were met was monitored by local managers, who were frontline state employees. Generally educated at a technical school or university, these frontline bureaucrats traveled endlessly to clinics and schools to register households, collect attendance information about children, and enter all of the numerical data they gathered into a centralized computer system, which was based in Lima. Juntos recipients who met the conditions received a transfer, on the *dia del pago* (payday) as local managers and mothers referred to it, at a preestablished collection point. Normally, this was a National Bank branch; but in places without a bank, the state ensured delivery by armored truck. In some Amazonian regions with limited road access, the state delivered the monetary incentive by boat or airplane. Increasingly, program users were given debit cards and expected to withdraw the monetary incentive from a National Bank ATM.

In all cases, the local managers orchestrated the payday, insofar as they communicated to the mothers on which day it was to occur, made it known who would receive the payment and who would not, and organized the system of queuing mothers waiting for the cash (this is elaborated in chapter 4). In the first trimester of 2012, 95 percent of households nationally met the program conditions, fulfilling their share of the coresponsibility agreement. In Cajamarca, between 96 percent and 99 percent of affiliated households were recorded as having met the conditions and received the transfers (Juntos 2012).

Institutional Ethnography: An Approach to
Accounting for Care and Power

This book presents findings from a ten-month institutional ethnography of the Juntos program. Research took place between September 2012 and July 2013 and was divided between Lima and Cajamarca. I did not embark on fieldwork knowing that I would conduct an institutional ethnography. I had originally set out to understand how women experienced Juntos in terms of time use and access to public space, which I had planned to explore through a household survey, interviews, and observations. Yet as my fieldwork progressed, I pivoted in response to what I found.

In my first months of fieldwork in Lima, I interviewed current and former policy makers and program administrators at Juntos and MIDIS. I benefited from my tenure as an affiliate researcher at the Instituto de Estudios Peruanos (Institute for Peruvian Studies), scoured the two main national newspapers for public opinion, and attended conferences and other events on the topic of socially inclusive development. Much of the narrative that I encountered from high-level Juntos affiliates conveyed the idea that Juntos was a largely successful program for delivering rights and citizenship to the rural poor. My interest in the gendered impacts of the program was met mainly with curiosity and sometimes with contempt; one policy administrator at MIDIS exasperatedly explained to me that Juntos was intended to benefit children, not women. Staff at the Ministry of Women and Vulnerable Populations and the influential national women's organizations told me about being excluded from the policy design and operational decisions regarding Juntos. This reality was an obvious source of contention and, in their opinion, explained a number of program flaws. The tension caused by the relative absence of engagement with the question of gender in spaces of policy making and administration would later inform my analysis of what I found in the communities where Juntos intervened.

I chose to conduct the portion of my fieldwork with Juntos recipients in the region of Cajamarca because it had the largest number of Juntos recipients, it was one of the top five poorest regions in the country, and most Cajamarcans speak Spanish as their first language (rather than an indigenous language), which would allow me to conduct all of the interviews myself. Upon hearing that I was interested in Cajamarca, staff at MIDIS tried to convince me to conduct my research elsewhere, suggesting instead two provinces in the central Andes where, in their words, I would see traditional indigenous communities in which Juntos had been highly successful. Cajamarca, they told me, was not actually poor. This assertion was commonly made by high-level policy staff in Lima. It was almost always connected to a disdain for the communities of politically engaged Cajamarcans who protested the local environmental and social abuses of the powerful extractive industry. After discussing the decision with local researchers and NGO staff, I decided to proceed with my study in Cajamarca, although this meant that my contacts at MIDIS no longer answered my emails and I was left to find another way into local-level program research.

Development organizations are often difficult for researchers to access without the support of a "gatekeeper" (Willis 2006), and I needed to find one of these in an area where Juntos intervened. In Cajamarca, Lewis Taylor, a British sociologist with a long history of research in the region, generously invited me to a fiesta at his house, where he introduced me to a host of other researchers, health-care and NGO staff, and other local authorities, many of whom came to be research participants or gatekeepers in my study. One of these was a judge who eventually put me in contact with the regional administrator for the Juntos program. The administrator invited me to the regional office and excitedly and patiently explained the ins and outs of program implementation. He also introduced me to the district and local managers, whom I eventually "job shadowed," following them around the districts they managed and as they completed administrative work and sent the mothers' compliance data to Lima.

I had initially assumed that, in Cajamarca, I would make contact and build relationships with Juntos recipients through program channels. This assumption was deflated very early on. I had been invited by a local manager to accompany him to a meeting of Juntos recipients in a tiny village called Tinca. At the meeting, he introduced me as "Doctora Tara," explaining to the room full of watchful mothers that I was working with the Juntos program and would be going around, house to house, "making sure that the mothers were meeting program conditions." I had not, of course, suggested anything of the sort. It was clear to me that for the mothers in the room, I was as good as a Juntos employee, the panicked expression on my face notwithstanding. As a result, it seemed all too certain that no one from that community or the surrounding villages was going to share with me her honest experiences of the Juntos program. I learned at least two important lessons in that moment—one, that I needed to be much more clear about my intentions, and two, that I was going to have to pivot in my research design.

Starting the next day, I began dividing my time between two distinct districts where Juntos intervened, focusing on the implementation practices of Juntos staff in one district and on building relationships with Juntos mothers and their families in the other. This is not to say that there was no overlap; I eventually interviewed local managers and related local authorities from both districts, and I spoke with Juntos mothers in both districts too. What this bifurcated approach permitted me to do was build trust with Juntos mothers in a way that would not have been possible otherwise. Let me illustrate, with another example, why this was important.

At the same fiesta where I established a connection to the regional Juntos office, I met Carla, who ran a number of grassroots projects oriented to meeting the needs of women and their families. Carla took me to a community where she used to work and had maintained a close relationship with a number of women, all of whom were Juntos recipients. She introduced me to some of these mothers and arranged my first interview with a Juntos recipient, a woman named Luz who traveled into the city every Saturday to clean the house of a middle-class Cajamarcan family. This early interview confirmed a number of hunches. The first was that I was going to have to establish a great deal of trust with the Juntos recipients I hoped to interview. Even though I had met Luz through a contact who was not related to Juntos, it was obvious that the responses she gave me were censored and shaped to present a rather more simplistic experience than that which I had begun to observe. It seemed to me that from Luz's perspective, I was interviewing her to find out if she was responsibly fulfilling her obligations as a Juntos mother.

Second, I realized that my carefully crafted interview script was not going to capture the contradictory dynamics that I was starting to observe in Juntos communities. For instance, why and how did Juntos mothers come to believe that in order to receive the cash payments they were required to grow gardens, participate in parades, and cook (unpaid) for the school lunch program—when none of these activities were officially mandated by program headquarters in Lima? These activities were a result of some of the obvious power dynamics at play that were not captured in the enormous body of CCT evaluations or present in the dominant narratives about program effectiveness.

Two months into fieldwork, frustrated and rather sure that my research was going nowhere, I explained the situation to a dear friend and colleague, Emily, over Skype. Her response—"Well, it sounds like you're doing institutional ethnography. Have you heard of Dorothy Smith?"—changed the course of my research. I immediately had Smith's and other institutional ethnography texts shipped to Cajamarca. Institutional ethnography is an explicitly feminist method of inquiry that illuminates how institutions organize people's everyday lives.[13] Smith developed institutional ethnography in response to what she identified as "the deep opposition" between the branch of mainstream sociology she had been taught as a PhD student and the deeply experiential political practices she discovered in the women's movement (Smith 2005). Rather than testing "expert"-generated theories or hypotheses, institutional ethnography strives to generate knowledge that is grounded in the standpoint of daily life.[14] Smith explained the distinction as follows:

> To write a sociology from people's standpoint as contrasted with a standpoint in a theory-governed discourse does not mean writing a popular sociology. Though it starts from where we are in our everyday lives, it explores social relations and organization in which our everyday doings participate but which are not fully visible to us. The work of discovery sometimes calls for research that is technical and conceptually outside the everyday language of experience; at the same time, it has been our experience that once the institutional ethnography is completed, it becomes a resource that can be translated into people's everyday work knowledge. Hence it becomes a means of expanding people's own knowledge rather than substituting the expert's knowledge for our own (Smith 2005, 1).

Central to institutional ethnography is a feminist attention to the work performed by people situated throughout the institution. Work is defined *generously* to include paid and unpaid labor alike. I approached the unpaid activities of Juntos mothers as work, including their efforts to meet program conditions and collect the payment, and the caring labors they carried out in households and community centers.

I also attempted to account for the work practices and processes of as many other institutional actors as possible; this included policy makers, program administrators, health-care staff, teachers, census takers, and regional Juntos staff. All of these actors (and indeed, many others) perform work upon which an efficiently functioning CCT program depends. During my research, I paid particular attention to the way that bureaucratic administrative tasks like checking boxes and filing paperwork connected the work of rural Juntos mothers to the decisions, actions, and inactions of more powerful actors in urban office buildings and boardrooms. My analysis thus stretched out from the local site of women's experiences and further and further into the many veins of the institution, tracing these connections at each stage to shed light on how the experiences of Juntos mothers were organized by social, political, and economic relations largely invisible to them.

There are institutional ethnographies of health care, education, and international aid; this book presents, to my knowledge, the first institutional ethnography of a CCT program. Over the course of ten months, in locations ranging from foggy Lima to the sparsely oxygenated communities of the northern Andes Mountains, I mapped the implementation of Peru's CCT program, holding women's experiences at the center of my inquiry. I triangulated the information I collected from differently situated actors through observation, semistructured and informal interviews, focus groups, and textual analysis. In Lima, I interviewed high-level decision makers, including the minister of the Ministry of Development and Social Inclusion; the executive director of Juntos and members of the now defunct Juntos Executive Committee; policy and program administrators at MIDIS and Juntos headquarters; and actors at major women's organizations, including the vice minister of the Ministry of Women and Vulnerable Populations and the executive directors at Flora Tristan and Manuela Ramos, the two largest nongovernmental organizations serving women in the country.

At the Juntos regional headquarters in Cajamarca, I interviewed the regional director, the district coordinator, and the four local managers overseeing the districts in which I conducted fieldwork. I accompanied local managers on most of their major work practices, including hosting community meetings, auditing household compliance with conditions, and entering data into the computer system. I also attended a regional staff training. To gain a better understanding of how the government targets the CCT program, I conducted participant observation with the regional census team as they prepared a community for a forthcoming survey.

In the communities where Juntos intervened, I interviewed health and education staff and substituted for an absent English teacher over a three-week period at
a local high school, an experience that gave me valuable insights into the quality
and availability of education services. I attended meetings with Juntos recipient-
volunteers called Mother Leaders, sat in on sewing circles, played with children,
accompanied women while they harvested alfalfa and quinoa, and generally hung
about. I conducted my most substantive interviews with Juntos mothers at the tail
end of my fieldwork, once I had established trust and was able to ask questions
grounded in the many dynamics I had observed over the previous seven months.[15]

Institutional ethnography allowed me to make a number of empirical discov-
eries grounded in the everyday experiences of women who receive conditionally
provisioned social support. In the next section, I introduce a few concepts that are
vital for making sense of these findings.

CONDITIONS IN CRITICAL PERSPECTIVE

In the following sections I introduce two critical conceptual tools that informed
my fieldwork and have guided my analysis. The first of these is a feminist ethic
of care—an approach to understanding the world that recognizes the centrality
of caring to healthy and productive individuals and societies. The second conceptual tool is power—or more specifically, the disciplining power of governing
techniques, especially when these are used to improve the well-being of populations. I introduce care and power here in order to help the reader trace them as
connecting threads that run through the subsequent chapters, and through the
future research and practical policy experiments that I hope this book will inspire.

Care

Care is difficult work, but it is the work that sustains life.
JOAN TRONTO, *MORAL BOUNDARIES*, 1993

While both men and women all over the world experience poverty, women experience poverty at higher rates than men, especially as mothers (UNDP 2003; UN
2015). One of the driving factors of this gendered disparity is the unequal distribution of care work.[16] The term *care work* signifies the labor involved in the
direct care of persons, in both paid and unpaid capacities (see Razavi 2007a).
Care work is "work" because caring requires expenditures of time and energy.[17]
It includes activities that involve direct physical contact and emotional connection, such as feeding, bathing, consoling, encouraging, teaching, and accompanying dependents on visits to the doctor. Some activities, like shopping, washing
clothes, cleaning, and preparing meals, are related to care work because they create the preconditions for caregiving (figure 4). They are imperative components
of providing care even though they may be done without physical proximity to
dependents (Razavi 2007a, 6).

FIGURE 4. Juntos recipient Luz performing care work. Photo by the author.

Feminist economists have illustrated the ways in which care, far from being optional, is inseparable from all dimensions of development. Care is essential for human survival, affects the availability and quality of the productive labor force, and influences the rate of economic development (Razavi 2007b, 379). Economist Susan Himmelweit contends that it is unrealistic for development policy to ignore care work, because the decisions that ordinary people make about care work and seeking paid employment are inseparable. She is worth quoting at length: "There is increasing recognition that such decisions not only have short-term impacts on the labor market and the economy as conventionally understood; they may have even more important long-term implications for society as a whole, because the quality of care affects the type of workforce an economy can look forward to in the future, the supportive relationships that can be sustained between generations and the social values that can be maintained" (Himmelweit 2005, 2). In other words, care is necessary for the development of human capital. Questions about who gives care, who receives care, and who finances care work are central to the effectiveness, sustainability, and fairness of development policy.[18]

While the benefits of care work are dispersed broadly and profit society as a whole, the costs of caring are disproportionately borne by women (Razavi 2007a, 12). Of course, who does care work and how it is financed varies historically, regionally, and culturally. Care is provided by a variable and shifting combination of actors, including individuals, community organizations, the state, nonprofit organizations, and markets.[19] While the gendered division of care work varies from context to context, women tend to do more paid and unpaid care work all over the world. To be sure, some caring labors, such as childbirth and nursing, are tightly bound to the natural bodily functions of womanhood. Yet outside of these, the lifelong gendered disparity in responsibility for care has precious little to do with biology. Rather, arbitrary social and political norms describe caring as women's work.

The distribution of care work has serious implications for the well-being of caregivers. Care ethicist Joan Tronto suggests that "caring is often constituted socially in a way that makes caring work into the work of the least well off members of society. . . . [I]f we look at questions of race, class, and gender, we notice that those who are least well off in society are disproportionately those who do the work of caring, and that the best off members of society often use their positions of superiority to pass caring work off to others" (1993, 113). By attending to questions of care, "we are able to cast in stark relief where structures of power and privilege exist in society. Because questions of care are so concrete, an analysis of who cares for whom and for what reveals possible inequities much more clearly than do other forms of analysis" (Tronto 1993, 175).

While women do more care work than men across the developed and developing world and in urban and rural spaces, economic and social policies do shape the circumstances of care and who performs it. For instance, when governments make cuts to social services, paid care work that was performed by women in the public and private sector, such as in health clinics and day-care centers, becomes *unpaid* care work carried out by women in households and, in some cases, community centers. In places where government investment was never adequate, women have always accomplished the survival of their families through unpaid care work in their households and communities. The social policy architecture— what social services are available and who they target—influences the gendered face of poverty. As Shahra Razavi, chief of research and data at UN Women, once put it, "How society addresses the issue of care has significant implications for the achievement of gender equality, by either broadening the capabilities and choices of women and men, or confining women to traditional roles associated with femininity and motherhood" (Razavi 2007b, 379). While less often discussed, the pervasive idea that care is "women's work" also prevents men from accessing purpose and identification as loving fathers and carers within their families and communities.[20]

In this book I am particularly interested in the relationship between social policy and unpaid care work. While unpaid caring typically takes place in households and between family members, it also occurs between friends, neighbors, and community members and in public, private, and nonprofit settings outside the home, such as community centers, soup kitchens, and day-care centers. Unpaid care work is not remunerated—which is not to say that it occurs without a cost.[21] Unpaid caregivers shoulder financial obligations and must cope with forgone wages and missed opportunities (Folbre 2006). The amount of time required to accomplish care work influences whether an unpaid caregiver is able or willing to engage in paid employment (Himmelweit 2005, 19). This varies by context: while technological advancements have made washing clothes and dishes and preparing meals much quicker in developed countries, low-income and rural households in developing countries are unlikely to have access to these amenities. Access to paid domestic labor and well-developed infrastructure—such as potable water, electricity, and transportation that enables individuals to travel to grocery stores and pharmacies—also affects the amount of time spent on unpaid care work.[22] The amount of unpaid care work women perform is largely hidden; this is because it typically takes place in the private sphere (i.e., households), and because it is not recognized as "productive" labor in most aggregate measures of economic activity, such as the gross domestic product.[23]

CCT programs reorganize care in a way that experts believe will best produce future citizens equipped with the skills and good health to participate in the labor market and contribute to and benefit from economic development (see Ruckert 2010). For the most part this is done without any explicit acknowledgment of the role of unpaid care and unpaid caregivers in the success of these programs. In an attempt to correct what I show is a harmful omission, the chapters that follow draw attention to the technical realms—policy documents and auditing measures—that are conspicuously inattentive to the spaces in which care is accomplished and to the mothers responsible for caring. This conceptual grounding in care is imperative to making sense of the empirical evidence I present about the hidden costs and unjust outcomes wrought upon women when aid is made conditional.

Power

An accepted and reasonable conclusion to draw from a review of the quantitative evidence on CCTs is that they are powerful tools for changing poor people's lives for the better. It is far less common to think of CCTs as a means for exercising power over the desperately poor. Very little is known about specifically *how* CCTs achieve the high rates of compliance that they do. This question, while infrequently asked, is important because the populations targeted by CCT programs are among the most marginalized and vulnerable. While behavioral economics is interested in the mechanics of achieving behavioral change in individuals and groups, it does not tend to dwell on the broader social implications of these mechanisms. CCTs are a governance mechanism; they are a tool used to shape the behavior of certain populations to produce a desired outcome. It is worth considering, and I do so over the following chapters, the coercive power of incentives. I set up this notion—of the coercive power of incentives—early in the book in order to train attention on the unintended and sometimes unjust effects of conditional aid, and I hope that it will be a useful framework for interpreting the evidence I present in each chapter.

To understand the social implications of conditionality, I turn to critical development studies, and to a particular body of work that treats governing as a set of activities through which power dynamics are produced and reinforced (Ferguson 1990; Rankin 2001, 2002; Englund 2006; Li 2007). Governmentality studies explore the sometimes obvious, often subtle mechanisms used to shape the behaviors of populations to create a desired outcome, whether better health, higher literacy rates, or rural development. Governance interventions are typically driven by a concern for the well-being and prosperity of individuals and populations (Foucault et al. 1991). Regardless of intention, governing the behavior of others necessarily involves an exercise of power (Foucault 1982). Power is often exercised in mundane and barely visible ways: "At the level of population, it is not possible to coerce every single individual and regulate their actions in minute detail. Rather, government operates by educating desires and configuring habits, aspirations and beliefs. It sets conditions, 'artificially so arranging things so that people, following only their own interest, *will do as they ought*'" (Jeremy Bentham, quoted in Li 2007, 5, original emphasis). This is not to say that government interventions force unwitting or helpless individuals to do things that would otherwise be of little or no personal interest.

Take, for instance, the issue of smoking. Fifty years ago, smoking was not merely permissible but fashionable. Today, equipped with research proving the harmful impacts of tobacco use, authorities in government and health institutes devise large-scale interventions to prevent addiction and curb consumption. The grotesque photographs printed on cigarette boxes and billboards in some countries and the regulations restricting smoking in restaurants, airplanes, and some parks communicate that smoking is not only unhealthy but also disgusting and antisocial. While these governance mechanisms do not succeed at modifying the behavior of all smokers everywhere, they have been highly effective at "educating desires and configuring habits, aspirations and beliefs" on a large scale. Many people who quit smoking and enjoy better health likely feel grateful for the intervention. Many nonsmokers do too; having prior knowledge of smoking's adverse impacts, they never took up the habit in the first place and can now enjoy smoke-free public spaces. The smokers who resist changing their behavior might resent being labeled as disgusting or having their freedom restricted in public places. They might also contest the authority or legitimacy of public health experts to govern their lives. This example draws attention to a key insight from governmentality studies, which is that governance involves an exercise of power.

The regulation of smoking is a relatively positive example, but there have been many other attempts to improve a given population's health and well-being that illustrate the darker and less subtle ways that power can operate. In Peru in the late 1990s, the Fujimori government staged a large-scale family-planning intervention intended to alleviate poverty in rural indigenous communities. With funding from the United States government (the US Agency for International Development) and the support of Peruvian national women's organizations, the campaign sought to increase poor people's access to a range of contraceptives, including voluntary surgical contraception (sterilization). Yet individuals in the poor and mostly rural indigenous communities targeted by this program reported that in some cases, local health professionals persistently pressured them to undergo the sterilization procedure. Other female victims described being forcibly restrained and anesthetized after giving birth, at which point health staff performed the procedure without the woman's knowledge or consent.[24] Over a four-year period, between 260,000 and 350,000 mostly indigenous women and some men were forcibly sterilized (Boesten 2010). This example, while extreme, highlights the potential for purportedly well-intended governance interventions to operate through coercive power—to devastating effect.

This critical analysis of power and governance has a number of implications for how we understand the use of conditions to alleviate poverty. Shaping the behavior of populations to create a desired outcome is precisely the work CCTs are deployed to do. In order to explain how power operates in programs that implement conditions, I draw on two related conceptual tools from governmentality studies. The first concerns discipline, by which I mean the regulation of behavior (Foucault 1977). In a number of institutional settings, governments discipline individuals' behavior by regulating how and where they spend their time and how they move their bodies. Social scientists have shown that discipline is often accomplished through use of surveillance. French philosopher Michel Foucault wrote about institutionalized discipline in the prison system (Foucault 1977). In prisons, the government regulates the behavior of inmates by controlling the spaces they can access, the schedules they follow, and the activities in which they can and cannot participate.

When a government disciplines the behavior of individuals, it exercises power. This is not to say that power is only ever top down. The people whose behavior is being disciplined also deploy tactics of resistance (Scott 1985; see also Li 2007). Of course, the prison is an extreme example. But disciplinary power functions in many institutions where authorities seek to create high-functioning, productive citizens, including schools, factories, and welfare programs. In this study of CCTs, the notion of discipline trains our attention to the ways that authorities regulate the behavior of rural mothers by imposing a schedule of conditions, closely monitoring these women to ensure that the conditions are met and levying sanctions when they are not. It also trains our attention to the unequal power relationship between development experts and the poor mothers who are subject to their expertise. While studies of development often focus on the purported deficiencies of the poor, my purpose is to draw attention to the power-laden relationship between poor mothers and the policy makers, technocrats, and frontline program implementers who set and enforce program conditions, shining a light on how these relationships shape the experiences of CCT recipients.

If CCTs discipline women to act in accordance with a governance project, a related question concerns the intentions and outcomes of the project itself. A handful of studies have drawn on theories of governmentality to show that CCTs are intended to produce compliant, productive female subjects who mother responsibly and interact, often for the first time, with financial markets (Luccisano 2006; Hossain 2010; Meltzer 2013). I am interested in the productive work of CCT programs that is unintentional and that largely goes unseen. Attempts to govern rarely work out precisely as planned, and even the best-intended and well-funded development interventions frequently fail to meet their original stated aims.[25] Even when they do succeed, well-intended interventions generate unintended consequences. Social scientists have shown that routine failures and unintended consequences are not aberrations of the development process but, rather, a logical outcome of what happens when planned development interventions encounter the messy, lived world of politics, bodies, social relations, and environment that may not have featured in program design (Ferguson 1990; Li 2007).

When experts in institutions like government bureaucracies, think tanks, NGOs, and private foundations are tasked with solving problems of poverty, their analyses and proposed solutions often favor a nonpolitical, technical approach that avoids grappling with the seemingly intractable political and economic structures and systems that drive and sustain inequality (Ferguson 1990; Li 2007). Anthropologist of development Tania Li calls the practice of framing questions of poverty, inequality, and ill health in apolitical terms "rendering technical" (Li 2007).[26] This term is useful because it draws our attention to what experts include and exclude when they make decisions about what needs to be improved and how. Apolitical, technical problems beget apolitical, technical solutions. As a result, interventions devised for an issue that has been rendered technical often focus on reconfiguring the capacities and behaviors of poor people instead of transforming the political systems and economic policies that keep some people rich and others poor (Li 2007, 7).

CCTs are one such example of a depoliticized, technical development approach. The programs are premised on the assumption that poverty is the result of misguided individual choices, a problem that has been matched with the technical solution of incentivizing children's mothers to make better choices. While use of health and education services certainly plays a role in improving life outcomes, a number of relevant political questions that locate the drivers of poverty *outside* of the household are excluded from both the framing of the problem and its solution. Take for instance the availability of decent paid labor, or inequitable patterns of investment in education, health care, and infrastructure across rural and urban spaces. By excluding political-economic drivers of poverty in the design of this intervention, CCTs frame poverty as a result of the irresponsible behavior of individual mothers (Molyneux 2006; Bradshaw 2008).

This framing and the disciplinary practices that CCTs sanction produce a number of unintended consequences for the poor mothers who are targeted by cash transfer programs. The first is extensive care work. Chapters 3 and 4 illustrate how mothers are disciplined to comply with program conditions, only to find themselves in the ironic situation of taking their children to underfunded and short-staffed schools and health clinics that are not equipped to deliver an adequate level of service. The state wastes women's time by requiring them to walk and wait for services that are sparsely distributed and often difficult to access in the rural countryside. The technical manner in which CCTs are monitored and evaluated makes women's extensive care work invisible; there are no questions asked about the availability and quality of services, or about what is required of women to access them.

In chapter 6, I show that mothers comply with a host of shadow conditions imposed on them by CCT staff, teachers, health professionals, and local government, all of whom have the institutionally sanctioned power to do so. The CCT disciplines women's behavior to the extent that they comply because it is the reasonable thing to do, despite the demands on their time, well-being, and dignity that many of these shadow conditions entail. While these unforeseen outcomes are certainly unintended, they should not be treated as aberrations. Rather, these hidden costs are a logical outcome of imposing conditions in a place where the state fails to adequately invest in health care, education, and infrastructure, and where urban, "whiter" professionals have more power than poor, indigenous, rural women beneficiaries. The unintended consequences discussed in this book are rarely captured in mainstream program evaluations, in large part because they fall outside the technical boundaries drawn around the problem and its solution—few evaluators are looking for them.

I had some reservations about drawing on governmentality theory. Many governmentality studies are based on textual analyses that can miss the messiness and contradictions of processes of implementation and resistance (Pat O'Malley et al. 1997, cited in Rankin 2001, 23). As a result, analyses in this field are susceptible to totalizing accounts that leave little room for pragmatic responses or even hope. As someone who insists on bridging the seemingly separated spaces of academy and policy, I find that pragmatism and hope are essential. Many scholars of governmentality maintain that coming up with "improved" policy proposals is not the purpose of critical studies, and that critique for critique's sake is essential. I do not disagree with this. On the other hand, it is difficult to study CCTs and not think about the dynamics of power that governmentality studies theorize so well.

Is there a place for critically oriented studies of policy? I position myself within a contingent of critical-development-studies scholars who suggest that there is. Geographer Katherine Rankin makes a case for using ethnographic methods to enrich our understanding of governmental strategies. She suggests that starting our inquiry "from the standpoint of the oppressed" provides a basis for challenging dominant regimes of power (Rankin 2001, 23). And Li reflects on the imperative to challenging hierarchies of expertise: "This is the purpose of critique: not to replace government by something else, as yet undefined, but to 'enhance the contestability of regimes of authority that seek to govern us in the name of our own good' (Rose 1999, 59), to question truths not in the name of greater or final truth but as a matter of continuous vigilance" (Li 2010, 3). My hope for this book is that it advances a critical account of a well-intended development intervention that doesn't paralyze but, rather, prompts difficult reflection and radical imagination for a more just future.

CONTRIBUTIONS OF THIS BOOK

This book makes three central contributions to development and social policy studies, through an analysis of conditional cash transfers that accounts for care, power, and geography. The first is an understanding of how conditional aid is implemented. Most academic and policy research studies examine the impacts or outcomes of development interventions; far fewer investigate the practices and processes of implementation. Yet it is at the level of implementation that we are able to capture hidden or unexpected dynamics of how outcomes are produced. This gap has led social scientists to call for additional meso-level accounts of development that illustrate how interventions function across scales and that offer detailed explanations of social change (Currie-Alder 2016).

This book situates cash transfer recipients' experiences within a much broader web of practices, processes, and decisions that stretch across time and space, linking Andean households to clinics and schools and to offices and boardrooms in far-away Lima. The focus on implementation allows our understanding of CCT outcomes to be informed by the social and geographical contexts in which Juntos operates. Implementing policy across unevenly developed and rugged territory is no simple feat, and the challenges posed by geography necessarily shape how the work gets done. Frontline program workers, health and education staff, and local government authorities easily escape studies that focus solely on program outcomes within households. In contrast, a focus on implementation reveals these myriad actors, their work, and the context in which they do it as key determinants in women's experiences of development. In this way, the book is less concerned with *if* conditionality works and instead illustrates *how* conditionality works.

The second contribution of this book is an evidence-based challenge to the "measurement imperative" pervading the contemporary study and practice of development. The dominant trend in development studies demands quantitative evidence of impact on specific aspects of human well-being. Randomized control trials are the measurement tool par excellence, with proponents insisting that this method is synonymous with rigor (Karlan and Appel 2011). Yet this preoccupation with quantification stands at odds with many of the concerns of feminist scholarship, including the much messier and harder to quantify stuff of social relations, intersecting inequalities, and power (Buss 2015). This book brings ethnographic evidence and an analytic focus on care, power, and geography to bear on dominant data trends.

Most analyses of CCT programs are aspatial, neglecting to account for the landscapes over which implementation occurs (Ballard 2013). In contrast, this book provides an illustration of what happens when technical interventions and the metrics that feed them do not account for the landscapes that women traverse—and the labor it takes to do so. In this way, it reveals the hidden costs of a narrowly quantitative approach to measurement and evaluation that renders invisible women's extensive care burden and the deeply rooted social and economic drivers of poverty.

Finally, this book contributes a "thick description" (Geertz 1973) of the hidden costs of women's participation in conditional cash transfer programs. In a number of nonfeminist circles, a common response to my research has been: "Oh, CCTs, but there is so much data on those!" The review of data that I presented above indicates that, to an extent, this is true. Yet there is a very real difference between sex-disaggregated data and a gender analysis. While there is plenty of sex-disaggregated data on CCTs that provide us with important indicators like how many girls versus boys attend school, there are far fewer *gender* analyses examining how CCT programs not only affect the social and material inequities between women and men but also explain why such inequalities exist and what it might take to undo them.

The research in this book builds upon the seminal feminist work on CCT programs that unpacked a number of normative implications of the programs and, in particular, disrupted the widely held assumption that giving cash to women is a straightforwardly empowering feature of policy design (Molyneux 2006; Bradshaw and Víquez 2008; Tabbush 2009). The ethnographic evidence presented in the following chapters puts flesh on the bones of these important arguments. The seemingly mundane details of mothers' walking and waiting, interactions with local authorities, and participation in shadow conditions illustrate the coercive power of incentives and the ultimately unjust conditions fostered by this fashionable mechanism for development.

In the chapters that follow, I present an analysis of conditionally provisioned aid that is alternative to mainstream accounts in terms of both methodology and conceptual approach. It is a view from the margins. With this book, I hope to provoke a broader discussion about how we approach care and what that means for the people who provide it, most of whom are women. I also hope that this discussion spans the oft-disconnected realms of policy making and academic research. I have conducted research and participated in projects of improvement in both worlds and have seen firsthand the dire need for these two communities to be in productive conversation.

CHAPTER OUTLINES

The next chapter in this book illustrates how a narrowed focus on a handful of quantitative metrics permitted the substance of a well-intentioned social policy to be evacuated. The chapter is situated in the air-conditioned office buildings and conference rooms of Lima, where development experts at Juntos and MIDIS make decisions in the context of a global "measurement obsession" (Liebowitz and Zwingel 2014). Policy makers spoke to me about the state's responsibility to provide poor people with quality health and education services, which they knew the state did not provide. Yet by narrowing program focus to conditionality, they were able to produce impressive statistics related to service uptake and present Juntos as a success story. By depoliticizing and rendering technical (Li 2007) the problem of poverty, policy makers set into motion a set of processes and practices that masked the very exclusions Juntos sought to redress.

Set in the more isolated areas where Juntos intervenes, chapter 3 uncovers the ironic impacts of conditioning aid in underdeveloped places. It addresses two questions: why do poor, rural people not attend health and education services of their own volition? And when the cash incentive does drive the intended behavioral changes, what do poor women and their children encounter at schools and health clinics? By documenting the everyday ordeals rural mothers face in meeting program conditions, this chapter sheds light on what statistical evaluations fail to capture: institutionalized discrimination and the uncomfortable realities of poor-quality services. I argue that in making aid conditional, the state—ironically—compels women and children to confront the material realities of their exclusion.

Chapters 4, 5, and 6 explore the gendered dimensions of power to which conditionality gives rise. In chapter 4, I explore rural women's mobility and access to state services and how these are exacerbated by the demands of the CCT. Rather than the smooth surfaces, simplistic transactions, and easily mobile development subjects presumed by policy makers, the experiences of CCT recipients reveal uneven geographies and the embodied, tedious work of "walking and waiting." I contend that the requirement that women walk and wait for assistance from the state effectively "puts them in their place," reminding them of their lowly social status.

Chapter 5 further explores the various forms of additional labor women perform to make the CCT an "efficient" program. Local managers rely on both support from clinic and health staff and a select group of CCT recipients called Mother Leaders to aid them in enforcing conditions. While reliance on such help was unplanned at the national level of policy making, I show how Juntos is unviable without the work of these women. With this detailed analysis of the slippages between paid and unpaid labor on the frontline state, I offer a window into the gendered assumptions underlying so-called inclusive development, laying bare a reliance on women's time and willingness to discipline their neighbors to make up for persistent underinvestment in public institutions and services.

Chapter 6 documents and analyzes the myriad additional tasks that women perform as Juntos recipients, above and beyond the officially required program conditions. I refer to these tasks, which also feature in other CCTs, as "shadow conditions." While they are invisible in official documents, these activities are integral to program implementation and experienced by Juntos mothers as part and parcel of their coresponsibilities. This chapter illustrates how in the real world of bodies, uneven development, inequality, and discrimination, conditionality becomes a tool for various, more powerful groups to implement their own projects of improvement among less powerful groups.

In the conclusion, I reflect on what a conditional approach to aid means for social policy and development more broadly. Dominant actors in international development and global health urge the implementation of "adequate" cash transfer programs to enhance human capital, eradicate poverty, and reduce inequalities. Yet poor, rural women's experiences illustrate that conditionality is an unjust means for achieving these goals. I consider here how women's experiences might reorient optimistic discussions about the potential for *unconditional* cash transfers to drive what some have imagined as a "new politics of distribution" (Ferguson 2015). As I argue in this book, without a substantive investment in improving the basic conditions of people's lives, cash only alleviates some of the costs of caring.

2

Setting the Conditions

I have been struck again and again by how important measurement is to improving the human condition.
BILL GATES, ANNUAL LETTER, 2013

As insiders know, the production of good things is not pretty. Workers are caught in a web of demands that compel them to deviate from formal and idealistic rules. Yet for public consumption, practitioners must present glossy versions of how they work. These illusions are essential for occupational survival. When the work is messy, workers have to clean up well.
GARY ALAN FINE AND DAVID SHULMAN, "LIES FROM THE FIELD."

In October 2012, the affluent Lima neighborhood of Miraflores was adorned with eye-catching purple-and-orange posters and banners advertising Social Inclusion Week. The week, which was intended "to call attention to poor and vulnerable populations and their opportunities for development," marked the one-year anniversary of the Ministry of Development and Social Inclusion (MIDIS 2012d).[1] The theme for the week was "women as partners in development," and a number of posters depicted female figures in Western and traditional indigenous dress.[2] MIDIS proclaimed that the week would "pay homage to the women users of social programs, who are agents and *partners* in the progress of their households and communities" (MIDIS 2012d, original emphasis).[3]

Social Inclusion Week was one of several moments in the country's history where women have been called upon to participate in improving the nation. The organized week bore a striking resemblance to a Mothers' Day celebration in the early 1990s when then-president Alberto Fujimori also paid homage to the nation's women, praising them as self-sacrificing mothers and "heroines" (Boesten 2010). At the time, Fujimori called upon women in their caring roles to soften the blow of austerity measures in households and communities. In practice, self-sacrifice and "heroism" had a gendered cost; development scholar Jelke Boesten showed that for many low-income women, austerity meant assuming an even larger load of unpaid care work where the state had retreated, even as opportunities for paid work were shrinking. Poor Peruvian women "were perceived first as mothers and carers of other people, and only thereafter as citizens in their own right" (Boesten 2010, 39). While the intentions may have been good, this framing of women and their contributions had the effect of exacerbating women's marginalized economic status and masking their own unmet needs.

Two decades later, Social Inclusion Week provided a view into the more recent turn in Latin American development policy and how women featured in it. Following the election of President Ollanta Humala in 2011, social inclusion became the driving development paradigm in Peru, as it had in a number of other Latin American countries. By creating MIDIS, Humala fulfilled a campaign promise, charging the ministry with coordinating action across the country to fight poverty and social exclusion. MIDIS did so primarily through social programs but also through monitoring compliance with agreements, evaluating impacts, and sharing knowledge.[4] The government oriented its social inclusion policy toward achieving a situation in which all people throughout Peru exercise their rights, have access to high-quality public services, and are able to make use of the opportunities opened up by economic growth.

Central to the policy are ethnic and geographical dimensions: it holds that all Peruvians shall participate equally in their communities, regardless of their ethnicity or place of birth or residence (MIDIS 2012c).[5] The creation of a ministry devoted specifically to smoothing out long-standing patterns of geographical and ethnic exclusion was significant. MIDIS targeted the implementation of its programs to rural areas populated primarily by indigenous and campesino communities that had previously experienced neglect on the part of the state, which had failed to make investments in the basic services and infrastructure required for good health, economic prosperity, and well-being in those communities.[6]

One of the ministry's most striking accomplishments has been ensuring that previously undocumented rural residents possess state identification cards that permit them access to government services, including social programs and public health insurance. Among the initiatives that ID cards specifically allow *women* to access is Juntos, the conditional cash transfer program. Today, Juntos is Peru's farthest-reaching mechanism for social inclusion. In 2013, the program ensured that 1.5 million children attended school and had regular health checkups, and that over seventeen thousand pregnant women attended prenatal appointments (Juntos 2015b).

Peru is not exceptional in its use of a CCT program to implement a program of inclusion. In no small part because of World Bank support and financing, CCTs are the most widely used tool for promoting inclusive development in countries across the global south (Cecchini and Madariaga 2011). According to indicators for geographical coverage and service uptake, Juntos is reasonably considered a successful intervention. Yet it is worth considering how much these indicators actually tell us about the capacity of CCTs to include the poor. The women represented on the posters and banners for Social Inclusion Week provided a moment for critical reflection: how did they feature in social inclusion policy? Were the aspects of their own exclusion addressed, and were their contributions to a more inclusive Peru accounted for?

In the air-conditioned offices and conference rooms of Lima, policy makers and state bureaucrats at MIDIS and Juntos make decisions that affect how the CCT is rolled out in regions far away. I call these actors "experts." Some wield more power than others; the "high-level experts" that I interviewed hold or held a considerable amount of authority and influence, including the minister of development and social inclusion, the executive director of Juntos, members of the now-defunct Juntos Directive Council, and leaders of governmental and nongovernmental national women's organizations. Other experts are university-educated professionals at Juntos and MIDIS who are responsible for policy and program administration. They could also be called bureaucrats or technocrats. The aspirations of these experts are important to the story of Juntos, and to the fraught process of translating good intentions into a manageable—and measureable—intervention, and so this chapter begins with them.

GOOD INTENTIONS: INCLUDING THE POOR
THROUGH RIGHTS AND ACCESS TO SERVICES

Tucked deep within Lima's grungier city center, the windowless meeting space of the General Confederation of Peruvian Workers reverberated with the sounds of organizing in the adjacent rooms. Under fluorescent lights and flanked by red-and-white posters from Peru's long-standing labor union movement, a former member of the Juntos Directive Council spoke to me about poor people's rights.[7] Like others associated with Juntos in similar positions of administration and power, she emphasized that for the poor, the cash payment was a citizenship right: "You can't give these hundred soles like charity: 'Hey take this handout,' no? [Instead] you have to say, 'This is part of the government, it's your part!' Right? We deliver it, but it corresponds to the citizenship of our country! . . . And [Juntos recipients] shouldn't feel humiliated or mistreated or owing favors: 'Look, please, the hundred soles...' No, no, none of this. Rather, *it is their right.*"

In Peru, as elsewhere, many supporters of CCT programs spoke about the cash transfer as a citizenship right.[8] In another corner of the city among the big-box warehouses and dried-fish stink of the industrial sector, the director of the Catholic aid organization Caritás Peru, also a former member of the Juntos Directive Council, had similar views. Seated in a stuffed swivel chair beneath a simple wooden crucifix, he patiently explained to me that it was important that "the program's impact doesn't remain just an issue of economic subsidy, but becomes a process for reinforcing citizenship."

The difference between charity and a citizenship right in these narratives is significant because it delineates particular roles for the government and its citizens. First, charity is a voluntary, benevolent act toward the poor in which the giver's obligations derive from a higher moral purpose rather than the poor themselves (Spicker et al. 2007). From this perspective, if the CCT were charity, the state would not be under any obligation to provide it. Second, recipients of charity are traditionally conceived of as passive actors with little agency. Given that they have no claim to entitlement, the role of recipient is to await a handout. In a charitable arrangement, the less powerful are positioned at the behest of more powerful others. In contrast, citizenship rights imply an obligation on the part of the state. Juntos, like other CCTs, emerged out of a growing consensus in the mid-1990s regarding the need for government to actively participate in addressing the persistent poverty and exclusion of groups for whom "the market" had consistently failed to provide.[9] In Peru, as elsewhere, this shift has materialized in efforts to reach the poor through social programs.

Shortly after Social Inclusion Week, I attended a conference called "The Role of Women in Development," which was open to the public and raised a number of related themes. The conference was hosted in the theater of the French Alliance's stately colonial building, and besuited panelists from both government and civil society, spoke about the role of social programs in mitigating poverty. Among the panelists was the minister of MIDIS, a well-respected rural development economist. In addition to emphasizing MIDIS's approach to delivering rights and services, the minister stressed the role of the government in redressing inequality. She said, "We need social programs to stop being seen as a generous help from the state. It's the state's *obligation* to provide [social] services to those populations for which the state hasn't been able to guarantee exercise of rights or good opportunities. So while we aren't able to guarantee these things, we need to have social programs." The minister went further, insisting that in addition to social programs, the state was obligated to provide resources, including water, electricity, and health posts offering primary care: "There is a set of basic services that the state *has to* provide for the poorest populations, and it has to provide all of it."

This notion of state obligation was consistent with the idea of coresponsibility upon which CCT programs like Juntos are grounded. The state agreed to provide the social services that support health and education, and households agreed to make adequate use of these. Through implementation of this contract, Juntos strove to achieve its vision, "to have restored the basic rights of households[,] whose members have regular access to quality basic services in education, health and nutrition, corresponding to full exercise of their citizenship, and to have improved their quality of life and human capital development, thereby reducing the intergenerational transfer of poverty" (Juntos 2015a). While experts reproduced the narrative around poor people's access to rights and quality public services and the state's obligation to provide these, operationalizing these good intentions was another matter entirely.

THE POOR CONDITIONS OF HEALTH AND
EDUCATION SERVICES

While policy makers and bureaucrats at MIDIS and Juntos oversaw high-level administration of the CCT and made new iterations of the program's design and implementation as necessary, they did not control the quality and availability of public services that women and their children were incentivized to access. Health and education were the purview of the Ministry of Health (MINSA) and the Ministry of Education (MINEDU). In effect, Juntos stimulated demand for health and education services, while the distinct entities of MINSA and MINEDU were responsible for supplying those services. The configuration of this relationship had significant implications for how Juntos functioned on the ground, and for women's and children's experiences of the program.

During Juntos's early years (2006–2011), the program was housed within the Presidential Council of Ministers. In this cabinet, Juntos was governed by the Directive Council, which was constituted by representatives from MINSA, MINEDU, and other ministries, and by members of civil society. This institutional arrangement was designed to bring disparately situated entities into productive dialogue. According to the accounts of Directive Council members, the previous model of governance allowed the program to provide the health and education sectors with information regarding demand for services (e.g., where improvements to service provision were needed). In turn, the relevant ministries were supposed to be better equipped to attend to the matter of improving service supply.

However, Directive Council members reported that the coordinating potential of the council was never realized. In part, this was due to conflict over program ownership and budget. At the time, ministerial resolutions allocated 30 percent of Juntos's budget to health, education, and other relevant sectors, such that the Ministry of Health and the Ministry of Education each received 10 percent of Juntos's total budget (MINEDU 2009; MINSA 2006; see also UNDP 2006). Yet tensions arose because the funds were aligned with an agenda crafted by Juntos, and the health and education sectors were not granted the autonomy to allocate funds as they saw fit. Juntos presided over the use of funds through signed agreements, creating a hierarchical tension that complicated cooperation (UNDP 2006, 32). In an interview, a high-level development expert reflected on Juntos's frustrated efforts to implement improvements to health and education services: "The experience of Juntos *forcing* these sectors to make things better has been really bad in previous years. Around five years ago Juntos even had money that it gave these sectors, money to make the service offering better. And it didn't work at all. It didn't work at all. . . . It gave them the money and nothing happened."

Another factor that contributed to the Directive Council's inability to coordinate service delivery related to political culture. There was a perceived failure on the part of the council to explicitly confront the poor quality of services, as explained by another high-level development expert: "What was lost from this model? That there was a *space,* to take information about the precarious state of health and education services to the health and education ministries. But [the Directive Council] was never used for this. Rather there was much care taken such that it was never openly stated how bad health and education could actually be. So it was eliminated, because it didn't fulfill its role." When Juntos was moved to MIDIS in 2012, the Directive Council was dissolved and, along with it, the institutionally sanctioned space for dialogue between Juntos, MINSA, and MINEDU.

After the move, some attempts to coordinate the efforts of Juntos and the health and education sectors were made. One of these was a tripartite convention that assigned MINSA and MINEDU responsibility for providing an adequate supply of services in the places where Juntos intervened. However, despite the agreement, the supply of health and education services in many areas remained inadequate to meet the demand that Juntos generated. In an interview, a high-level expert at MIDIS expressed frustration at the situation:

> So what are we doing now? Because we noticed that you can encourage, encourage, encourage families to go [to the services], but if the school doesn't change, and if the health centers don't have vaccines, [children's health and education aren't] going to change. So yes, now we are having serious problems *with the [service] supply.* The service supply is insufficient, the service supply is poor quality. . . . [T]he sectors have to get on this. I'm pushing for it, but they aren't responding to me. And what's more, in all of the meetings I go to when I travel to the field, this subject comes up with Juntos users. Service supply. The doctor isn't there, the teachers aren't there, et cetera.

Yet it was not only that clinics and schools were often closed. Reports of discriminatory behavior on the part of health and education service providers toward Juntos recipients also made their way into the offices of policy makers in Lima. The high-level expert at MIDIS continued: "They treat them really badly, no? They make them come, and then they treat them badly. They say, 'Oh you are the Juntos women, come tomorrow! Because they pay you!' No? . . . And make sure that they don't negotiate, for example: 'Ah, if you don't do this, I won't sign off [verifying that you fulfilled the coresponsibilities].' There is *lots* of this."

Discriminatory attitudes toward the rural and indigenous poor were a problem not only at the level of service delivery but also in spaces where policy decisions were made. While the more technical frustrations that were related to budgets and interinstitutional coordination were more often voiced in interviews, the issue of institutional discrimination also surfaced. The former president of the Juntos Directive Council suggested that ability to coordinate services was also impeded by the discriminatory attitudes of political leaders, who were unconvinced of the imperative to improve the conditions of poor rural and indigenous populations.[10]

In the context of bureaucratic barriers and institutional discrimination, one visibly frustrated high-level development expert that I interviewed gave a bleak forecast: "These sectors don't have a plan of improvement. It's not going to happen." Those responsible for Juntos were understandably concerned about their inability to ensure that the program's target population would encounter high-quality services at schools and health clinics. What was the point of sending people to subpar services? In recent years similar concerns have become visible within program evaluation circles; researchers who were once unabashedly enthusiastic about the potential for CCTs to reduce poverty increasingly stress that long-term positive outcomes depend upon the provision of quality services (Cecchini and Soares 2015).

Poor quality notwithstanding, experts at MIDIS and Juntos continued to incentivize women and their children to use the health and education services available. This begged the question, On what grounds did experts justify the use of conditions?

HOLLOWING OUT THE POLICY: FROM "ACCESS TO QUALITY SERVICES" TO ENFORCING CONDITIONS

Policy makers knew that the public services available to the rural poor were inadequate, yet they continued to incentivize Juntos recipients to interact with them. This was perplexing, as a common argument for *un*conditional cash transfers in other parts of the world is that the poor quality and availability of services makes conditional grants unjustifiable.[11] During my fieldwork I often asked policy administrators if conditionality was necessary. What about an unconditional cash transfer? The common response—that conditions were necessary to increase health and education uptake—often elided the issue of service quality and shifted responsibility for overcoming poverty to the poor.

The following excerpt from a MIDIS document that outlines the government's approach to addressing exclusion and to building the case for Juntos illustrated this shift in responsibility:

> A sustainable reduction in exclusion requires a complex intervention. . . . But above all, it requires time: it is not possible to effect an immediate change in conditions that restrict the ability of people in the process of inclusion to take advantage of economic opportunities and enjoy high-quality public services. Nevertheless, there are Peruvian households today living in conditions of extreme poverty and vulnerability that cannot wait for new investment and programs designed to improve their lives. Furthermore, *these homes shackle future generations to the same conditions of exclusion, as they have never been able to feed their children adequately or to pay the costs of health care and education.*" (MIDIS 2012c, 9, emphasis mine)

In the document, MIDIS acknowledges that poverty and exclusion are complex issues relating at least in part to patterns of investment that limit some people's access to opportunities and key resources. Yet in the same instance, blame is located with poor parents and their failures to overcome the barriers to health and education. In interviews, high-level experts echoed these charges and suggested that conditionality was necessary to mobilize poor people to overcome geographical barriers as well. One high-level expert explained the importance of conditionality to me as follows:

> One of the pieces of evidence from which this program originates is that in the rural regions of Peru, many children are not using the poor service supply that exists. The gap in school attendance and use of health services between rural children compared with urban children is huge, and it doesn't reduce itself automatically. So we have to do something to ensure that rural children have the same opportunities as urban children. This is why it is basically a rural program; it's not that there aren't extremely poor people in Lima. There are. Lots. But these children go to school, because the school is four blocks from their house, and they receive teaching. The health post is ten minutes away; and [they can go] to the hospital. In the rural zones, this doesn't happen.

Instead of making it easier for rural families to access services, the state's response was to incentivize families to make the journey *in spite of* the difficulties. As stated by another high-level expert that I interviewed, "Supply of services is poor[,] . . . so you give incentives through a transfer so that [families] effectively meet the conditions."

Yet why, if services were poor, were rural families expected to use them?

Deservingness

One of the reasons why policy makers insisted on imposing conditions was related to public perception of deservingness. At the time of my fieldwork, there was an ongoing debate about Juntos in the Peruvian media. At the center of the debate was the question of what kind of behavioral change Juntos actually provoked. In particular, critics condemned the program for its supposed proclivity to foster dependency and for its unwillingness to invest in the types of infrastructure that would help the rural poor generate wealth themselves—for instance, irrigation systems to increase agricultural productivity (*El Comercio* 2013b, 2013a).[12] This claim, which was not unique to the Peruvian program, has been disproved by a number of studies (Arroyo 2010; IEP 2009).

Despite evidence that Juntos did not foster laziness, public anxieties about giving cash to poor people persisted. According to the accounts of experts at MIDIS and Juntos, the conditional aspect of the program attended to these concerns. A former Directive Council president suggested to me that "when [poverty] is accompanied by social assistance, you can create a lot of dependency and paternalism.[13] For example, 'I receive this because I'm poor and you have to give it to me, and I won't do *anything* on my part.' So I think that this type of [program] that comes with a commitment . . . on the part of the beneficiary is positive."

Conditionality was viewed as a way to ensure that the poor, rural, and indigenous communities that Juntos served displayed the appropriate levels of motivation to lift themselves—as the popular adage goes—out of poverty. According to another development expert I interviewed, "[MIDIS] shouldn't always be giving help and having people that don't want to make progress. [Poor people] can't live just getting, getting, getting." Anxieties about the poor's deservingness were pervasive, sticky, and contradictory; these views were often held by the very same authorities who insisted that social programs such as Juntos were a citizenship right.

Among experts at authoritative development institutions such as the World Bank, conditionality is widely viewed as a mechanism for managing public anxieties about dependency and deservingness, and achieving public buy-in (Fiszbein et al. 2009). These experts suggest that conditionality makes the redistributive aspect of the policy more "palatable" to taxpayers and voters: "It is possible, for instance, that taxpayers are more prepared to pay for transfers to those who are seen to be helping themselves than to other equally poor people who are seen to be lazy or careless. Some voters who object to unconditional 'handouts' may be less averse to 'rewards' to 'deserving' poor people who are investing in the health and education of their children" (Fiszbein et al. 2009, 60). This perspective understands conditionality as fostering a kind of social contract, "whereby society (through the state) supports those households that are ready to make the effort to 'improve their lives'—*the deserving poor*" (Fiszbein et al. 2009, 60, emphasis in the original).

Studies show that conditionality in and of itself, however, is not enough to achieve public buy-in. A World Bank analysis of sixty-five hundred newspaper articles about the Brazilian CCT found that the imposition of health and education conditions mattered to the public for a number of reasons (Lindert and Vincensini 2010). These included the perception that conditionality emphasized long-term impacts (whereas cash without conditions was limited to alleviating immediate poverty), ensured the adoption of parental behaviors deemed appropriate (sending children to school instead of work), and reduced the potential for the program to generate welfare dependency (*assistencialismo*). Interestingly, the public perception that conditionality mitigated the risk of dependency was neatly tied to a perceived connection to long-term impacts, which was the most important reason for imposing conditions. That said, conditionality increased public support for Brazil's CCT only *when it was monitored*. The monitoring of program recipients' compliance with conditions generated vital political legitimacy for Brazil's program.

My research suggested that data about women's compliance with conditions also generated legitimacy for the Peruvian CCT. Experts enforced program conditions, in spite of the poor quality of health and education services, at least in part because conditionality reduced anxieties about deservingness. My research also revealed another reason for the imposition of conditions, one that had to do with the metrics for success.

Impact Measurement

The policy makers and bureaucrats in Lima also incentivized women and their children to use the poor-quality services available because the key metrics for success encouraged them to. Juntos was subject to the results-based budgeting strategy of the Ministry of Economy and Finance, which monitored and promoted efficiency in public spending. Juntos, like other social programs, was required to produce particular kinds of data to prove that the public funding allocated to the program was money well spent.

The results-based budgeting strategy had a number of priority themes, including the incidence of chronic childhood malnutrition and maternal mortality, which related closely to Juntos's aims. Social programs affiliated with the strategy were required to show that they contributed to achieving targets related to those priority themes (MEF 2008, 11). For instance, in order to show that Juntos addressed chronic childhood malnutrition, the program was required to make progress relating to two indicators: proportion of children under thirty-six months with complete vaccinations; and proportion of children under twelve months of age who had completed the government-mandated set of growth and nutrition checkups.[14] The requisite proportion was determined by dividing the number of Juntos-affiliated children who had obtained their vaccinations or their set of checkups by the total number of children in the target population of Juntos recipients (MIDIS 2012a). Other targets imposed on Juntos were operational and related to the percentage of pregnant women registered within the first trimester of pregnancy; the percentage of children registered with Juntos within thirty days of birth; and the elaboration of management documents that outlined processes for household affiliation and monitoring conditions (often referred to as verification of core-sponsibilities), among other targets (MIDIS 2012a).

Notably, most of the targets were related to service usage, rather than quality. As a result, when Juntos demonstrated that it had sound processes for enforcing and monitoring conditions, its upper-level functionaries were able to claim the program's success and to secure continued financial support. After lamenting the state of health and education services in areas of Juntos intervention, a high-level development expert that I interviewed framed the success of the program as a matter of compliance with conditions: "[Juntos] is an incentives program so that boys and girls go to health and education. Continuously, and *all* boys and girls. And this objective is achieved. And this is what you must protect and preserve." Another high-level development expert that I interviewed referenced studies conducted by the World Bank that found a positive relationship between school attendance and completed growth and nutrition checkups. While acknowledging the very serious problems related to service quality, he emphasized that according to quantitative measures pertaining to service attendance, Juntos was a successful intervention, suggesting that "from this viewpoint, Juntos fulfilled its role."

The standard to which Juntos was held was related to a shift in institutional focus: Juntos went from striving to improve poor people's access to quality public services to making sure that poor people used services of whatever quality was available. A series of press releases in January 2013 on the Juntos website proclaimed that "the most important aspect of this program is that it mobilizes rural households to use health and education services in favor of their children" (UCI 2013). In interviews, experts spoke about the institutional turn in which enforcing and monitoring conditionality was emphasized: "I think the most important achievement of Juntos in the past year and a half has been the redefinition of its role—to focus on being a program that promotes human capital with a component of [poverty] alleviation, where the most important thing is verifying the behavior changes of the families, so that the boys and girls of these households actually use health and education services."

The quality of services, a much messier, more political and intractable issue to contend with, was constructed as someone else's problem. Policy makers and program administrators at the highest levels of MIDIS and Juntos insisted that service quality (or system strengthening) was the responsibility of the ministries of health and education—not the Ministry of Development and Social Inclusion, and not Juntos. I found this perspective to be prevalent. The following quote from a high-level development expert I interviewed illustrates the logic: "The Juntos program, what it does is ensure that the poorest people *use* the universal services. But the universal services have to get better. But the Juntos program can't do this. This has to happen *in the [health or education] sector.* Because the obligation of the Juntos program is to ensure that children *go* to school every day. What happens inside the school, we'd love to help. But this isn't Juntos's job. Juntos's role is to ensure that the poorest people are going to take their kids to school."

Speaking to me about the "precarity" of health and education services, a high-level expert directly responsible for the program insisted, "I can't do anything about this," and shared with me a guiding maxim: "Zapatero, a tus zapatos," or "Cobbler, stick to thy last."[15] Policy makers' frustration at their perceived inability to effectively coordinate services was understandable. Yet the implications of an approach that passes off responsibility for a vital component of this program were grim. Earlier in that same interview, we had compared experiences of elite education—upon learning that I was earning my PhD at Cambridge, she related having graduated from Peru's excellent private university to attend graduate studies at an Ivy League school in the US. Like others charged with administering the country's social inclusion policy, she benefited from a high-quality education, the likes of which was unavailable to the hundreds of thousands of people who qualified for Juntos.

FROM POLICY TO PRACTICE: COORDINATING
CONDITIONALITY AND GATHERING DATA

In order to be presented as a successful development intervention, Juntos was required to enforce and monitor conditionality. The Verification of Coresponsibilities Unit at Juntos headquarters in Lima was responsible for coordinating the conditional aspect of the program. I met with employees there one morning for what began as an interview with one staff member and turned into something more akin to a focus group. As I was led to the conference room by the original participant, additional staff seated at desks throughout the open floor plan were called or volunteered to join the discussion, until there were six of us, all women, seated around a large table in the conference room.

During the interview, the group spoke enthusiastically about traveling to rural areas of Juntos intervention, where they met with exemplary CCT recipients and related emotional stories about institutional attempts to involve the mothers in program implementation and local decision-making processes. Through these participatory experiments, most of which took place a few years before the interview, the staff learned about the women's lives: "In these . . . workshops that we went to in the regional headquarters, we listened to the mothers, and we ate lunch with them. We had breakfast with them, danced with them, we sang together. Everything. And we learned a ton, because it's one thing to *think* you know what the mothers think, and it's another to listen to the reasons why they do or don't take their child to school." These encounters, which staff suggested involved the "accompaniment" of Juntos mothers, informed the ways that the midlevel administrators thought about their work and the value of the Juntos program—they believed that Juntos played an important role in improving the quality of life and dignity of the families, with tidier and better educated children.

The participatory experiments did not last, however. In coordination with the increased institutional focus on conditionality discussed above, the work of the midlevel bureaucracy also shifted: "Now we've begun to refocus on the issue of compliance with coresponsibility, so that their children become more responsible citizens, because the mothers are now responsible for the education and health of their children, who, because of participating in the program, are going to be better people." During the interview, I inquired about how compliance with program conditions was monitored: "Well, this is all done with some forms that we elaborate here, for children's health and for education, and for pregnant women, so that they *attend*—they have to attend, right? What we verify is that *children attend*, from age six, or three in the case that they are in school starting at age three, [and before this their attendance] is verified at the [nearest] health post."

Verifying that conditions were met involved coordinating the frontline implementation work of Juntos staff called "local managers," who operated in the rural areas where Juntos intervened. Every two months, the Verification of

Coresponsibilities Unit sent a stack of verification-of-coresponsibility forms to the regional offices. The forms were large, white paper documents; a regional Juntos administrator told me that she and her colleagues referred to them as "bedsheets." The forms captured information that high-level experts needed to report regarding the prescribed indicators of Juntos's impact. They arrived at the regional offices with Juntos mothers' names and identity documents listed down the left side of the page, and a series of check boxes that solicited data from health and education institutions about service uptake: children's school enrollment, attendance, and graduation; women's attendance at prenatal appointments; and children's attendance at health checkups, also prompting input of height, weight, and vaccinations administered. In a final column, the forms prompted a "yes" or "no," corresponding to whether a Juntos mother met the required set of conditions. If "no" was inputted on the form, the mother would not receive the next cash payment. When the program recorded high rates of compliance with program conditions, which it regularly did, high-level administrators were able to claim Juntos's success.

In theory, at the beginning of every two-month Juntos cycle (the cash transfer being made every two months) local managers were meant to deliver the verification forms to health clinics and schools in the districts they managed. There, over the course of two months, health and education personnel who had been trained by Juntos to handle the forms would fill them out with the required information. At the end of the cycle, local managers would collect the completed forms and return to the regional capital, where they would input the information into a centralized computer system. As evidence presented in the following chapters illustrates, there were no data-quality or verification mechanisms in place whereby women could verify or contest the validity of information that their local managers entered into the system.

This arrangement formed part of the unsuccessful agreement between Juntos and the Ministry of Health and Ministry of Education discussed above. Given Juntos's inability to enforce the health and education sectors' compliance with the agreement, the arrangement requiring health and education professionals to record compliance information on the "bedsheets" was unevenly implemented throughout the country. In 2012, 88 percent of health establishments in the department of Cusco filled out the verification-of-coresponsibility forms, while 46 percent of education establishments did the same. By contrast, in Cajamarca, 0 percent of health establishments and 0 percent of education establishments honored the agreement that same year (Juntos 2012). Other regions fell between these extremes, with a substantial number of them falling at or near 0 percent.

A qualitative evaluation at health and education establishments undertaken by MIDIS indicated several contributing factors to noncompliance among staff. Rural clinics and schools faced a high rate of staff turnover, which caused a delay in securing representatives to fill out the forms. The staff at the Verification of Coresponsibilities Unit also spoke about this barrier:

Participant 1: What happens is that health or education staff rotate, change—

Participant 2: They rotate a lot, they rotate a lot.

Participant 1: But in the case of health, I think one of the problems is that many times the staff are [practicum students], they are about to graduate and they have to do a year of service in the communities, and so from time to time they rotate. It is not a person—a professional—who stays for many years.

In such cases, the local managers found themselves responsible for training new staff on how to fill out the forms, which was time-consuming. The MIDIS study found that in other cases, staff were unaware of the agreements and the requirement to fill out the forms; and in yet others, school and clinic personnel reported that they did not have time to do it. These observations speak to the perception among health and education staff that Juntos was unrelated to the remit of their own establishments (MIDIS 2013a).

In response, Juntos administrators emphasized that the central focus of local managers' work would be monitoring compliance with program conditions. According to a high-level development expert that I interviewed, "In the majority of cases internationally, the verification of coresponsibilities is done by the health and education sectors . . . but not [in Peru]. Here, Juntos does it, because the [health and education] systems are isolated, they don't work, and they don't enforce policy. So the strength of Juntos has to be to do verification of coresponsibilities through its field personnel." Practically, this meant that instead of "accompanying" Juntos mothers, to borrow the term from Verification of Coresponsibilities Unit staff, Juntos's frontline personnel were required to spend their time in the back offices of schools and clinics, rooting through attendance records and stacks of medical histories. Less time was to be spent listening to mothers' reasons for complying or not complying, and more time was to be dedicated to gathering the data requested by program headquarters in Lima.

WOMEN AT THE SERVICE OF THE STATE

How did women, the Peruvian state's "partners in development," fit into all of this? Central to Juntos achieving high rates of compliance was women's willingness to use the services as Lima required. Women made up 95 percent of all Juntos recipients, and the majority of MIDIS's program users overall were women. Juntos, like most other CCTs, had a policy preference for women to enlist in the program and assume responsibility for meeting the conditions. MIDIS did not, however, consider rural women to be a "target population" for its programs, and Juntos referred to women as program "users" rather than "beneficiaries."

During interviews, experts spoke about women's role in Juntos in a way that was unabashedly instrumental. The shiny new MIDIS offices were located on a busy, well-manicured boulevard in central Lima. In a boardroom located high above the whizzing traffic, Lydia and Armando, two besuited cabinet advisors laden with multiple, blinking Blackberries, labored to correct my unfortunate phrasing of Juntos as "directed" at women:

Armando: In reality, [Juntos] is directed at the *household.*
> *Lydia:* Right. Precisely because of the conditionality, it is the woman that is in charge of taking the child to school and the medical post, and for *signing* the [conditionality] agreement.

Armando: Exactly. I think something that might help you understand Juntos is that, for example, if you go on the MIDIS webpage, and you look for programs, right? . . . In Juntos, it doesn't say *women.* It says *households.*

In addition to putting me in my place, the two technocrats underscored a significant shift in Latin American social policy. In recent years, social assistance targets such as "children" and "women" have been replaced with "households." For many, this semantic shift was intended to acknowledge the nuances of poverty, especially that women and children tend to cohabit and share socioeconomic conditions (Serrano 2005; Barrientos et al. 2008; Barrientos and Santibáñez 2009). In principle, this is very sensible. Yet use of the term *household* also masked a number of inequities (Serrano 2005). In the case of Juntos, household members were selectively and unevenly implicated in program implementation and intended outcomes. For instance, as the technocrats at MIDIS indicated, Juntos audited *women's* compliance with program conditions—not men's, and not children's. At the same time, the explicit program objectives were all oriented to the benefit of children. Even in the case of pregnant women, the implicit intention was to improve the life chances of the unborn child rather than the expectant mother, as is the case with CCTs elsewhere (Molyneux 2006).

Feminist scholars have discussed at length the ways in which CCT design positions women as "conduits of policy" through which the state improves the lives of children (Molyneux 2007). My research with experts in Lima confirmed these design-related indictments. One high-level expert unabashedly defended the program's utilitarian approach to women: "Juntos, *uses,* literally, the woman as a means to get to the child. This, I know that it is very tough, that the feminists are not going to [like it] . . . but Juntos is not a program, nor is it designed, with an explicit gender component—i.e., the social construction that women and men are different is not here." She was quite right to speculate that feminists would find this approach to women and their labor objectionable—I left the interview more than a little prickled. To claim that the CCT was not gendered, however, was misguided. Juntos, like other CCTs, was not designed to improve gender *relations*—that is, the unequal relationship between men and women that systematically affords women less power. Juntos was, however, designed with a gender *awareness*—an understanding that men and women are assigned different social roles according to their biological sex (Molyneux 2007).

"Gender aware" approaches to development capitalize on gender norms, rather than seek to change them. In interviews, experts in Lima rationalized the gendered policy preference as a simple equation—little more than a matter of logistics. According to a member of the Juntos Directive Council, "It's the mother who dedicates herself to the child. And if this money is dedicated toward improving the child's conditions, the mother should administer it." Gender was important insofar as it related to the distinct social roles assigned to women and men; in this case it meant that women were the most useful means of achieving program aims.

It is well documented that equipping women with financial resources can empower them, and many of the world's best-implemented development interventions explicitly seek to have this impact.[16] When the question of women's empowerment surfaced in interviews with Juntos's high-level experts, however, it was framed as a positive externality of the program: unintended, albeit not unwelcome. One high-level expert explained to me that fostering women's empowerment (or, for that matter, anything else related to women's well-being) was not a part of her job description: "I don't work on social themes linked to women—*no*. If there are positive effects, great. But I haven't done a single thing directly so that this happens." It was very clear that Juntos did not give the cash to women in order to empower them; rather, women received the cash because experts sought efficiency in their investment.[17]

Did it matter that women were instrumentally folded into program design? A logistical approach to gender is not necessarily problematic in and of itself. Given the well-established relationship between poverty and gender inequality, there was, however, an unsettling contradiction that emerged in the ways that experts responsible for Juntos spoke about women. In Peru today, women experience poverty at higher rates than men owing to a number of interlocking political, economic, and social causes. Women are more likely than men to be illiterate and to experience violence at the hands of an intimate partner. They are less likely to participate in formal paid labor and more likely to engage in unpaid and underpaid care work. They are less likely to own land. Women are less likely to participate in politics at the local and national level and, as a result, less likely to have their needs represented when decisions are made. In light of these trends, the claims that Peru's farthest-reaching program for inclusion does not need to address the needs of women bears further scrutiny.

Policy makers in interviews and advertisements for public projects held women up as the state's partners in development. Yet as Juntos focused less on access to rights and quality services and more on the enforcement of conditions, "partnership" appeared to entail little more than women's compliance with a schedule of tasks imposed by the state. Take, for instance, the verification-of-coresponsibility forms. These monitoring tools solicited data that permitted the state to know which women had complied with the conditions and which had not. What it took for women to comply, or the reasons they might not have complied, was never recorded on these forms. There was no space for local managers to record how many times a woman had to travel to a health clinic before she found it open, or how far she had to walk, while pregnant and with a baby on her back or children in tow. The forms did not solicit data on the quality of attention she received, whether the clinic was clean or adequately stocked, or whether the technician or nurse there treated her with dignity. Regarding education, the forms did not solicit information about the quality of education received, whether the teacher showed up to work, whether the library had books and the bathrooms had running water, or whether students graduated equipped with literacy and other skills necessary to secure a job in the formal economy.

The forms laid bare what was left of a well-intentioned policy to include, once the more complex issues of delivering on rights and providing access to quality services were passed off as someone else's responsibility. The work of women was rendered invisible to the state, despite their contributions being heavily relied upon. How can we make sense of a situation in which an institutional attempt at social inclusion was evacuated of its more substantive aims yet still deemed successful?

THE "WILL TO INCLUDE"

Anthropologist of development Tania Li contends that when policy makers and development practitioners stubbornly press forward with a policy that has obvious failings, they demonstrate a "will to improve" (2007). For Li, the will to improve "draws attention to the inevitable gap between what is attempted and what is accomplished," and it also points to "the persistence of this will—its parasitic relationship to its own shortcomings and failings" (1). Li's work acknowledges the good intentions of experts committed to improvement while also insisting that we look at how and why intentions go awry.

We might understand inequality as produced and reproduced through economic policies, political processes, and social and cultural institutions that allocate resources and opportunities unevenly (Mosse 2010; Elwood et al. 2016). When well-intentioned experts aspire to tackle problems of inequality such as poverty, they enter into a process of translating aspirations into action. This involves making a seemingly unwieldy problem wieldy; policy makers must delineate a manageable area of intervention, both thematically (what will the intervention try to change?) and demographically (who will the intervention target?). This process often involves the sidelining of what Li (2007) calls "political-economic questions," the "questions about control over the means of production, and the structure of law and force that support systemic inequalities" (11). These questions get at the heart of why people experience poverty in the first place, and so when they are sidelined, ambitious development interventions lose their substance.

The Peruvian government set an ambitious agenda, one that included the rural poor; and Juntos's substantive aim to improve access to quality services was taken up by high-level and midlevel experts. Inequality in Peru has a markedly geographical character; while coastal Lima has benefited from generations of investment in infrastructure and services, rural Andean and Amazonian Peru—where Juntos's target population resides—has not received the same level of attention. As a result, the rural poor do not have access to the same level of care as wealthier urbanites. This reality was no secret. Yet when actors at the state institution were charged with including the rural poor, they were unable or unwilling to tackle the messy political-economic questions underlying the terrible state of health and education services in the rural countryside.

Instead of tackling the infrastructural and institutional conditions that made and kept poor people poor, the state focused its efforts at a scale that was much more manageable: the household. MIDIS framed poverty and exclusion as a lack of human capital, or capabilities. The root causes of persistent poverty and exclusion were to be traced to the failure of already poor parents to appropriately feed, educate, and invest in the health of their children. This view reflected the dominant contemporary approach to development driven by the World Bank that places children's capabilities at the center of poverty responses. In the 2006 *World Development Report,* the bank advocated making investments in children as a powerful mechanism for overcoming future inequalities at the same time as it evaded more "complex" political-economic questions, including land rights and taxation (Razavi 2007a). My document analysis and fieldwork with policy makers in Peru revealed that targeting the household had two important effects. First, it relieved the state of responsibility for creating the conditions in which poor people are made poor. Second, it gave credence to the view that children were shackled to poverty by the faulty behavior of their own parents.

Eliding complex dilemmas in favor of a focus on households and the behavior of the individuals within them was an example of what Li (2007) refers to as "rendering technical." She uses the term as shorthand for the set of processes by which political-economic questions are depoliticized and made "amenable to a technical solution" (Li 2007; see also Ferguson 1990; Schwittay 2011). While rendering seemingly intractable problems like poverty technical makes them more manageable, it also explains why so many well-intended development interventions fail. Development experts in Peru acknowledged that requiring poor households to use low-quality services limited the capacity of the program to deliver real change. Yet by narrowing the program focus to enforcing conditionality—and passing off responsibility for service quality to other experts located in other ministries, they were able to generate impressive compliance and service-uptake statistics. Equipped with these authoritative data, experts were encouraged to press on with an attempt to include the rural poor that they themselves recognized as flawed.

The case of Juntos highlights how the metrics applied to improvement can bolster and facilitate persistence in the face of policy shortcomings and potentially even failures. What we might call "the will to include" was in fact facilitated by a much larger trend in contemporary development policy and practice: a measurement obsession. In order to illustrate this contention, I turn to a body of literature that critically evaluates the data-oriented turn in development.

SYSTEMATIC BLIND SPOTS AND
THE MEASUREMENT OBSESSION

In poor countries we focus on health, agriculture, and family planning. Given a goal, you decide on what key variable you need to change to achieve it—the same way a business picks objectives for inside the company like customer satisfaction—and develop a plan for change and a way of measuring the change. You use the measurement as feedback to make adjustments. I think a lot of efforts fail because they don't focus on the right measure or they don't invest enough in doing it accurately.

BILL GATES, ANNUAL LETTER, 2013

For a variety of practical reasons, policy administrators systematically sidelined questions of equity and focused instead on a handful of metrics they knew to be poor indicators of the changes they originally aspired to effect. When interviews and even routine reading of local newspapers so easily revealed that Juntos's more substantive aspirations had been hollowed out, how is it possible that the program still markets itself as such a remarkable success? Clearly there is a blind spot here, but how was it produced?

To explore what I mean by blind spot, let us consider medical anthropologist Salmaan Keshavjee's analysis of "realms of programmatic blindness," in which he draws attention to "the original aims of projects that get lost or ignored" in pursuit of ideological adherence (Keshavjee 2014, 15). Keshavjee's ethnography details what happened in post-Soviet Tajikistan when foreign NGOs attempted to bring health care to the poor by creating markets for delivery of health products and services. This attempt was grounded in the neoliberal ideology of the day, which posited that free and private markets were the most democratic and efficient way of providing care. Yet as the intervention unfolded, data suggested that people's health was not improving as hoped. Instead of changing course, the NGOs stubbornly pressed forward with the creation of new health care markets. While acknowledging that the attempt was well intentioned, Keshavjee showed that, in the end, loyalty to an ideology obscured the original aim of the intervention itself. Priority was given to building markets, rather than to ensuring that poor people had access to health care. The poor were faced with markets selling health services they could not afford.

While Keshavjee wrote about an obsession with markets, a different set of political-economic forces was at play in the case of Juntos and the broader trend of making aid conditional. In Peru, experts knew that the inadequate quality and availability of health and education services was a barrier to achieving Juntos's aim of including the rural poor. However, the narrowly defined metrics for Juntos's success permitted them to replace a substantive vision of inclusion with a more manageable approach that ensured poor people used services, quality notwithstanding. We might understand the way Juntos unfolded as the result of a fixation with measurement, one that extends far beyond Peru.

Measurement, in the words of legal scholar Doris Buss, "includes the production and mobilizing of quantitative data, but also the array of reporting processes, monitoring systems, and paper trails" that have come to mark the everyday practices of a society smitten with numbers and auditing (Buss 2015, 381). In global health and development, "evidence-based development" and "results-based financing" determine which problems, and which solutions, receive funding (Liebowitz and Zwingel 2014). This shift reflects the reach of economic and corporate logic into the governance of social spheres (Merry 2011). Consider, for instance, the rise of "venture philanthropy" (Merry 2011) and the exceedingly influential philanthro-capitalist actors whose tastes and logics reflect years spent amassing wealth in commerce and tech, and who now turn their attention to solving the problems of poverty, disease, and environmental degradation. In his 2013 annual letter, Bill Gates, arguably one of the most powerful actors in global health and development today, made a case for why he believes that the kind of measurement practices found in the business world are imperative to solving poverty and the global disease burden. He suggested that measurement provides a productive feedback loop: the data it generates allow policy makers and development practitioners to identify the scope of a particular problem, whether they are making progress toward resolving it, and if not, when to change course. Taking this cue from the business world, funders of development interventions demand proof of a problem and evidence of results in order to ensure that their investments are opportunely located (see Merry 2011).

To be sure, the "demand for data" turn in development responds to legitimate concerns about efficiency and waste in development spending. Yet skeptics of this turn suggest that the burgeoning demands on policy makers and development practitioners to produce evidence of impact constitute a "measurement obsession" that needs to be critically assessed (Liebowitz and Zwingel 2014). First, what constitutes evidence in this trend is often limited, having been generated by a handful of numerically oriented indicators designed to facilitate comparison across widely different contexts (Merry 2011; Liebowitz and Zwingel 2014).[18] Equally problematic, these quantitative indicators are assigned an aura of scientific or "objective truth" (Merry 2011; Liebowitz and Zwingel 2014). Feminist scholars have raised a number of concerns about what the imperative to measure means for gender equality and other matters of social justice. One of their primary concerns relates to the capacity of quantitative metrics to capture the things that matter to women.

They point to an important and oft-overlooked question: what truths do numbers not capture?

Numeric indicators are orientated toward simplification: they "convert complicated contextually variable phenomena into unambiguous, clear, and impersonal measures" (Merry 2011, 84). On the one hand, this means that statistics are particularly useful for identifying patterns and facilitating comparison. On the other hand, this means that they are less apt to capture the messier, more complicated aspects of social life. For instance, statistics might tell us how many women have experienced violence by an intimate partner. Yet they are less apt to identify unexpected drivers of violence, to explain connections between seemingly unrelated phenomena like violence and women's access to transportation, or to identify, from the perspective of women, what elements of available support need to be maintained or improved and why. Liebowitz and Zwingel (2014) suggest that simplification "results from the exclusion of social dimensions that cannot easily be translated into categories, not because they are unimportant, but because they are rather complex and fluid" (356). As a result, statistical renderings of problems of a socioeconomic nature rarely provide the nuanced and contextual information that helps us understand what drives them. One of the great risks in the persistent demand for rapid and continuous quantitative data on program outputs is that our attention is diverted away from qualitative data that captures vital dimensions of social well-being—that is, the root causes and structural aspects (Buss 2015).

The measurement obsession produces a "self-fulfilling imperative: create indicators that are measurable and then require that social justice work be directed, even pigeonholed, to achieve progress on said indicators" (Liebowitz and Zwingel 2014, 363). This dynamic was evidenced as policy makers and development practitioners in Lima navigated the fraught terrain of translating a substantive policy of social inclusion into a successful development intervention. While experts continued to speak of the Juntos program's rights-based vision, when it came to confronting their inability to deliver on these more substantive aspirations, they hid behind a handful of quantitative metrics. Recall that program financing was tied to these key indicators. By narrowing program focus to conditionality, they were able to produce impressive statistics related to service uptake and present Juntos as a success story. This move focused attention on women's compliance with conditions and, at the same time, diverted attention away from what the state did or did not do to ensure that mothers and their children encountered adequate services.

CONCLUSION

The quantitative measurement obsession that shaped program implementation in Lima obscured the conditions that produce poverty and the gendered costs of compliance. At the level of policy and program administration, turning a blind eye to political-economic questions was incentivized. Experts were conditioned to focus on changing the behavior of individual mothers, rather than on addressing the persistently poor quality of health and education services. While some of the institutional dynamics among MIDIS and the health and education ministries are unique to Peru, the broader policy narrative is not. Globally, statistics indicating impressive levels of compliance feed narratives about the success of CCTs, even though compliance is hardly evidence that these programs are delivering on the loftier aspects of their stated missions. Nonetheless, the pressure to focus on numeric data not only comes from national-level results-based budgeting but also the development banks and other external funding agencies that provide governments with the technical and financial support to implement CCTs and other social programs.

To be sure, tackling inequitable allocation of resources, institutionalized discrimination, and other complex drivers of poverty is difficult work. Yet the exclusion of such matters from the design, implementation, and measurement of development interventions limits the potential of these interventions to achieve their own stated aims. Moreover, it can produce a host of unintended consequences (Ferguson 1990); the messy questions do not, in the words of Tania Li, just "go away" (2007, 124). Social policies that are blind to gendered, racial, and geographical elements of exclusion often end up reproducing the very inequalities they intend to address (Paredes and Thorp 2015). In light of this analysis, my next step in this book is to shed light on these blind spots using data derived from long-term ethnographic fieldwork. Research in the rural areas where Juntos was implemented illuminates complexities and hidden costs that the measurement obsession would have us not see. The following chapter shifts location to the rugged Andes mountains, where frontline state employees enforced conditions and where compliant mothers accessed services.

3

The Ironic Conditions of Clinics and Schools

We can't expect people to run towards care when the care isn't good.
PAUL FARMER, "*FAILURE TO COLLIDE: EBOLA AND MODERN MEDICINE*,"
2015

One sunny afternoon in Sonsonate, I was approached by a Juntos mother named Paloma. She was the first person I had met in the village, and we had developed a close relationship. I often started and finished my days chatting with her and a variable combination of her seven children in the small courtyard of her humble home. Looking much more serious than usual, Paloma asked if I would volunteer to teach English at the secondary school her children attended and that she had once attended herself. She explained that it would be a temporary arrangement, just until the school director filled the vacant position. After chatting it over with her, I agreed, and Paloma promptly whisked me over to seek consensus from two fathers in the parents' association, who were busy with shovels making improvements to one of the school buildings.[1] The men's nods of approval secured, Paloma led me to the director's office. After a brief meeting in which the director implored me to make a monetary donation, which I politely explained I could not provide, I was introduced to the other teachers and provided with my schedule. I was to start the next day.[2]

The Sonsonate secondary school was built through the unpaid labor of community members, who identify that effort an act of *mit'a,* voluntary public service, with great pride. But community members were unable to supply the school with some important equipment that the state had neglected to provide. The toilets were not serviced with running water, and there was nowhere in the school to wash one's hands. The school had a small, locked room in which staff stored boxes of outdated textbooks, but there was no library at the school, or anywhere else in the village, where students could find books on subjects of general interest. Moreover, the reading materials available didn't reflect the realities of rural livelihoods or the contributions of rural people. The English textbooks were clearly written for an urban student body; the vocabulary provided for students to use when answering the question "What do your parents do?" included *pilot, doctor,* and *accountant,* professions that none of the students' parents—subsistence farmers, construction workers, or migrant laborers, held. It was about as disconnected as the textbook's section on technology; I never encountered a single student at the school who owned a computer, and the one in the director's office was not available for student use.

My three weeks spent teaching at the school helped me better understand the context in which Juntos mothers met program conditions, as did my observations of and conversations with women in clinics and day-care centers, municipal halls, and community centers, and in households and on *terrenos* (plots of land). Mothers like Paloma had a different view of conditionality than the experts based in Lima. These mothers' experiences provide key insights into questions that much of the quantitative research on CCTs overlooks: Why do poor, rural people need a "nudge" to attend health and education services? And when the cash incentive does drive the intended behavioral changes, what do poor women and their children encounter at health and education services?

TEACHER SHORTAGE

Before being approached by Paloma, I had wondered why the schoolyard was so often occupied with seemingly idle children during regular hours of instruction. As it turned out, over a period of more than two months, an ongoing "teacher shortage" (*falta de profesores*) meant that over half the secondary students in Sonsonate, Santa Ana District, missed classes in English, communications, and biology. The reason cited by the school's director was that "there was no budget." During my stint as a substitute teacher, I observed that depending on the grade, students could spend up to three hours out of a five-hour school day without classes. Their mothers, nearly all of whom were Juntos recipients, ensured that they arrived promptly at school in order for them to pass hours in the courtyard patch of gravel and brush, chatting or kicking around a deflated soccer ball.

The issue of idle children and inadequate staffing that I encountered at the school in Sonsonate was not limited to this one school. The regional capital city, Cajamarca city, also suffered a teacher shortage, and this too was identified by education staff and frustrated parents alike as a budgetary issue. Around this time, the local newspaper reported that the regional government had petitioned the Ministry of Education for 24 million soles (at the time US$9,184,878) in order to contract with enough teachers to fill the vacant spots (*El Panorama* 2013). According to mothers whose children attended the secondary school in Sonsonate (which also served a number of surrounding villages), the teacher shortage was an annual occurrence. Teacher shortages, however, were only one of a number of reasons for which the quality of education in rural Peru was commonly character-ized as *pésima,* or "terrible."

Absenteeism—teachers simply not reporting to work—was another persis-tent issue in Cajamarca and elsewhere in the country. A survey conducted by researchers at Harvard University, the World Bank, and the Peruvian think tank Grupo de Análisis para el Desarrollo tracked teacher absenteeism at primary schools in Peru. Their findings included a strong connection between geography and absenteeism. According to the study, "Teachers at public schools in higher-poverty districts are absent twice as often as other public school teachers, and for teachers at remote public schools (measured by distance to a paved road), absence rates are two and a half times those of other public school teachers" (Alcázar et al. 2017, 124).[3] Reasons for absenteeism included remoteness (rural communities are hard to reach and involve extended absences from family); underresourced classes and unpleasant working conditions; poor salary; and weak community ties, or limited sentiments of accountability toward the local community (Alcázar et al. 2017). In wealthier countries, an absent teacher is likely to be replaced by a substitute. This was not the case in rural Peru. "In a developing-country setting, where substitute teachers are uncommon, absence of a primary-school teacher may have various consequences—doubling up of classes, idle time for students, and even student dropouts if absence becomes frequent enough. But learning is not likely to be one of them" (Alcázar et al. 2017). Notably, Juntos mothers were required to send their children to school, regardless of whether the teacher showed up for work.

Even when the schools were fully staffed, Juntos mothers raised the issue of poor-quality instruction. The students in my classes were enthusiastic, volunteer-ing answers and requesting extracurricular classes. However, even in the upper-level classes, students' level of language acquisition was strikingly poor. This was not through any apparent fault of their own. The students reported that their previ-ous teacher, who had gone on to teach other subjects, did not know how to speak English—a point I was later able to confirm with that teacher. At the time of my research, local and national newspapers frequently reported on the exceedingly low number of teachers able to pass the qualifying professional exam. For instance, in a rural region that neighbored Cajamarca, of 2,125 teachers who stood for the qualifying English exam only 25 of these passed. The local Ministry of Education representative responded with a disheartening dose of pragmatism: "The results are alarming, only 25 passed the exam, but what are we going to do? We have to fill 500 spots" (*La Republica* 2013).

Placing blame on teachers for poor-quality instruction would be misguided. Public school teachers in places like Santa Ana operate in an underfunded sys-tem that does not adequately invest in training and resources, particularly in rural areas. In *The Education Trap in Peru: When Education Reaches Many and Serves*

Few, researchers Arlette Beltrán and Janice Seinfeld (2013) of the Universidad del Pacífico in Lima underscored the inadequacy of teacher training and poor salaries attached to the profession as central drivers of persistently poor educational outputs. Provocatively, they suggested that the only solution to the persistent problem of poor education was to remove all of the unqualified educators; any teacher or director who could not pass a pedagogical evaluation could be reassigned to an administrative position. They also implored the state to ensure that schools meet minimum infrastructural standards, supplying water, lights, an Internet connection, a library, whiteboards, and a guaranteed six hours of instruction daily.

In Cajamarca it was immediately apparent how the failures of the state affected children. The results of a national standardized test provided to second grade students in public and private schools revealed that only 30.9 percent of students in the country registered at a satisfactory literacy level, meaning that they understood what they had read (MINEDU 2013). In Cajamarca, only 19 percent of students registered at a satisfactory level of literacy.[4] When those same students were tested in math, 12.8 percent of students nationally and 9.5 percent of students in Cajamarca were able to resolve numeric problems indicating an adequate level of skill, such as: "There are 26 pencils in a box. 14 are red and the rest are blue. How many pencils are blue?" Nationally, almost half of all students were unable to identify simple numeric relations, like which number in a scrambled sequence was the largest (3, 8, 6, or 5?), indicating the most basic grasp of math. In Cajamarca, this percentage was 57.7. Some regions faired even worse than Cajamarca; of all the regions tested, Cajamarca ranked twentieth out of twenty-six in reading comprehension and fifteenth out of twenty-six in mathematics. The results indicated a significant geographical gap: urban and coastal areas registered higher scores than the rural Andean sierra and Amazon regions—places where the state uses Juntos to ensure that parents send their children to school.

To be sure, the Peruvian government has undertaken a number of efforts to improve the state of education over the past decade and a half. The administrations preceding Humala invested in the construction of new schools and, through initiatives like Juntos, reduced the rate of student desertion and the number of students receiving good-quality subsidized lunches. However, substantial improvements to educational output—other than attendance—have been largely elusive. Following an extended period of news media coverage of the teacher shortage, the Ministry of Education announced the government was dedicating 446 million soles (US$170,763,485) to improve school infrastructure in over two hundred schools located throughout the country (*El Comercio* 2013c). The ministry was also in the process of implementing reforms in order to improve the quality of instruction students received, including in rural areas. The extent to which these investments were successful remained to be seen.

Juntos mothers sent their children to school knowing that the quality of education they would receive there was poor. Most of the mothers I spoke with in

Cajamarca were largely unaware of the discussion about education taking place on the national level; they were, however, exceptionally keyed in to what was happening locally. Juntos recipient Paloma spoke to me about the teacher shortage one afternoon as we walked back from her small plot of land. Paloma, who had a bundle of ears of white corn larger than her own body secured to her back, told me that before Juntos, many families didn't send their children to school. Instead, the children helped their parents cultivate the land and raise animals, a common practice across Latin America's smallholder farms. Nowadays, she told me, women are obligated to send their children to school, and so everybody did it, "but there are no teachers!" Sharply identifying the irony of the situation, Paloma wittily quipped, "Perhaps it's the teachers' attendance that should be monitored." Other mothers echoed Paloma's sentiments.

In light of such evidence, we can hardly blame these women for asking, Who is really responsible for poor outcomes? When children become adults who are unequipped to take advantage of economic opportunities (to borrow language from development experts), who should take responsibility?

These women's perspectives challenge the very premise of conditionality and the supposed necessity of a "nudge" to ensure that households uphold their end of the bargain in sharing responsibility for overcoming poverty. Persistent staff shortages, low quality of instruction, and inadequate infrastructure are manifestations of the state's failure to redress persistent inequalities in the distribution of basic resources (Oliart 2003). While women upheld their end of the bargain by sending their children to school, the state failed to provide the infrastructure and human resources necessary to provide a quality education. Yet, notably, while women's compliance in meeting conditions was monitored, there was no simultaneous audit of the state.

In addition to their comments, women's actions, too, demonstrated a great deal of responsibility for the education of their children. Aside from securing a substitute teacher (at no cost to the school), Paloma and other mothers and fathers from Sonsonate decided to forgo their subsistence tasks and traveled to Cajamarca city to protest the teacher shortage outside the Department of Education. Not long after, the local newspaper reported on an organized group of parents protesting a sustained case of absenteeism on the part of teachers and the school director in a neighboring district (Cruzado 2013). My findings corroborated evidence from elsewhere in Peru that documented the significant efforts expended by rural parents to ensure their children received a meaningful education (Figueroa et al. 2010). Research among mothers in the Mexican CCT program registered similar concerns about teacher absenteeism; there, mothers astutely proposed a reduction in teachers' salaries to correspond with the fines women faced for not doing what was expected of them (Rivero 2002, cited in Molyneux 2006, 435). The point raised by mothers in Mexico and Peru troubles the assumption undergirding CCT policy, that poverty is a result of poor people's irresponsibility. Paloma was but one of the many mothers I met who assumed the responsibility for improving their children's access to education, even when the state was apparently failing to do the same.

DISCRIMINATION IN SERVICE ACCESS

When CCTs successfully increase children's uptake of health and education services, they also expand women's interactions with public services. It is well established that women's exposure to public spaces and actors can lead to increased self-esteem and empowerment, at least at the local level. While women's well-being or empowerment was not an aim of Juntos, it is worth exploring the nature of experiences CCT recipients have when they use public services. To be sure, I observed indicators of empowerment that have been more intentionally explored by a handful of studies in Peru and elsewhere, including increased purchasing power within their communities and a more positive outlook on life, especially as it related to their capacity to provide for their children (Alcázar et al. 2016; Correa Aste and Roopnaraine 2014; Latapí and la Rocha 2008).[5] My observations indicated that some Juntos mothers interacted confidently with public services and, in particular, with the education system. Paloma was an exemplary case of this: she participated in the parents' association, protested the teacher shortage, and successfully inserted me into a teaching position at the local school.[6]

Yet it was unclear to me, and the jury remains out—in the broader albeit limited research on women's empowerment and CCTs—on whether Juntos was a catalyst of this participation. A number of women like Paloma arrived at their interactions with public service providers as already relatively empowered individuals. In her case, Paloma had experience as a community leader in other social programs, took advantage of local trainings and microproductive projects, owned a small plot of land in her own name, and had a husband widely recognized in the community for treating her well. Not all mothers came to Juntos with these same experiences.

But even mothers like Paloma were not immune from features of the public services system that were grounded in prejudice. For campesinas, discrimination at the hands of public service providers is a regrettably common experience.[7] Such experiences include being ignored, made to wait, and being addressed disrespectfully. For example, Juntos mother Grimalda was very well respected by other mothers in the village. She was always smiling and her three children were cheerful and affectionate with their parents. Like all the other Juntos mothers I spoke with in Sonsonate, Grimalda disliked the director of the secondary school, a mustached man from the city who distinguished himself from the school's rural families on the premise of being "a good Christian." Mothers frequently commented that "the director doesn't do his job," and my own observations supported their claims. During the three-week period when I taught at the school, I bore witness to several occasions in which the director was absent from work, sometimes even leaving teachers and students locked out of the school.

Mundane abuses of power were commonplace. Mothers reported that the director corruptly charged them a fee for access to their children's enrollment and graduation certificates, which Juntos required the women to provide. When the mothers protested, the director laughed at them, and so the women paid the fees. If they refused, the mothers risked suspension from the Juntos program on account of failure to prove compliance with program conditions. On multiple occasions I saw mothers made to wait while the director sorted through paperwork on his computer, the only one in the school (and to my knowledge, the surrounding villages). On one illustrative occasion, Blanca, a slight, quiet woman in the full, calf-length dark skirt and white blouse typical of campesina dress, approached the doorway of the director's office and, without entering, asked politely if someone would please unlock the gate so that she could leave. Without making eye contact, the director snapped, "I have other things to do!" Blanca was also ignored by his young female secretary, who never looked up from her desk. After waiting a moment, Blanca retreated to wait silently by the locked gate.[8]

Commonplace acts of interpersonal discrimination and unsanctioned fee-charging were indicative of larger patterns of inequality. Social scientists Martiza Paredes and Rosemary Thorp situate the poor quality of present-day education services in rural Peru within the historical context of discriminatory patterns of public funding and social policy (Thorp and Paredes 2010; Paredes and Thorp 2015). In the early twentieth century the Peruvian state increased its near-nonexistent spending on education in the rural Andes in order to civilize and assimilate indigenous populations through a curriculum promoting literacy and personal hygiene. Prejudiced attitudes against indigenous and campesino people cut through educational policies and laid the foundation for grievous mistreatments. In some of the worst incidents, young women were humiliated and sexually abused by their teachers (Thorp and Paredes 2010). Despite increased investment in education, literacy rates in the region barely improved. This example illustrates how "poverty traps" work. Nothing was done to modify deeply ingrained discriminatory attitudes and beliefs about the inferiority of campesino and indigenous people; and as a result, "while the resources did get delivered the outcomes were perverted" (Paredes and Thorp 2015, 8).

This historical policy environment provides important context for contemporary attempts to "include" the poor and marginalized. Juntos required children to attend underresourced schools, generating perverse outcomes that included attending classes without teachers, using toilets without water, and finding libraries without books. For their mothers, the situation involved confronting discrimination and humiliation at the hands of school authorities. Poor women quite rightly pointed out the gross irony of this arrangement: Juntos effectively increased demand for services, without making those services any more desirable.

CONFRONTING HEALTH CARE

Regarding health services, Juntos recipients confronted even worse conditions of access and quality. Some of the most salient issues came to the fore during a Juntos meeting in Labaconas. The meeting took place at ten o'clock on a rainy morning in the municipal hall. It was attended by approximately forty Mother Leaders, elected village-level representatives of Juntos recipients who, among other things, served as liaisons between Juntos's local managers and the households in their jurisdictions. The two local managers responsible for Labaconas District had summoned the Mother Leaders from the surrounding hills to attend the meeting in the district capital. They arrived wearing wide-brimmed white sombreros and colorful shawls that they had likely knit themselves, and while chatting to one another they took seats in rows of plastic chairs. The local managers, easily identifiable in their fire-engine-red Juntos jackets, stood at the front of the hall. They were accompanied by the perpetually campaigning district governor and health staff from the surrounding clinics, including a newly appointed middle-aged male chief of staff, a young male technician, and a female nurse, all of whom wore the Western dress of urban dwellers.

When the meeting began, the local managers and health staff instructed the Juntos mothers to use health services when pregnant and on behalf of their children, which was framed as a matter of responsible behavior. In turn, the mothers queried the availability of services in their area. My field note from that day reads:

> At half past ten the meeting starts, and the health chief begins by telling the quietly seated mothers not to come to the health post at night unless it is an emergency, not to ask for medicines, and not to show up expecting to be attended. Health staff, he says, will attend them from 7:30 a.m. to 7:30 p.m. He is aware that during the past six months women have been coming to the health post during open hours and not being attended; he assures them the municipality has contracted more staff to resolve the problem. A mother named Felisa addresses him from the rows of seated women, apologizing quietly and politely for the bother, and asks if they could possibly get a doctor at the health center in the district capital. The health chief replies that the health center has been downgraded from a "center" to a "post," so only provides primary care. Felisa says that just two weeks ago she was told at the center to take her very ill mother to Cajamarca [city] for treatment, at which point "they didn't even give me a pill." Felisa wasn't able to take her mother all the way to the city "because she didn't have the money" [*por la economía*]. The health chief responds that women should always have some money saved for emergencies. Solanda, to my left, says quietly to her neighbor: "And how do we do this?!" A woman with long plaits called Juana requests a turn to speak; in a firm tone but using all of the formalities, she says that she is from Lotan village, where there is often no one working at the health post (the staff from this post is also absent from the meeting). Juana asks what the mothers can do, can they come down to the district capital? And could they please have some health training to deal with issues themselves? She recounted that the other day a mother in her village gave birth alone because the nurse wasn't there. One of

the other health staff interrupts to say that the nurse no longer works there, at which point Juana apologizes for the bother and takes her seat.

This meeting provided a view into rural women's experiences of accessing poorly distributed and resourced health care services, and the economic barriers mothers face in overcoming them. The landscapes in which Juntos was implemented were not like the urban spaces of Lima or even the city of Cajamarca. In rural Peru, women's access to care—for themselves and their families—was limited by the distances they had to travel in order to reach a health facility and by the lack of roads and public transportation. Despite the very obvious geographical and infrastructural barriers they faced, rural mothers encountered very little empathy from health staff; the health chief's response to Felisa's account of trying to access care for her ailing mother is a typical example.

For women like Felisa, who was poor enough to qualify for Juntos, this journey would be a time-intensive and costly affair. An average journey from where Felisa lived would entail three or more hours on foot from her village to the district capital, payment for travel by combi (which could include transferring to a different vehicle partway through the trip) or shared taxi depending on availability, and resulting in a journey of one and a half to two and a half hours to reach Cajamarca city, followed by the cost of an inner-city combi or taxi travel to the hospital. Felisa was responsible for the care of young children and would most likely have to bring them along. This would multiply transit, food, and lodging expenses. Once at the hospital, Felisa's family would likely queue for hours to be attended. Low- and no-income people, including Juntos recipients, were forced to queue out front starting at three o'clock in the morning for a chance to be attended. The Cajamarca public hospital was staffed for outpatient care only in the mornings; in the afternoon, the doctors attended to higher-income patients at the modern, more expensive private hospital on the other side of the city. Given the prolonged amount of time required to seek treatment, the family would likely need lodging for the night (or more, depending on whether internment was required) and would have to eat in restaurants, which were expensive.

The health chief implied that Juntos recipients ought to be able to generate savings for use in unforeseen circumstances such as those Felisa confronted, yet mothers' accounts suggested that in most cases this was an unreasonable expectation. Mothers frequently referred to the cash payment Juntos provided as "a little bit of help" (*ayudita*). In addition to covering unforeseen costs with it, mothers spent the cash on a variety of things requested of them by local managers, teachers, and health staff, including photocopies, school supplies, enrollment and graduation certificates, uniforms, medication, meat, and fruit, as well as travel to places where they could purchase these things. Suniva, a mother of three school-age children and a Juntos recipient of five years, voiced a contention I heard often: "Two hundred soles are a little bit of help. People think you can live off of this, but you cannot." While women said that they were thankful for the money, a little bit of help was indeed little. All told, two hundred soles ran out quickly.

To access this bit of help, women were required to meet the seemingly straightforward health conditions imposed by Juntos: pregnant women were to attend prenatal appointments, and mothers had to bring children under the age of five to regular health checkups. The state of health care in rural Peru complicated women's capacity to accomplish these tasks efficiently. Clinics were frequently closed during regular hours of operation, a reality I found evidence of in my travels with local managers, in conversations with mothers, and in regular reports in the local and national newspapers. Closures were the result of staff absenteeism and high turnover, both of which are chronic problems in the rural countryside. In a World Bank–commissioned study on education and health-professional absenteeism in Peru, researchers visited approximately one hundred schools and one hundred clinics on two separate occasions. In 81 percent of the schools they visited, teachers were present on both occasions. Health staff were present for both visits in only 56 percent of facilities, one-third of staff were present on one visit, and a full 10 percent were absent on both occasions (Chaudhury et al. 2006). Low wages and difficult working conditions were oft-cited reasons for why health staff disappeared from the job, particularly in remote communities. Current and former health staff spoke to me about missing their families and not being equipped with the medical supplies necessary to do a good job. Local newspapers reported on chronically short-staffed clinics throughout the region, where technicians and nurses refused to travel tiresome distances for such low-paid work.

The consequences of absenteeism were particularly acute in rural areas because the absence of one or two health staff could result in the clinic being entirely closed for service. Juntos mothers were eligible to receive the cash incentive only when their attendance at appointments was recorded by health staff and registered by local managers. If a mother descended from the hills with her children to attend an appointment and found the clinic closed, she was required to make the journey again (figure 5). In order to comply with program conditions, women could be forced to travel for hours on foot to a health clinic several times just to check the box for a single prenatal exam or child's checkup.

My observations corroborated findings from research elsewhere in the country underscoring the gross waste of women's time generated by poor-quality health services (Ewig 2010, 142). To be sure, wasting time in this way might not be so problematic if Juntos mothers had time to spare. Since most Juntos recipients do not participate in the formal labor market, some observers might assume it is reasonable to ask unemployed women to make a few extra trips to a health clinic. In fact, women in the Andes spend on average fourteen to eighteen hours a day on productive and reproductive labor, do more agricultural work than men, and multitask, caring for children while spinning wool and pasturing animals (Deere 2005). Their contributions to family and community well-being in rural Peru are

FIGURE 5. It was a three-hour walk to reach the health clinic in the valley below. Photo by the author.

extensive and significant, even if they are largely unpaid. Fulfilling the conditions Juntos imposed upon them constituted additional hours of labor. The time women wasted attempting to meet program conditions was time reallocated from sub-sistence agriculture, tending flocks, caring for sick and elderly dependents, help-ing children with schoolwork, or engaging in economically productive activities. These largely caring activities not only buffer families' experiences of acute poverty but also contribute to building and maintaining human capital—Juntos' explicit aim. The irony, and tragedy, of this situation was that CCTs were deployed to orga-nize women's caring labor in a way that development experts—who do not share rural women's predicaments—deemed preferable to women's own arrangements.

WHY DO WOMEN COMPLY?

Given the poor quality of services and the personal cost of meeting the conditions that Juntos imposed, why did women comply? My observations and Juntos moth-ers' accounts indicated that women tried their best to fulfill the conditions because the cash had a positive material impact on household economies. It enabled them to meet some of the needs of their children and other dependents. Juntos recipient

Santos, who cared for her young grandson, told me that Juntos was an important resource because local work was scarce: "if not for this little bit of help it would be very difficult. There's nowhere else to get [money] from. There is no work." Another Juntos recipient, Josepa, recounted how happy she was when the census takers finally arrived at her house, so that she could register for the CCT program: "As they say, it's a little bit of help, miss. Maybe to buy a little something . . . as there's no work. And, well, miss, if not, where do we [get money]?" Much like that of Santos, Josepa's appreciation of the cash payment—and fear of losing it—was grounded in her financial concerns as a single mother.

Reliable sources of income, however small, were valuable because there were few options for rural women otherwise.[9] Cajamarca, like much of the rest of Andean Latin America, was subject to the "growing distress" of the peasant economy (Deere 2005). Women like Santos and Josepa operated in an economy that incentivized men to migrate out of the region in search of agricultural work. A consequence of this was a rise in female-headed households as temporarily or permanently abandoned women were left to juggle care work with access to paid labor, if there was any to be had. Juntos provided a consistent source of income that helped women to care for their families. Women welcomed a "little bit of help" when help was scarce.

To say that women appreciated the cash is not the same as suggesting that they complied with the conditions uncritically. Their compliance was not evidence of support, let alone enthusiasm. When women referred to the cash as a little bit of help they educated the listener on its limits. They were demonstrating awareness of the pejorative assumptions made about Juntos recipients by higher-income people with whom the mothers interacted in clinics and schools and the district capital, where they went to collect the payment. Paloma explained this dynamic in an interview:

> I have the twins, plus Marcos and Juan, who are all studying. Four [children]. And one hundred soles for four children, well it doesn't cover everything [no alcanza]. Sure, it's a little help, but that's it. It doesn't cover everything. When we say, "Ok, let's go and queue so that they give us the hundred soles," the rest of the people say, "Look at those welfare recipients [pensionistas], how they're coming. They're doing really well getting a gift, the hundred soles." And they say, "Why [doesn't Juntos] give it to us, if we are the ones working?" That's what they say. . . . We hear them say it.

In referring to the transfer as a little bit of help, mothers worked to dispel assumptions among non-Juntos recipients about the women's deservingness and the material conditions of their lives. As noted earlier, the cash transfer permitted mothers to purchase necessities, access services, and make modest investments that would otherwise be difficult or impossible, including basic medicines, school uniforms, extra protein, local transportation, and small livestock. The cash transfer did not, however, compensate for the lack of employment opportunities or level of government neglect in the rural countryside.

Mothers' accounts and my observations also suggested that women complied with program conditions because using health and education services—even those of poor quality—was the responsible thing to do. Development and social-policy research examining the gendered design of CCTs in Mexico and Central America challenged the assumption that giving money to women was straightfor-wardly empowering by pointing out that CCT program design positioned mothers as responsible for their children's poverty (Molyneux 2006; Bradshaw and Víquez 2008; see also Chant 2008). Narratives about responsibility pervade the program from design to implementation. In Peru as well as other countries where CCTs are implemented, conditions are commonly referred to as "coresponsibilities," implying that the state and CCT recipients are jointly responsible for overcoming poverty. In the villages where Juntos was implemented, responsibility narratives circulated broadly. While women and even local managers regularly lamented the inadequacy of health and education services, these critiques were not explicitly framed in terms of the *state's* unmet "coresponsibilities."

In contrast, women's responsible or irresponsible behavior was frequently and explicitly in question. The choices of poor, rural women were often framed in terms of responsible and irresponsible motherhood by urban, middle-class experts in antipoverty programs, by doctors and nurses in health clinics, and by teachers and directors in schools. I frequently observed local managers implor-ing women to meet the program conditions as "responsible mothers," which they almost always did. These narratives have significant social power, functioning as they do to discipline women's behavior. Women themselves commented on their own or their neighbors' demonstration of responsibility as they cared for their children in the ways expected of them by the state.

To be clear, I am not suggesting that the mothers who participated in Juntos were so entirely constrained by the disciplining power of "responsible mother-hood" that they acted without agency. To the contrary, decisions taken by women like Paloma, who fought to improve the conditions of her children's school, or made pointed comments made about the limits of "a little bit of help," stand as evidence of the ways in which Juntos recipients exercised agency. These were the most common ways that I observed women push back against a program that frequently made some aspects of their lives more difficult, even while it alleviated burdens elsewhere, and I am quite sure that there are others.[10]

What I am suggesting here is something quite different: that women's compli-ance with the burdensome and ironic demands of the state was informed by mate-rial constraints and disciplining social dynamics that ought to be taken seriously. Bear in mind the popular assumption by behavioral economists that poor moth-ers fail to use adequate services because they lack the motivation to do so. I am suggesting an alternative explanation: that poor mothers are already highly moti-vated and have their own reasons for complying. These alternative explanations for why women comply undercut the assumption that poor mothers simply need the motivation to access services that are otherwise perfectly adequate. In taking these alternative explanations seriously, it is possible to challenge the authority that compliance metrics grant to policy makers and program designers. Women's high rates of compliance do not prove that the quality of services provided by the state is adequate; all they prove is that desperately poor families do indeed need every little bit of help.

The chapter thus far has addressed two issues that the dominant body of evidence on CCT programs largely does not: what Juntos recipients encounter when they access education and health services on behalf of their children, and why, in the face of poor services, women decide to comply with program requirements. I return to the question of women's compliance in chapter 6, where mothers' participation in a range of unsanctioned "shadow conditions" sheds light on the coercive power of cash incentives.

CCTS OVERLOOK WOMEN'S HEALTH

Who will provide care for the care provider?
AMMA DARKO

Juntos was concerned only with women's use of health services at a specific stage in their life course—when they were pregnant. Even then, program conditions were oriented toward the well-being of future children; nowhere did they focus on mothers themselves (Molyneux 2007). While Juntos mothers in Labaconas and Santa Ana dutifully whisked their children to growth and nutrition checkups, their own health needs remained unmet by the services available to them. Take, for instance, Yesenia, the Juntos mother of two whose experience opened this book. Yesenia had been diagnosed with breast cancer and was unable to access treatment anywhere within a ten-hour journey of the village where she lived. Her greatest concern revolved not around her own well-being but around who would care for her children if she were unable. By all accounts, she already was the sort of "responsible mother" that the state hoped to shape through use of behavioral incentives (Molyneux 2006; Bradshaw 2008). Yet when faced with a grave illness, she was presented with a host of economic and geographical barriers to care. The question of who provides care for care providers is not only practically relevant— given that their labor sustains the well-being of others—it is also morally relevant. If we take seriously the contention that the inequitable distribution and insufficient recognition of care work are tightly linked to gender inequality, then care providers' access to care is also an issue of justice.[11]

Ninón, a frail and kindly Juntos mother, shared a number of Yesenia's motherly concerns. I interviewed Ninón outside of her home, perched in the sunshine on an earthy stoop. Ninón had been on bed rest for the better part of a year after a serious stomach operation. Abandoned by her husband many years previously, she was responsible not only for the care of two children but also for her elderly mother and her severely disabled brother. In places like rural Peru, where institutionalized care is sparse and expensive, poor women often assume responsibility for sick, disabled, and elderly family members who depend on them for survival. Ninón's ability to carry out this care work was compromised by her own ill health. As we chatted, she confided that she didn't attend all of the Juntos meetings, on account of her health, and was unsure whether Juntos would suspend her from the program. While local managers were not sanctioned to expel women on account of missing meetings, it bears noting that Juntos policy did not make exceptions for women who failed to meet health and education requirements because of illness.[12] This raises the question of whether policy makers and program designers considered the significance of the work that women do, particularly as it extends beyond biological reproduction. What of their other care work and the good health necessary to accomplish it?

The lived realities of women like Yesenia and Ninón trouble the narrowly focused view of women's health embedded in CCT programs. Cases such as theirs illustrate that the targeted program design, which seems so sensible in theory, produces exclusionary and unjust ironies in practice. This is perhaps most striking when we consider the notion of coresponsibility. Certainly, a woman who cries because her cancer will affect her children, more than she cries for her own fate, stands as a rebuke to the view that poor people raise poor children because they are unmotivated.

RESPONSIBILITY AND THE STATE

Women's accounts of poor-quality services bring empirical backing to critiques other researchers have made about the capacity for CCTs to generate long-term positive impacts. While some of these critiques generate from quantitative studies of educational and health outcomes among children and youth (Murray et al. 2014; Cecchini and Soares 2015; Andersen et al. 2015), others look at social spending patterns (Lavinas 2013; Lavigne 2013). Social spending is what the state spends at its various levels of government to provide the public and private goods and services necessary to guarantee the social rights of the population; it does this through allocation of resources, redistribution of income, provision of preferential goods, and promotion of economic growth (Martínez and Collinao 2010, as cited in Lavigne 2013). Recall the high levels of absenteeism in clinics and schools, and the low salaries and difficult conditions cited by those skipping work: these are manifestations of inadequate social spending.

Development economist Lena Lavinas (2013) draws on comparative social-spending data across Latin America to show that while many CCT programs have increased the demand for health and education services, state governments have not met that demand with a proportionate investment in improving service supply:

It is true that total social spending has risen sharply in Latin America. Between 1990–91 and 2008–09, according to ECLAC, average annual per capita expenditure went from $318 to $819, and the size of social spending as a share of GDP rose by 6.6 percent, accounting for 63 percent of all public expenditure in 2008–09, as against 45 percent in 1990–91. The trend certainly looks very positive. Nevertheless, this growth has been unbalanced: monetary benefits have registered greater increases than other modalities of public provision, such as spending on education, healthcare or housing. . . . [M]onetary income transfers—either contributory, as in pensions, or means-tested benefits—accounted for over half the overall increase in public social spending, rising as a share of GDP by 3.5 percent between 1990–91 and 2008–09. *By contrast, spending on health rose by only 1 percent over twenty years, and on housing by a mere 0.4 percent.* (Lavinas 2013, 20, emphasis added)

Social spending in Peru is considerably lower than the Latin American average. In 2012, Peru spent 9.4 percent of GDP on social goods and services, compared to the regional average of 19.0 percent (ECLAC 2014). Since Juntos was created in 2006, overall social spending has increased. However, spending on health care and education have remained fairly steady. For instance, since 2006, expenditure on public health care as a percentage of GDP has fluctuated between 2.392 (in 2006) and 2.847 (in 2012).[13] Yet during this period, Juntos dramatically increased the number of children regularly seeking health services (Perova and Vakis 2009). In this respect the aggregate social-spending data paint an even bleaker picture than my observations in rural Peru, suggesting not only that health care has not improved but also that it may be getting worse as rural care providers are increasingly overburdened. This data underscores a "flagrant contradiction in governments establishing CCT programs that require medical visits, when they have made little effort to provide better public healthcare" (Lavinas 2013, 21).

Only people situated at the bottom of the social hierarchy would be expected to contend with discrimination and subpar social services for a small (albeit not insignificant) cash stipend. It is important to recognize that this reflects a clear historical trend, in which the Peruvian state attempts to improve the life conditions of marginalized rural and indigenous populations without attending to broader political, social, and economic structures that perpetuate inequality. When the state fails to attend to unequal patterns of social spending and discriminatory beliefs, its interventions often prove ineffective and, in many cases, harmful (Paredes and Thorp 2015). While it would no doubt be politically unpalatable, there is good reason to think that the "intergenerational cycle of poverty" might truly be broken if the state were to address its grossly inequitable patterns of investment in the rural places where indigenous people live and the urban places where mostly nonindigenous elites live.

The 2016 *World Social Science Report* contends that tackling inequality requires a focus on how specific dimensions of inequality, whether gender, racial, spatial, political, cultural, or environmental, affect the life chances of particular groups.

The report draws on data gathered globally to suggest that "the treatment of groups affects the well-being of individuals and their uptake of services that may help to reduce inequality, such as health and education. This means that reducing group-based inequalities can improve life chances for individuals, and increase the effectiveness of direct and indirect measures intended to address specific aspects of inequality" (ISSC et al. 2016, 8).

Unfortunately, "the institutional and cultural structures that sustain these [group] inequalities are often ignored and rarely addressed by the designers of change" (Paredes and Thorp 2015, 1). As it stands, the applause that governments receive for efficiently increasing service uptake masks what Lavinas stingingly called a "downsizing of social protection in the name of the poor" (2013, 40). In failing to meaningfully improve or perhaps even maintain the accessibility and quality of services available to rural families, Juntos compelled women and their children to confront the very markers of their poverty and exclusion. The everyday lives of Juntos mothers have much to tell us about how this contradiction plays out: in households, on footpaths, in clinics, and in schools. If the state ensured a reliable, good-quality, and culturally appropriate supply of health and education services, women and their families would almost certainly use them. What reason would they have not to? As it stands, the assumption driving CCTs—that poor people make irresponsible decisions and require incentives to make better ones— is not based on adequate evidence, at least in rural Peru. Services there have never been good enough to test such an assumption.

CONCLUSION

Doctor and anthropologist Paul Farmer once said, "We can't expect people to run towards care when the care isn't good" (Farmer 2015). CCT programs, however, operate on the assumption that we can and should. The woefully ironic condition of clinics and schools begs the question of whether policy makers imagined that rural, indigenous populations were deserving of anything better than what was already on offer. In Peru and elsewhere, development experts impose conditions to ensure that poor people use health and education services on behalf of their children and to reassure the more powerful, tax-paying public that the poor are not being given a handout. Yet spending any substantial amount of time with rural mothers and their children reveals experiences that undercut the logic of conditionality. For instance: much like the middle-income and wealthy women in my own neighborhood, the poor mothers of rural Peru want to see their off-spring thrive. A key difference in rural Peru is that women are afforded far fewer of the resources necessary to do so. In becoming defined by the anxieties, rigidities, and requirements of powerful groups and institutions, a well-intentioned policy of inclusion became a mechanism for delivering poor people to underfunded and ill-functioning clinics and schools.

The poor condition of health and education services in rural Peru was widely conceded. The health chief in Labaconas acknowledged the six-month period in which the district clinics were understaffed, and farther up the chain of command in Lima, experts at Juntos and the Ministry of Development and Social Inclusion regretfully confirmed the inadequacy of rural services. Local managers tended to express the most empathy with women who had difficulty accessing health services, because these managers walked similar routes and frequently grappled with clinic closures when enforcing and monitoring conditionality. And yet, local managers continued to require women and their children meet the program conditions. At the end of the day, frontline Juntos staff were still responsible for implementing a successful program, and high rates of compliance enabled them to claim success.

Of course, the imperative to implement conditional programs of social support originates externally. State governments are encouraged to implement CCTs by authoritative external development agencies like the World Bank and the Inter-American Development Bank (World Bank 2017; IDB 2009). To be sure, it is reasonable to suggest that these external agencies might not be aware of the poor quality of services in rural Peru. Yet there are plenty of data available. Take, for instance, the established global survey of the quality, equity, and efficiency of education systems carried out by the Organization for Economic Cooperation and Development's Programme for International Student Assessment. Peru consistently ranks near the bottom of the list; in 2015, it ranked sixty-fifth out of seventy countries (OECD 2016). Even lacking the kind of ethnographic data I've presented here, such surveys should give pause to the champions of CCTs. When ignorance of such readily available data results in requiring the rural and indigenous poor to use bad services, it is hardly an acceptable excuse.

This chapter has presented evidence of a significant lack of support for care work of the (poorly) paid and unpaid varieties. By looking behind high rates of program compliance, we see that the state neglected not only to account for the ways in which low-income, rural, campesinas labor to care for their families, but also to support them in that labor. Supporting them would require a critical look at the investments made in adequately remunerating teachers and medical staff, particularly in "last mile" communities. While the salaries afforded to teachers and medical staff were often not enough to entice them to work, the cash payment provided by Juntos effectively ensured that women and children arrived at clinics and schools. We know this is so because women's compliance with conditionality was monitored. But as this chapter has illustrated, compliance data does not tell the full story.

4

Rural Women Walking and Waiting

Managing poverty can be very time-consuming.
RUTH LISTER, *POVERTY,* 2004

People living in the most rural parts of Peru do a lot of walking and a lot of waiting. They walk to their *terrenos* (plots), to the health clinic, to school, and to the market. They will walk all day to visit family in another village. Many of the rural families that I spent time with in this study thought it was funny when I could walk some of these distances with them. They would tell one another "¡Ella puede caminar!" (She can walk!) with an equal mix of bemusement and pleasure. Rural Peruvians also do a lot of waiting. They wait for combis (private minibuses), for attention from bureaucrats, and for politicians to fulfill promises. They wait for the state to build roads, install sewers, provide potable water, extend electricity service to houses, send more doctors, and contract more teachers. They wait for the economic prosperity from the boom they've been hearing about to trickle down into their pockets, too. In unevenly developed places like Peru, walking and waiting are features of rural people's daily lives.

I began to grasp the significance of walking and waiting for cash during a crisp, achingly blue-skied day on the cusp of the rainy season. I was accompanying a Juntos local manager to a meeting he had called with mothers in a village called Colmica in the district of Labaconas. Colmica was not reachable by road, and the local manager had borrowed a dirt bike from the municipal government to get there. We traveled up rugged dirt paths, and when the course became steep, I would dismount and the local manager would gun the engine to jolt up the hill. After about an hour the bike was no longer able to make the climb, so we continued on foot through grasshopper-green pastures and the kind of crisp skylines achieved only when the oxygen is that thin (figure 6). Our (partially motorized) journey from the district capital to Colmica's village hall took approximately two and a half

FIGURE 6. Local manager Paulino ascends the hill on foot. Photo by the author.

FIGURE 7. A sudden and dense seasonal fog. Photo by the author.

hours. The meeting itself lasted just shy of three hours. At its close, the local manager and I exited the small, electricity-less community building into a fog so dense
it was impossible to see three feet ahead. The mountains, the district capital below,
and the house a short way down the hill had all disappeared, entirely whitewashed
by the weather. The fog was disorienting. It had become impossible for the local
manager and me to successfully (not to mention safely) make our way down the
mountain on our own. Cliffs, streams, and animals were unidentifiable until you
were already upon them. The *teniente* (village lieutenant, or elected chief) offered
to lead us. I recall at one point stumbling into the path of a large bull, whose presence and proximity I was made aware of only through its arresting *moo* (figure 7).

The environment and its propensity to change at a moment's notice shaped
rural women's experiences of earning and collecting a cash incentive. The mothers
who attended the meeting also returned home in the fog. Had the fog descended
before the meeting, the women's attendance would still have been required.

Part of the appeal of CCTs as a method for reducing poverty is their alleged efficiency. With the use of a simple cash incentive, poor people change their behavior.
Yet in practice, conditionality introduces hidden costs that are not accounted for
by this simple equation. We have established that Juntos's impact evaluations did
not capture information about the poor quality of the health and education services, or about what it took for women to meet program conditions in the context
of uneven development. If we were to view CCTs from the perspective of women,

would we still find them to be efficient? There are a number of long-standing feminist insights about poverty and time that have recently gained more mainstream attention, and these are worth exploring here. Women experience "time poverty" at a rate much higher than men (Antonopoulos and Hirway 2010). This is largely because women do unpaid care work in their households and communities, in addition to paid work in the formal or informal economy. If development interventions do not take into account women's unpaid labor, they have the potential to exacerbate gendered inequities (Elson 1995). Taking these feminist insights to heart, we might ask: What are the hidden costs of imposing conditions in unevenly developed places?

To answer this question, I take to heart the conviction of feminist geographer Isabel Dyck, who insisted that we pay close attention to women's more mundane, everyday undertakings, lest women and their activities "slip into the shadows" (Dyck 2005, 234). The pages that follow shed light on two of Juntos mothers' more mundane activities: walking and waiting. Mothers traveled, mostly by foot, to meet program conditions, to ensure the local manager had the correct information, and to collect the cash incentive. While the landscapes they moved through were breathtakingly beautiful, they were steep and subject to bright sun, heavy rains, and dense fog. Juntos did not make allowances for weather conditions, transportation shortages, or conflicts of interest that made women's travel uncomfortable, onerous, or costly. Women's walking and waiting draw our attention to the gendered inefficiencies of imposing conditions on social support.

WALKING AND WAITING

On a bright morning in the northern Andean dry season, Juntos mothers who had fulfilled their coresponsibilities traveled from their respective villages to the district capital of Labaconas in order to collect the cash incentive. Juntos dispensed cash from the municipal hall because there were no banks or ATMs in Labaconas. I had arrived from Cajamarca city in a combi, which was unusually full of opportunity-seekers from the city: microentrepreneurs loaded with boxes and plastic sacks who came to hawk their wares in an impromptu market that spread throughout the plaza.[1] Their presence transformed the public space: what was usually a tidy, serene square became a colorful and chaotic explosion of cooking pans and mops; men on loudspeakers selling "curative" Amazonian medicines, secondhand clothing, and cheap plastic toys; and vendors preparing fried guinea pig and ceviche (fish or snails cooked in lime juice, chilies, and onion). My field notes from the day recount that this was the scene from eight o'clock in the morning until four o'clock in the afternoon:

> At the far side of the bustling plaza, a few hundred campesinas, many with babies secured to their backs, stand queuing in four thick lines that stretch along both sides of the municipal hall [figure 8]. The women's white sombreros and full, black woolen

FIGURE 8. Waiting. Photo by the author.

skirts distinguish them from the handful of state and municipal employees in West-ern-style jeans and windproof jackets. A bright blue armored Hermes truck is parked out front, and a uniformed armed guard stands by. It carried the Juntos payments up into the mountains [figure 9]. Other than the municipal authorities, entrepreneurs, and security guards, there are very few men around. Large white posters labeled "Jun-tos Current Registry" are fixed to the wall on either side of the municipality doors. The registry lists the first name and surname, identity document, village, and institutional identification number of every Juntos recipient [figure 10]. The door to the municipal-ity remains shut, and municipal employees stand guard. Local managers give queuing mothers paper tickets that will eventually allow them to enter the hall in small groups. It is hot, bright, and chaotic; every time a group of mothers is allowed through the doors, there is a lot of pushing and shoving, and the local managers yell: "Understand! There is nowhere to sit!" and "Get in line!" The queues are patrolled by a vigilant female municipal worker in Western dress who informs local managers when she notices a mother cut in line. As they enter the building, mothers are filmed by a male security guard who points the camera at them and tells them to remove their sombreros.

At this point, mothers tell me that they have been queuing for hours. Many wom-en traveled to the capital in groups of three to five, several neighbors together. One group of women from Chan Chan left their village at 5 P.M. the previous day; they walked for four hours and spent the night in front of the municipal hall. One Juntos mother, called Aurelia, says that they have to come the day before because, with the time spent queuing, they couldn't make the trip in a single day. Other women left their communities at 3 A.M. to arrive at 6 A.M., or left at 2 A.M. to arrive at 5 A.M.

FIGURE 9. The district square on "payday." Photo by the author.

A young mother named Cenobia, her infant wrapped around her back with a colored shawl, says the mothers are unhappy because the women who live closer arrive late and cut in, while Cenobia and her neighbors "form a line but then are the last to collect." Other mothers are chastised by the local manager, who is circulating through the queues telling mothers not to let others cut in, that they should defend themselves. Cenobia, among others, protests that it is not their fault; there should be help to prevent this. The local manager responds that there are only two local managers for a thousand women, and furthermore, that the armored truck employees want to leave because the mothers are blocking the entrance to the municipal hall. The local manager threatens to take photos of the mothers who do this, saying that they'll be kicked out of the program and the photos will serve as proof of why—and if they don't queue nicely, the payment will be every three months instead, and then every six. A mother named Flor approaches with an infant on her back and produces a photocopy of a birth certificate; the local manager accepts it but tells her it is too late for her to collect the payment now; it will have to be for next month.

Halfway down the queue, five mothers huddle together; they tell me that after collecting the transfer they will make the three-hour walk to their village, where "we left our children!" Gladys says that she is tired, and they all laugh when I ask if they will rest once they return home. This time the payment took place on Friday and not Sunday, and they asked me, "Why would that be?" The sun is at full peak now, and it is less comfortable to be outside. A group of six mothers who left their village at 1 A.M. complained that "[the local manager] doesn't take into consideration that

FIGURE 10. The list of compliant mothers on public display. Photo by the author.

we have our babies, it is hot out, and there is no shade." They've also left their other children at home, and their husbands are working in the fields. Sara tells me that her father is very old and she has left him alone with no one to care for him. A quarrel erupts behind us over who has cut in line.

Inside the municipal hall there are more queues. Here, mothers stand in orderly lines to collect their payment from four uniformed cashiers, who are seated at a long table set out at one end of the room and flanked by armed guards. Inside it is cool, quiet, and organized—a sharp contrast to the heat and chaos on the other side of the doors. Collecting the money is all done manually, not electronically. When signaled, a mother approaches the desk, and a cashier takes a paper receipt with the mother's name on it from a book and hands over four fifty-sole notes, or the equivalent sum in twenties. Mothers must have their national identity document with them; an armored truck employee periodically calls out to all of the women to have their ID in hand. If he doesn't see it, he inquires brusquely: "Where is it? Have it ready." A woman called Sidra has forgotten hers, and the cashier doesn't allow her to collect the payment. I wonder how long she had to walk, only to be turned away; returning to where she'd come from to retrieve her ID seems to be an unlikely option. Once the women collect the cash, they tuck it into their skirts and exit through the doors back outside.

The way women travel and the queuing required of them reveal the starkly gendered dimensions of mobility and access to state services (Massey 1994; Radcliffe 2015). On Juntos paydays across the country, thousands of women's bodies re-pattern the Andean hills and Amazonian valleys, spilling out of households and pastures, traversing footpaths, windy roads, and rivers, ultimately concentrating into queues that spread from cash points like spiny fingers from a hand. This systematic movement of female bodies illustrates how Juntos "disciplined" (Foucault et al. 1991) women's mobility, requiring mothers to be physically present in some places rather than others and making them navigate the landscapes in between. Juntos disciplined women's movements so that they arrived at the places experts thought they should be, but it did not facilitate their ease of arrival. Women walked because the state did not provide poor, rural people with public transit, and women walked at night because the journey was so long that they could not arrive on time otherwise.

The scene at payday illustrated both the walking that women were required to do, and the waiting that was sandwiched between journeys. In order to receive the cash incentive, many of the women queued for half a day after beginning their walk before dawn or even the night before. Queuing is an exceptionally banal thing to have to do, but it is not inconsequential. Drawing on an extensive ethnography of poor people's waiting in the welfare offices of Buenos Aires, Argentina, anthropologist Javier Auyero (2012) writes about queuing as a mechanism for the production and reproduction of unequal power relations. He contends that welfare recipients learn their subordinate social position through waiting for welfare benefits. In part, this is because welfare recipients are subject to the desires and whims of low-level state bureaucrats who have more power than they do. If poor people want government assistance, they must wait patiently for the state bureaucrat to facilitate it. As a result, in the hours and hours of waiting for services, mostly without complaint, welfare recipients learn to be "patients of the state."

Through Juntos, the state shaped *gendered* patients—women who were responsible for their children's poverty and, therefore, responsible for waiting. To be sure, most CCT programs' gendered policy preference for female recipients could generate empowering—albeit unintended—impacts at the household level.[2] However, contrary to much mainstream thinking about development, giving women cash does not automatically empower them (Chant and Sweetman 2012). For the mothers who walk and wait for Juntos, the cash comes with significant demands on the women's time and mobility. It also requires them to confront their subordinate social status in a very public way. As researchers have noted in other countries where women queue to receive cash transfers, waiting can produce feelings of shame and humiliation for the CCT recipients whose poverty is on display (see Balen forthcoming).

Whether or not waiting has empowering or disempowering effects is influenced by the spaces in which it takes place (Auyero 2012). The municipal hall and surrounding plaza where people received their payments were parsed into spaces of unequal access for the mothers waiting and for the actors managing women's waiting. While women waited, they were exposed to the natural elements.[3] On this particular day it was bright and hot. During wet season it was cold and rained so hard that roads became impassable. Being patient meant watching urban professionals move freely to access basic comforts. These more powerful actors (local managers, security guards, municipal authorities, National Bank cashiers, myself), identifiable by uniforms and Western dress, could come and go in and out of the municipal hall, seeking a seat, a toilet, shade, and respite from the noise and jostling. The hundreds of campesinas queuing for the cash incentive were denied this option. The local managers, municipal workers, and employees of the armored truck company barred Juntos recipients' entry to the municipal hall except when it was their turn to collect the transfer. As a result, the mothers queued without access to toilet facilities, seating, or shade. The armored guard and his camera helped the local managers discipline women's behavior. When uncomfortable mothers began to wait *impatiently,* local managers used threats of suspension that would be backed by video surveillance.

Women queue for so long in part because Juntos is implemented in rural areas largely devoid of banking infrastructure. As a result the state goes to great (and admittedly admirable) lengths to ensure that the cash transfers reach their intended recipients. This includes armored trucks summiting Andean mountain roads, boats navigating Amazon River branches, and floatplanes landing in yet more isolated communities. Owing to the increase in demand for financial services generated by Juntos, the National Bank was opening new branches and installing ATMs in previously unserviced places, and Juntos was gradually switching over to automated payments. In these cases, mothers with bankcards and access to an ATM still traveled great distances to collect the transfer but could spend less time queuing. Many illiterate women continued to rely on local managers for help navigating the financial system.[4] Local managers assisted women by entering pin codes to withdraw the cash, and women waited in queues for this support.

It is worth interrogating which aspects of Juntos we might associate with cash transfers in general—including unconditional cash transfers—and which aspects we should associate specifically with conditionality. The next sections more closely examine what it takes to implement the conditional aspect of Juntos, focusing specifically on the work that mothers do to ensure they receive their earned incentive.

MOTHERS "MANAGING UP"

Before payday, actors throughout Juntos had to complete a number of necessary work tasks. These tasks related to implementing conditionality. Local managers had to maintain an up-to-date Juntos database, which they referred to as *el sistema* (the system). A properly maintained database had the correct information about where a mother resided, how many children she had and their ages, and whether they were enrolled in school and, if so, in what grades. To keep the database current, the local managers collected copies of birth certificates, school enrollment and graduation certificates, and identity documents. The database was used by staff at Juntos headquarters in Lima to produce documents called verification-of-coresponsibility forms, which were used to monitor women's compliance with conditions. Every two months, staff in Lima sent these forms to regional Juntos offices. The forms arrived with women and children's names already listed under their respective villages of residence. Once the forms arrived, local managers were responsible for using them to monitor women's compliance with conditions.

The local managers traveled to clinics and schools, recording information about whether pregnant women and children had used the required services. The hope was that they had; during the month following the previous payday, the local manager spent her or his time traveling between villages reminding women of what they were required to do. Once the forms were complete, the local manager returned to the regional headquarters to input all of the information "into the system." If the local manager registered a mother's compliance in the system, her name would later appear on a printed roster of women who would be eligible to collect two hundred soles on the next payday.

From Lima, implementing conditionality could seem relatively straightforward. Juntos headquarters sends out forms, and shortly thereafter the database is updated with information about the targeted population's service usage. Yet focusing narrowly on the data the forms provide has led many analysts to gloss over the time and effort it takes on the part of mothers to comply with conditions and ensure that their compliance has been registered. From Cajamarca, implementing conditionality looked far more onerous. Local managers were responsible for managing an unwieldy number of households. In Santa Ana District, two local managers shared responsibility for 1,710 households. In Labaconas District, two others were responsible for 1,004 households.[5] The majority of these households were not located in easily accessible, compact residential neighborhoods. They were dispersed across unevenly developed landscapes where transportation and modern communication technology was an infrequent luxury. As a result, it was not possible for local managers to independently maintain a current database and monitor whether program conditions had been met. Local managers required the help of the mothers they managed.

In addition to accessing health and education services, Juntos mothers were also required to "manage up"—that is, perform additional, time-burdensome tasks to ensure that local managers accomplished their monitoring work. If women did not manage up, they risked not receiving their cash incentive. The time women spent managing up subsidized the cost of implementing a conditional cash transfer in spaces of inadequate state investment. Managing up is another form of unpaid work that women do for the CCT. It is worth our attention because it would not be necessary if Juntos did not insist on monitoring women's compliance with conditions.

Managing Up at Meetings

One way that women managed up was by attending meetings. Local managers summoned mothers to meetings in order to communicate information about paydays, availability of health and education services (e.g., if a "clinic" is downgraded to a "post" and therefore no longer staffed by a nurse), changes to program conditions (e.g., when Juntos increased the age for school attendance from fourteen years to eighteen years or graduation), and to solicit women's participation in other activities that were usually unrelated to Juntos. These meetings could be viewed as a necessary and efficient communication tool in a context where there were few other options. These households did not have computers or Internet access, so sending out mass emails was not an option. By making meetings mandatory, a local manager could communicate important information to all of the households within a surrounding village while expending only a few hours of her or his time.

Juntos's reliance on meetings looked different from the perspective of the mothers required to attend. Women in Juntos are often also beneficiaries of other social programs, and so they attend meetings on a continual basis. In addition to Juntos, women were often at meetings for the Glass of Milk (Vaso de Leche) Program, the Qali Warma National School Lunch Program, the National Cuna Más Program (an early childhood development initiative establishing community day-care centers), the Techo Propio Program (My Own House, which provided subsidized house construction), and parents' associations attached to the preschool, primary school, and high school. The Juntos meetings placed an additional demand on women's time and took them away from other responsibilities, including those that earned them an income (figure 11).

Juntos recipient Marisela lived in a simple home with a packed-earth floor in the same village she had been born in. She was a mother to four children, aged twenty, twelve, seven, and four. Her eldest, a daughter, had married straight out of secondary school and was a mother herself to a three-year-old girl, who Marisela also helped care for. Marisela had been in the Juntos program for five years. The cash incentive supplemented the modest income she generated from selling produce from her plot of land. Every day Marisela prepared lunch for the *peones* (farmhands) that helped her to cultivate her plot. When Juntos called a meeting that conflicted with her food preparation, Marisela felt compelled to prioritize the meeting. In interviews, Marisela, like other Juntos mothers, told me that attendance at meetings was mandatory and that local managers threated them with suspension from the program if they failed to attend.[6] According to Marisela, "Well, when [the local managers] tell us there is a meeting, we have to go, because they say that they'll suspend us, which frightens us. . . . And sometimes we have to leave behind our chores and go, back and forth."

Local managers assured women's attendance by requiring them to use their national identity documents and a signature or fingerprint. Hermina, mother to five school-age children, explained how women's attendance at meetings was

FIGURE 11. Gladys returns from taking her herd to pasture. Photo by the author.

monitored and the conditions under which this was done: "Yes, [the meeting facil-
itators] give [the attendance list] to the local manager, [showing] which mother
participated and which mother didn't. And in the case that we miss one—well,
we are excused once, but if we aren't there at two or three meetings, they punish
us. . . . Everything is punished if we don't do it when we are supposed to."

Asking women to sign in was a mechanism of surveillance that ensured that
women spent their time in ways that helped the local manager implement conditionality. The meetings were not mandatory in any "official" sense. The verification-of-coresponsibility forms did not have a line of check boxes prompting
local managers to report on whether women had attended meetings. Yet the use
of surveillance techniques such as sign-in sheets bolstered the impression that the
cash incentive was tied to attendance. Local managers had the power to create this
impression and to enforce it. If a local manager chose to inaccurately register a
mother in the system as not having met the program conditions, she or he could.

Juntos recipient Josepa lived with her two young boys in her parents' modest
home on a wide brown hill in a small village in Santa Ana. Juntos meetings were
held in a neighboring village down below Josepa's home, where the schools and
health clinic her children attended were also located. The journey up and down
the hill took about thirty minutes in each direction on foot, which is how Josepa
and her young boys traveled. Josepa's eldest son was in primary school, so she
made the trip at least twice daily to drop him off and pick him up. I once made

the journey with her. We had lost track of time while eating granadillas, a delicate, pulpy fruit with a crispy orange shell, from the tree in front her house and had to rush as a result. While chuckling bemusedly, Josepa commented that I was quick (for a noncampesina, presumably), and I thought that she was being kind, rather than truthful; she would have made it down the hill in half the time had she left me with the granadillas. Whenever the Juntos local manager called a meeting, Josepa made an additional trip. She often heard about meetings at the last minute and, as a result, had to drop her other tasks and hurry down the hill:

> *TC:* Is it easy to get to the meetings?
>
> *Josepa:* No! We live far away. For those who live close, well, they are right there. I have to move quickly and sometimes I'm late. Sometimes they don't tell me in advance [when there is a meeting], and then my friends come down the hill and pass the house, calling out to me, "Let's go to the meeting!" . . . Yesterday I was terribly sick with a cold, a terrible cough, and, well, I went anyway, running down the hill; and so much *worse* that made my cough.

Josepa's running down the hill illustrates how effectively the CCT disciplined women's behavior. When local managers called a meeting, women subordinated their own needs and interests to the whims of program staff. Evaluations of the Mexican CCT reported similar findings. There, too, cash transfer recipients described having to weigh the costs of engaging in paid labor or meeting program coresponsibilities (González de la Rocha 2006).

There was no prescribed number of meetings that local managers might call; in theory, they could call as many or as few as they would like. I was often told by local managers and other authorities from government and privately run social programs that mothers increasingly refused to attend meetings that were not called by Juntos. Local managers and the other program workers suggested that it was because attendance at Juntos meetings was attached to the cash incentive. The social program workers related this situation with resentment; their attempts at communicating information were thwarted by women's refusal to participate. As a result, they established arrangements with local managers to summon mothers to meetings under the guise of calling a Juntos program meeting. I attended one such meeting that had been called by a Juntos local manager on behalf of the Cuna Más worker, and I heard about several others. Local managers do this favor for a variety of reasons, including that they believe it is important for women to participate in the activities of the other program, or because they might need a favor in return.

To be sure, some meetings would be necessary whether the cash transfer is conditional or unconditional. At the very least, women would need to be informed about where, when, and how they could collect the payment, particularly if the cash is delivered manually. Yet many of the meetings I observed were called in order to align women's behavior with conditions. Yet others were used to request women's participation in activities that had little to do with the specific aims of the Juntos program (see chapter 6). The unregulated manipulation of women's time would be eliminated or at the very least reduced if Juntos were not conditional. As it stood, the current arrangement constricted women's autonomy to make their own decisions about time use in light of their own knowledge about what was best for themselves and their families.

Managing Up to Demonstrate Responsibility

In addition to attending meetings, mothers also did a great deal of work to verify that local managers had the correct information on file, to make the latter's work easier. Since policy makers typically think that local managers gather information on their own, women's work constitutes another instance of managing up. Juntos headquarters required confirmation that mothers had met the program conditions. Recall that the two local managers assigned to each of the two districts, Santa Ana and Labaconas, were responsible for managing 1,710 and 1,004 households, respectively. If each of these households had an average of three children, these local managers monitored whether 5,130 children in Santa Ana and 3,012 children in Labaconas attended health appointments or school, and whether an additional number of pregnant women attended their prenatal appointments. If the local managers failed to register this information in the system, Juntos would not release the payment.

In chapter 2, I discussed the failed agreements between Juntos and the Ministry of Health and the Ministry of Education that resulted in local managers having to complete additional paperwork. The agreements stipulated that health and education staff would fill out the Juntos verification-of-coresponsibility forms. In clinics this was supposed to occur when children and pregnant women attended the required checkups. In schools, the director or other staff person was supposed to use attendance records to fill out the Juntos forms. In practice this regularly failed to happen. According to Lina, one of the local managers: "As you've seen in Santa Ana, nobody helps you. Despite the fact that there is a signed agreement and this work is theirs to do, nothing. 'No, no, no, everyone does their own work, here are the histories,' they tell us: 'Do what you have to do, the clinic is all yours.' And they don't help us. . . . They say that they have too much work; they are very busy and they don't have time."

As a result, local managers were left to track down the necessary information on their own. This amounted to a significant burden on their time. Clinics and schools were located far apart, and local managers generally faced the same lack of transportation infrastructure as the women they managed. There was also the sheer number of children and pregnant women whose appointments had to be recorded.

This additional work, and the strategies local managers devised to accomplish it, had ramifications for mothers' managing up. One common strategy I observed was

FIGURE 12. Juntos recipients "managing up." Photo by the author.

for local managers to summon women to a central health clinic or municipal office, where local managers would fill out the coresponsibility forms on the spot. Such strategies, while helping local managers meet their own professional responsibilities, wasted women's time. The following vignette describes a scenario in which mothers were required to manage up. Over the course of two and a half ten-hour days, Juntos mothers queued in the courtyard of the health clinic in the district capital of Santa Ana. Directed by their Mother Leaders, who had been instructed by the local managers, to walk down to the clinic, women collected their medical histories from inside the building and stood waiting for the two local managers to input their information into the large coresponsibility forms (figure 12).

> The queues of mothers with small paper folders in hand stretch across the outdoor courtyard and spill into an unordered mass at the far end, enveloping two local managers who are seated at a desk under an awning that provides the only available shade. At 10 A.M., many women have their babies wrapped to their backs and have been on their feet for hours—the queue moves very slowly. Nearing the front third of the queue, Juntos mother Govinda tells me she has already been waiting for two and a half hours. The scene is noisy and chaotic, jostling bodies and crying babies. There is a nurse who brusquely patrols the courtyard, yelling at women to get in line and advising local managers not to attend to those who cut in.
> As the local managers decipher and transfer information between forms, mothers hover around and speak all at once, holding their histories out and asking to

be attended. Juntos mother Estrella stands in front of the desk, taking her turn. Estrella's name is not on the list for her village; the local manager asks her a series of questions to determine if she might be assigned to another village. Other mothers interrupt the questioning, asking to be attended, and the local manager pleads with them to wait their turn: "Please, listen to me!" They don't pay her any attention, and she says more forcefully: "Are you going to shut up?!" For a moment things become quieter, and the local manager makes a note of Estrella's name and village and promises to investigate later. Estrella exits the line, her program status unknown. Some of the mothers are missing information on the medical histories they present, such as their children's height and weight. These women are sent back inside the clinic to see if a staff person will fill out the health history, after which point they must get back in the queue and start again. The nurse continues to pester the women about getting in line.

It is hot, and the mothers, with their babies, stand uncomfortably in the sun. A couple of women begin to quarrel over another having cut in line; one local manager calls out, "What is going on?!" and the other yells, "Get in line! This isn't a line, it's a mob!" at which point she turns to a mother named Ynes and tells her in a flat voice that her daughter is underweight and marks a number on the form. Ynes collects her health card and disappears back into the clinic. Carla, who has been in the queue since I arrived three hours earlier, is questioned about where she currently resides; she reveals that she has moved to Cajamarca, which is not allowed (Juntos does not intervene in urban centers). The local managers consult, and one makes a "cut it" gesture with her hands to signal "no," and Carla walks away.

A baby screams, and another several start to cry. Some other women laugh. It is very loud. The nurse wants to know if the local managers will attend to the last person or if the remaining women should come back later. They say they will attend them a while longer, and the nurse says, "Yes, ok, but until what time, because the children are dying of hunger and the women want to leave and feed them." The local managers decide to attend the queue until 1 P.M., and then come back and finish at 2 P.M., leaving those women who have yet to be attended to wait. At this point there are only eight or ten mothers left.

With all of the walking and waiting, the scene at the health clinic bore striking similarities to the Juntos payday. Waiting for hours for the local manager's attention was a tedious and uncomfortable exercise for the mothers, many of whom had walked for hours to arrive there, and many others who had come with babies on their backs. At a later event at a municipal office, local managers similarly monitored women's compliance with health conditions. Rather naively, I questioned a fussing baby: "What's the matter, dear?" Her mother, Sol, turned to me and said with understandable impatience: "It is because we have been here since ten." The local manager had directed Sol to arrive at ten in the morning, which she did. However, the local manager arrived three hours late, at 1 P.M. When she arrived, she did not apologize for making the mothers wait. The local manager set straight to business: she took a seat at a desk and proceeded to summon the mothers one at a time to stand before her. She then set to transferring information from the medical histories the women had brought into the broad, white Juntos forms.

Some mothers waited for hours at the central clinic only to learn that the local manager had already been to their village and retrieved the information they required. As a result the mothers had waited in vain. In other cases women were unclear about which conditions they were actually required to meet. Other mothers waited, only to be informed by the local manager that they, too, had waited in vain because their children were all over five years of age (at which point Juntos monitored school attendance). In other cases, local managers informed waiting mothers that they would be suspended because their children had not attended all of the required health appointments. It was clear from the confounded expressions on the women's faces that they had been under the impression that they had done everything correctly. In such cases there were a number of possibilities for what had gone wrong. The mother may not have known or understood what was required of her to meet the health conditions (for instance, how many health appointments her children had to attend). She also may have forgotten to attend an appointment (the health clinic staff did not phone women to remind them of their appointments, a common practice in better-resourced health systems). The mother may also have delivered her children promptly to all of the required health appointments but the nurse had failed to properly record her attendance.

Sometimes women managed up because the local manager asked them to. In other cases, women managed up to make sure that the local manager had the correct information about their compliance with conditions. Juntos recipient Leocadia stood out from most of the other Juntos mothers because she wore Western dress. She arrived for our interview in trousers and a delicate colored scarf, the type that was made in a factory somewhere, rather than the *tejidos* women wove themselves in the villages. Leocadia was illiterate and cleaned a wealthier family's home in Cajamarca city on Saturdays to support her two children. The father of Leocadia's children was abusive. In order to escape him, Leocadia had moved her children from one village to another. In theory, Leocadia could have been expelled from Juntos for earning a salary that placed her household just above the imposed income threshold. Recognizing the risk but also needing the extra financial support the cash transfer offered single mothers, Leocadia went to great lengths to maintain her status as a Juntos recipient.

One persistent issue that Leocadia faced was that she and her children were still registered with Juntos in the village where their father resided. In addition to stipulations about income, Juntos had rules about residency and required mothers to present paperwork proving that their children were enrolled in school. Confronted with unresolved uncertainties and a complicated residency situation, Leocadia frequently sought out her local manager to make sure that her information was correctly registered "in the system" and that she would not end up erroneously suspended. I talked to Leocadia about her status.

TC: Have you ever been suspended?

Leocadia: No, I always [do what I'm supposed to]. They haven't suspended me yet. Who knows until when? [*laughs*]

TC: I've been told sometimes there are errors and some women end up suspended even when they've done [what they are supposed to].

Leocadia: Yes . . . sometimes [mothers] present a whole bunch of documents, and in the end it's like there was nothing at all in the system. In these cases we have to be [vigilant]. For example in my case, I collect [the transfer] in [a different village]. So I go to meetings here, but my name appears on the list over there. As I don't see or communicate with the [local manager] there, sometimes I go to find her. I go to the other village and I ask her if I'm missing anything, or if I've done something wrong. So she looks in the system and she says to me, "You are fine" or "You are missing this thing." And if I am missing something I go and bring it to her again.

Leocadia traveled three hours by foot and combi to reach the village where she was registered. The need for her to return there also meant that she might confront her abusive ex-partner. Yet as Leocadia noted, if she chose not to manage up in this way, she risked losing access to a consistent source of income that helped her meet her children's needs.

In rural Peru, moving was not an uncommon occurrence. Women migrated to find better schools for their children, to escape abusive relationships, or to seek family support after being abandoned by their spouses. Leocadia was willing to move to a new village, to live on her own, and to undertake poorly paid and often undignified domestic work in order to improve her children's opportunities. Had the cash transfer been unconditional, Leocadia would have confronted a different situation. An unconditional cash transfer would enable women like Leocadia to provide for her family in a (not uncommon) situation of violence while eliminating the need to waste her time. It would not eliminate all of her problems, but it would alleviate some of them.

Managing up involved paperwork. Retaining active status as a Juntos recipient required women to provide their local manager with photocopies of birth certificates, confirmation of school enrollment, graduation certificates, national identity documents, and "proof of residence" forms to indicate that they lived in a place that Juntos recognized as poor. Sometimes this involved a terrible runaround. The local manager could request that a mother produce a photocopy of a document that she did not have on hand; it might be at home in her village, which was located several hours away on foot. Managing up often also required women to navigate services and circumstances unfamiliar to them and to draw on resources and skills that they might not possess. During a verification of health coresponsibilities in Santa Ana, Juntos recipient Edelmira made four trips between the municipal office where the local manager was stationed and the photocopy shop. Each time, she returned with paperwork that did not satisfy the local manager. Like many Juntos recipients, Edelmira was illiterate and was unable to decipher what was on the paper. Edelmira paid for all of the unsatisfactory copies out of her own pocket. After the fourth trip, the local manager asked Edelmira to put the document on a USB, which is almost certainly a tool most Juntos mothers have never heard of. Edelmira's bewilderment was obvious, yet the local manager failed to acknowledge it and Edelmira left the office.

Local managers confessed to me that when mothers provided them with photocopies, the local managers often misplaced them or forgot to deal with them. Juntos recipients were not privy to what happened with their paperwork once the local manager tucked it into a backpack and returned to the city. As a result, for Juntos mothers the process of earning the cash incentive was mysterious. When their efforts to clarify or correct their program status were unfruitful, many women reported that it was as if "there was nothing at all in the system." It is little wonder that mothers like Leocadia and Sol walked and waited above and beyond what was necessary to attend health appointments and deliver their children to school. Mothers managed up because there was no other option. The enforcement and monitoring of conditionality in unevenly developed places required women to manage up. Conditionality was contingent upon women's willingness to walk and wait for stretches of time that would be unthinkable to ask of wealthier women or men in places made easier to navigate because they were better resourced.

Earlier in the chapter I suggested that in requiring women to walk and wait for social support, Juntos produced gendered patients of the state. Women's managing up illustrates that it was not only that Juntos made women patient. Managing up was a productive labor upon which Juntos relied. Women's walking and waiting were part of how local managers implemented Juntos. The women's labors were necessary in order for the state to implement a cash transfer that was conditional and tightly monitored.

This gendered labor—which was necessary from an administrative point of view—was unpaid and often demeaning. People "get a sense of [themselves]" while they wait in queues for state services (Corbridge 2007, 196). Put differently, people learn and relearn where they fit in society when they are made to wait for goods and services to which they are entitled or might simply just need. Provided they had met the program conditions, women had a right to the Juntos payment. The way that policy makers and program administrators in Lima talked about Juntos as a right trickled down to regional program staff, and some—but not many— mothers also related to me that Juntos was their right. Yet the walking and waiting and the circumstances under which these activities were carried out reinforced a system that "privilege[d] rank over rights" (Corbridge 2007, 196). Walking and waiting, sometimes to receive payment, sometimes to manage up, gave women a sense of their subordinate position in relation to all of the other people with whom they interacted. When women's labors failed to materialize in state records—having disappeared into the ever-mysterious system—they got a sense of their subordinate position then, too.[7] Women's time, needs, confusion, and dignity were of little import to the frontline state workers who came from the city to enforce the state's preferred schedule of caring and to monitor women's compliance with it.

We might say that women's walking and waiting "put them in their place." Like societies in many other parts of the world, Peruvian society is deeply hierarchical. Poor, rural campesinas occupy some of the lowest social rungs. To be sure, they occupied this position before Juntos arrived in their communities. Imposing a conditional program of social support simply reinforces their subordinate social position.

CONCLUSION

Most research on CCTs questions *if* the programs achieve high levels of compliance, rather than *how.* CCTs are not efficient when viewed from the perspective of the mothers who walk and wait for "a little bit of help" from the state. Juntos was rife with gendered inefficiencies. The time that mothers spent walking and waiting bolstered the administrative capacities of the Juntos program. This was time that could have otherwise been dedicated to subsistence farming, to assisting children with schoolwork, to weaving or cooking or helping a neighbor, to leisure. Juntos's gendered inefficiencies were made visible to me only after I accompanied women in their more mundane, everyday activities. Yet it was not only that mothers were asked to support a well-intentioned program and that their time was sacrificed, or even wasted, in the process. The wasting of women's time had the unintended consequence of putting women in their place.

This chapter could be read as evidence of failure in the implementation of an otherwise good policy. In this sense, the generalizability of my observations about managing up hangs on yet another empirical question—whether local managers' shortcomings were due to local discretion or to how the CCT was designed. It could be that mothers needed to manage up because their individual local managers were lazy or recalcitrant, or because these managers believed that the women had nothing better to do. An alternative explanation is that CCTs are designed in a way that makes it impossible for local managers to do the job that experts in Lima think they are doing. It could be that CCTs are designed in a way that relies on the unacknowledged contributions of women's unpaid labor. To examine these possible explanations, we must look at what it is that local managers are expected to do, as well as what they actually do.

5
_____

Paid and Unpaid Labor
on the Frontline State

My first opportunity to observe a local manager's work routines involved waking up at two o'clock in the morning. Local manager Paulino had asked me to meet him at a petrol station on the edge of Cajamarca city, from which a combi would depart in the darkness at three o'clock for Labaconas District. The shuddering old minibus was packed with dozing travelers, many of whom would disembark at one or another of the tiny villages tucked between the hairpin turns of the only road connecting Cajamarca to Labaconas. Over the course of two hours, as the combi snaked its way through the mountains, Paulino told me how he came to work for Juntos, what the work entailed, and what it meant to him personally. Efforts to evaluate social programs often focus on these programs' intended beneficiaries. Yet when we gloss over the people who implement social programs, or fail to take their experiences seriously, we miss an opportunity to identify unintended consequences and broader social impacts.

In previous chapters, I discussed how local managers relied on Juntos recipients to walk and wait and manage up in order to implement and monitor conditions. Did local managers in Cajamarca rely on mothers to help them do their jobs because they were lazy or felt entitled to make such requests? Or was this a larger institutional issue related to program design, in which case we could understand walking and waiting and managing up as instances of the state's reliance on women's unpaid labor? Conversations like the one I had with Paulino in the combi, and with other local managers over meals and in the clinics, schools, and Internet cafes where they did their work, helped me to answer these questions. In the following pages, I offer an unflinching account of just how difficult it is to be a Juntos local manager in a rural mountainous region. In addition to humanizing a cohort of workers who might otherwise be perceived as "bad actors," I hope to make a broader point about what we should expect to happen when policy makers require local workers to monitor and enforce conditions under impossibly difficult circumstances.

On an unusually bright day in the Andean rainy season, one of the local managers in Labaconas District invited me to attend a meeting in Tinca village. At the meeting, Juntos recipients were to elect a new committee of Mother Leaders, and the local manager was to guide this process. The local manager had often explained to me that "the Mother Leader is the local manager in her community." I was curious about these women, especially because I could not find very much information about them on the Juntos website or in the available research on CCT programs. The little information that I could locate described Mother Leaders differently than the local manager had. Generally Mother Leaders were introduced as an informal subset of "exemplary" CCT recipients who served as elected representatives of Juntos-affiliated households (Juntos 2011). In policy documents produced by the World Bank and the United Nations Development Programme, Mother Leaders were described as a resource for achieving program aims (Grosh et al. 2008; UNDP 2006).[1] I would eventually discover that Mother Leaders could be accurately described in all of these ways. By listening to local managers talk about their work, and by observing it in action, I was able to document these and several additional ways that the state relied on women's unpaid labor.

The meeting in question was held in a sky-blue village hall perched atop steep green fields already well fed by the recently begun rainy season. The village was located well above the district capital, and the local manager and I traveled there partway on a dirt bike, lent to the local manager by the mayor, and partway on foot, when the narrow footpath leading to the village became otherwise impassable. The village hall was dark and cool, a single room with a packed-earth floor. At the far end was a smokeless stove (*cocina mejorada*), which had been installed by a joint government and NGO initiative intent on improving women's health. The stove sat unused, however, and the women explained that "it doesn't work." A worker from that initiative later told me that many smokeless stoves sat unused because they had not been designed to accommodate the pots that women used for cooking—the stoves were too small.

The hall was furnished with a long table, a handful of wooden benches, and a small window through which the only light poured in. Women wearing muddy rubber boots arrived at the hall from the surrounding hills while, at the same time, drawing raw wool into a single strand of yarn and winding it on tall wooden *palitos* (sticks)—which they continued to do throughout the meeting. Twenty Juntos recipients attended the meeting, some of whom brought very young children; a few male partners sat along a bench near the back. Throughout the meeting five of the women bustled around a smoky stove (positioned beside the rejected, smokeless version), preparing a lunch of savory lentils and cabbage, which we all shared afterward. The following vignette is from my field notes, which begin by describing the selection of the new Mother Leaders committee.

> The local manager stands at the front of the room to present the six women currently serving as Mother Leaders. He asks the six women if indeed they want to elect new leaders; three are in strong agreement, the other three appear to be less so, but in the end they decide to go ahead with the election. All of the mothers in the room are talking among themselves, and the men in the corner raise their voices requesting the women to listen up, por favor! The seated men also reproach the women who are entering and exiting the hall preparing the lunch, telling them they will have time to cook later and that they should show some manners, which "they obviously don't have." The women disregard the men's comments and continue cooking. A number of mothers suggest potential nominees, at which point the local manager urges those nominated to come forward. They do, albeit most of them rather timidly.
>
> Gesturing to the nominees one by one, the local manager asks for a show of hands to determine who will occupy each of the six positions. One nominee, a woman named Lourdes, who is older than the rest, tells the local manager that she has been ill and is tired, and worries she wouldn't be able to do the walking required; apologizing, she says she'd prefer not to be considered. A younger woman, named Rosa, is nominated for treasurer, but the local manager elicits from her the information that she is illiterate and suggests the women elect someone else. They do so, and Rosa is given a position that doesn't require literacy. She will be a "vocal," a committee member who travels from house to house communicating information verbally. The friendly woman seated to my left is Maria. She tells me that she is twenty-nine years of age and a mother to three children. After watching me scribble notes in my field book, Maria volunteers that she is illiterate "and doesn't know anything" (no sé nada), with the kind of giggle I came to learn accompanied statements that were funny and not funny, alike. When the election is over, the new Mother Leaders return to their seats.
>
> The local manager then raises the issue of health and education conditions (co-responsibilities), and speaks for fifteen or twenty minutes about how important it is that mothers meet these. If they do not, they will not receive their two hundred soles. He talks first about education and how their children need to study to "keep progressing." Afterward he transitions to nutrition, bringing up the municipality's guinea pig project for Juntos mothers. He makes a joke that the women must give the child the guinea pig's leg and the father the head, not the other way around, which elicits laughter. He then brings up the forthcoming reproductive-health training at the municipality in Labaconas. He says that it is important for the Mother Leaders to attend, because there are a lot of pregnant women who "continue having more and more babies."
>
> The local manager tells the mothers not to let other people call them lazy or tell them that they don't work for their Juntos payment (soles). A number of women chime in, confirming that they've weathered these accusations, and that it isn't true, they aren't lazy. Finally, the local manager speaks about the responsibilities specific

to Mother Leaders. They are expected to be "very self-sacrificing" despite their work not being remunerated. The Mother Leaders speak up in agreement with this; several women comment that they must travel very far to get to the meetings that local managers frequently call.

The meeting provided a view into the relationship between local managers and the select group of CCT recipients called Mother Leaders. It also indicated the importance of this relationship to Juntos's capacity to operate in the isolated and unevenly developed places that it did. In fact, the large body of research on CCT programs reveals very little about the people who carry out local-level program implementation or how they carry it out. As a result, we have an incomplete understanding of how unintended impacts are produced.

This chapter zooms in on two sets of actors formally and informally tasked with local-level program implementation—local managers and Mother Leaders. In this this book I have already introduced local managers and illustrated some of what their work entailed. In this chapter I delve deeper into what they were expected to do and what they did. Mother Leaders receive limited attention in policy-oriented literature; and where they *are* discussed, they are not the focus of the study (IEP 2009; Vargas Valente 2010; Molyneux and Thomson 2011). To my knowledge, no comprehensive academic analysis of Mother Leaders exists.

In the villages of Cajamarca, Mother Leaders were far more visible than they were in the literature on CCTs, and the role they played was significant. Given this, the sporadic and passing references to Mother Leaders' in the literature is surprising. Why do we know so little about them? Mother Leaders' work is not formally recognized in policy; analysis at that scale could quite easily miss them. Similarly, surveys or structured-interview research that approached program recipients as a homogenous group could easily overlook Mother Leaders. In contrast, evidence presented here illustrates the work practices and processes required to implement Juntos and, in doing so, uncovers additional layers of gendered labor and social costs.

Before I turn to the relationship between local managers and Mother Leaders, it is necessary to establish the existence of the gap that Mother Leaders helped local managers fill. This requires a look at what Lima expected local managers to do and the conditions under which they were expected to do it.

LOCAL MANAGERS

The Juntos experts we met in chapter 2 relied on a range of local managers to implement the program in its rural areas of intervention. Frontline state workers, whether bureaucrats in urban welfare offices or project implementers in rural villages, mediate the relationship between the state and its citizens (Lipsky 1980; Mosse 2005; Goetz 2001; Hossain 2010). This role imbues them with significant power at a local level. Frontline state workers are authorized to make decisions that affect the lives of the people they are intended to serve, and sometimes their unauthorized decisions make just as great an impact. This includes assessments of poor people's eligibility for government benefits and sanctions, as well as state workers' choices influencing the treatment poor people receive as they participate in state-sponsored programs (Lipsky 1980). The decisions that these workers make are influenced by their own biographies: their gender, ethnicity, and social class. These and other identities shape how they relate to the beneficiaries of the programs they implement and, in turn, how beneficiaries experience the state (Watkins-Hayes 2009; Hossain 2010; Radcliffe and Webb 2015).

In the case of Juntos, frontline state workers and the mothers and children they managed belonged to distinct social classes. Local managers often were technical-school- or university-educated, lived in urban district or regional capitals, and wore Western dress. Before finding employment with Juntos, many worked as teachers, nurses, or professionals in other social programs. Local managers belong to Peru's "new middle class." Many of them came from poor families and were the first to receive secondary or postsecondary education. They spoke proudly of the sacrifices their parents had made to see their children "progress" in life (*seguir adelante*). It was evident from my observations and in conversations with the local managers that their personal histories and professional identities shaped the way that they carried out their work and interacted with the mothers they managed.

Hundreds of miles and mountains away from Juntos's head offices, local managers encouraged women to meet program conditions, work that they often referred to as making sure mothers "changed their behavior." They visited clinics and schools to verify that mothers had met the required conditions, and they managed data related to affiliations and suspensions by "entering the system" (*entrar el sistema*) on computers at the Juntos head office and in Internet cafés. Local managers advised women when payday would take place, and then they supervised the occasion. They coordinated with health and education staff and other social services to ensure that babies had birth certificates, that children were enrolled in school, and that health staff knew when the local managers would be monitoring women's compliance with conditions.

While these tasks may seem fairly straightforward, the unevenly developed landscapes over which Juntos was implemented made the work time-consuming and complex. Local managers' implementation work was geographically spread out over Cajamarca city and the countryside. Cajamarca is a city of 218,000 inhabitants, and because of its close proximity to the world's second-largest gold mine, the city had a number of "developed" comforts, such as public and private hospitals, an international school, taxis, a modern shopping mall, and Internet cafes. Yet outside the district and regional capital cities, the countryside lacked modern infrastructure and was largely isolated from urban resources. Local managers traveled frequently between the rural communities they managed and Cajamarca city, where they reported to their superiors, attended professional development train-ings, accessed administrative infrastructure including computers and the Internet, and spent time with their families. As a result, much of local managers' work was spent in transit, either on the treacherous, winding mountain roads that connected urban and rural spaces, or on the quiet, steep footpaths between villages.

Every month, the local managers drew up a schedule detailing their forthcom-ing trips and implementation activities. However, they rarely kept to this schedule, as circumstances in the field were unpredictable. Sometimes paperwork sent from Lima was delayed, or whatever Internet access was available in the district capital went out, or they were not able to track down records for new births because the health clinic was closed.[2] One local manager, Elena, described to me the unpre-dictability of her monitoring work in the district of Labaconas, which took her between that district and Cajamarca city:

> During the first training session, they told us that we could work accumulating hours: for example, if the month has twenty-two workdays, I could work these straight through, including Saturdays and Sunday, and the eight remaining days could be taken as days off, also accumulated, no? I could maybe visit home, do whatever I like. But when it came to down to it, the work wasn't like that. For example, we're in the countryside for six days, eight days, then [for some reason] we have to use the [Juntos online user database] system, so we come to Cajamarca because in Labaco-nas there isn't Internet; and when there is, it is very slow and hardly works. So I come back, I'm in Cajamarca for two, three days, and then I go back again, and then come back again, and that's what it's like. . . . Because all of the information that we gather in the countryside has to be entered into the system. And this is our work in Juntos.

In order to effectively monitor conditions, local managers were required to be adaptable and resourceful. Implementing Juntos was physically and temporally demanding, and the requirements of the work had gendered costs for the local managers and their families. Local managers were required to spend long stretches of time away from home, which had negative implications for their family life. Of the three female Juntos local managers with whom I interacted closely, one worked while eight months pregnant, another found it difficult to manage childcare, and the third confided that she had no idea how her female colleagues with babies were able to get their work done at all. Given the structure of the work, she imagined that if she were to have children she would have to quit her job. The male local managers who had children, and a spouse at home to assume caring responsibili-ties, did not have to quit their jobs in order to have a baby, but they did lament the infrequency with which they saw their families. My observations were consis-tent with a trend identified by other feminist scholars of international develop-ment: the historic domination of the public sector by male employees conditioned organizational practices and processes to reflect men's traditional roles and needs, which largely excluded reproductive responsibilities (Goetz 1997).

To arrive at their respective districts, local managers traveled in combis, privately owned minibuses that were infamous for having intoxicated drivers and for traveling at high speeds over treacherous mountain passes. Within the districts, much of local managers' time was spent visiting villages, many of which are accessible only by foot. During the period of my research, Juntos purchased motorcycles for the local managers to use between villages. They were expected to get training in Cajamarca city on how to operate them. Paulino, one of two male local managers in my fieldwork sites, was very pleased about this; he had already been using the motorcycle provided to him by the district government in Labaconas, and he knew how to operate it.[3] Female local managers were less enthusiastic. One of the local managers had no intention of using the motorcycle because it frightened her, and another said that she would learn, but that it was scary because it was so large. Local manager Lina described the travel that Juntos required of her:

> Unfortunately, there isn't always transportation in the places where I work. Only on Thursdays. But now they've given us a motorbike, just recently this month. Thank God, so now we'll go on the motorbike. But before, I did my work walking. Fifteen hours, twelve hours. Sometimes there is a combi [in which to travel to a central village], so then we have to leave at three or four o'clock in the morning to get to the educational institution to verify coresponsibilities. So we manage with whatever we've got, be it combi or motorbike or even on foot to get the job done.

The rumbling combis were not equipped with Wi-Fi, and so the time spent in transit could not be dedicated to advancing in their work. The hours spent in travel to and from the villages were additional to those considered official working hours; the legally sanctioned eight-hour workday very often became a twelve- or fifteen-hour workday.

In order to capture the data on compliance that policy administrators in Lima required, local managers had to arrive on time at clinics and schools by any means available, even when this required them to rent rooms in family homes in the district capital or sleep in village health posts that were not equipped as overnight accommodations (i.e., did not have proper beds). Renting accommodations in the field placed a significant financial burden on local managers, all of whom also rented or owned homes in the capital city, where their families resided. Local managers often remarked that once the costs of lodging and food were accounted for, they were unable to accumulate any savings. Local manager Lina described the days-long routes she traveled to monitor women's compliance with conditions:

> Yes, I stay over[night], I stay up there, Tarita. I stay in the health posts. My route is Cajamarca to Santa Ana, Santa Ana to Seladin, I go through Seladin to Chan Chan, three and a half hours walking. In Chan Chan I verify coresponsibilities in education, and in health. I do that all afternoon and into the night, and then I stay there overnight in the health post. From there I go up walking five hours to Palo Blanco, Nuevo Hallaqui, Matirca, verifying in these communities. So then I start over in

Palo Blanco and from there go up to San Pablo, again! Another route. I go up from Santa Ana through Bombacana to San Marcos, which is about ten hours. And then from there I come down again, until I arrive at the district capital, and then back to Cajamarca, and start on another route.

The local managers' direct supervisor, Ofelia, described the imperative to collect the data: "The local manager has to verify coresponsibilities. They have to go from sunrise to sunset, in the sun, rain, shade, hail, no hail: it doesn't matter, *they still have to go.*" When experts claim that CCTs are efficient, they typically are not counting the time, expense, and physical effort required of frontline staff to verify conditions in regions that receive disproportionately little investment in basic infrastructure.

When I arrived in Cajamarca, Juntos management had recently implemented a new procedure to monitor and cut down on staff absenteeism. Local managers were required to "clock in" when in Cajamarca city, and to have local authorities such as the school director or mayor sign a paper acknowledging their presence when in the field. The regional Juntos administrator, the local managers' direct supervisor, and three local managers had all told me on separate occasions that instead of traveling in the countryside between communities, some local managers had been turning off their mobile phones and "hiding at home." Some members of management were sympathetic about this alleged practice, acknowledging that local managers' work was extremely difficult. Ofelia explained to me how it looked from her perspective:

There's a percentage of [local managers] who don't get to all of their communities—for example, in Cospan. Sometimes as a [supervisor] I'd say, "This guy doesn't work! He doesn't enter the coresponsibilities [information] properly!" So I went to Cospan, and there wasn't a motorbike! I had to walk for seven hours. Do you think with the salary they pay me that I'm going to go there? I'd kill myself! No! So, since then I was able to understand that, as a [supervisor], I couldn't always be so demanding—because *we don't see* how the [local managers] suffer in the field, the hours they have to walk, how *terrible* it is.

The demands placed on local managers were obvious to me, too, but I never observed a local manager hiding from work or dishonestly filling out verification-of-coresponsibility forms when she or he had not actually monitored women's compliance. In light of my conversations with local managers and other local Juntos staff, and also my broader observations about the political economy of northern Andean Peru at the time, I'm convinced that local managers had clear motivations for showing up to work and, as they frequently said, "getting the job done."

First, they believed that the mission of their work—helping families overcome poverty—was important, even though they were also critical of how they were required to spend their time. During a conversation in a small, Van Gogh–themed café in Cajamarca city, local manager Elena explained to me that her own social position informed how she approached her work: "I was born and grew up in the *campo* (countryside), in a rural area, so I admire campesinos because I am also campesina, my parents are campesinos. When I return home, my father has his cows, his fields—and I always return there. I like the campo because it is my home, it is my reality. So I feel proud when I see campesino people progress, when they get ahead in life, you know?"

A second source of motivation is that many local managers belong to Peru's new and precarious middle class.[4] Many new middle-class families are just a little above the poverty line, and a shock such as loss of employment would be devastating. Other than work in the new social programs such as Juntos, employment opportunities were limited in Cajamarca. Even the gold mine, Yanacocha, was laying off employees. Juntos's local managers worked on a three- or six-month contractual basis, and the possibility that the contract might not be renewed was not worth risking.[5] Local managers were close enough to poverty, whether because it was the subject of their work or because they had been born into it themselves, that showing up to work was the reasonable thing to do.[6]

MASS-PROCESSING COMPLIANCE DATA

In Lima, experts at MIDIS and Juntos emphasized that the most important work local managers did was, first, to make sure that women and their children used health and education services and, second, to "verify coresponsibilities" (monitor women's compliance), as the local managers referred to it. According to the accounts of local managers, monitoring women's compliance with program conditions at all of the health and education facilities in their districts took approximately a month. The number of schools and clinics they had to visit in each city and village varied. For instance, the health center in the district capital of Santa Ana served hundreds of families, while a small post in an isolated village served far fewer. As noted earlier, in Santa Ana District two local managers shared responsibility for managing 1,710 households. In Labaconas District, two others were responsible for managing 1,004 households. This meant that the two pairs monitored the compliance of 1,710 and 1,004 women, respectively. Yet the most important figures for understanding the scale of the local managers' monitoring work have to do with how many children and pregnant women lived in those households. Local managers were required to track the service usage of every pregnant woman and every child under the age of nineteen residing in a Juntos-affiliated household. If, on average, every mother enrolled in the Juntos program had three children, this would mean that local managers monitored the school attendance and health service usage of 5,130 children in Santa Ana and 3,012 children in Labaconas. The number of pregnant women whose attendance at prenatal appointments they monitored would be in addition to these two figures. By all accounts, local managers were required to mass-process the mothers and children they managed.[7]

FIGURE 13. Monitoring conditions in education. Photo by the author.

Local managers deployed a number of creative strategies in order to accomplish this mass-processing. When staff at clinics and schools did not cooperate in producing the attendance records and medical records that local managers required, the local managers worked around them. For example at a high school in Santa Ana District, the school administrator was upset that her own children did not qualify for Juntos. As a result, she refused to facilitate the local manager's monitoring work. In response, the local manager deployed what other local managers confirmed was a common strategy—soliciting the attendance information from the students themselves. On one such instance, I observed the local manager ask a small group of students in the school courtyard to summon their peers, and we sat on a bench and waited for them to crowd around us. The local manager pulled the large paper verification-of-coresponsibility forms from her backpack and, taking up a pencil, proceeded to call out the students' names one by one (figure 13). She operated methodically. After calling out a name, she would wait for the students gathered around us to confirm whether that individual was enrolled and attending class. Depending on their response, she would check "yes" or "no" in the corresponding box.

Local managers also used this strategy when they perceived that school administrators failed to keep accurate or updated attendance records. The local managers insisted that children "didn't lie," and that asking them to report on their peers was much quicker than navigating school records. While this method of data collection saved local managers time, it was also, from the perspective of Juntos mothers, fraught with opportunities for error. On a number of occasions I watched the local manager record a "no," only to have that student appear running from within the school to correct the erroneous information. Had the student not heard from her peers that she had been marked as no longer attending school, the girl's mother would have been suspended from the Juntos program.

In previous chapters I discussed how frequent clinic closures and absenteeism made it difficult for Juntos mothers to obtain care and meet program conditions in a reasonable manner. The unreliable nature of services also negatively affected the time and effort local managers had to expend on monitoring conditions. On several occasions I accompanied a local manager to a health post only to find it locked up and deserted during "open" hours, with the responsible staff absent. The consequence of this was that the local managers had to return the next day and try again, returning to the clinic until they were able to obtain the data that Juntos required. Even when the health posts were open, local managers encountered complications in collecting the required data.

On a warm day in May, two local managers, Lina and Silvia, and the new local-manager trainee, Felipe, monitored conditions at the central health clinic in the district capital of Santa Ana. Over the course of the previous two days, the local managers had asked mothers from the surrounding villages that were managed by either Lina or Silvia to wait in lines with their children's medical histories so that the local managers could transfer the information into the verification-of-coresponsibility forms. Even after asking mothers to manage up, local manager Lina was still missing compliance data for a number of women and children. As a result, she had to ask the clinic to allow her access to medical files, in which she and the trainee, Felipe, would attempt to locate the missing information. The following field notes describe what this entailed:

> We are inside the building, in the obstetrician's office, which has a painted indicator on the wall of the work done there: "Women's Health." The nurse on duty tells Lina that she doesn't have time to help her because she has to attend a delivery, so Lina asks for her book to see the list of births for the past two months. The book is a simple, lined notebook, filled out by hand. Lina and the new local manager start filling out the Juntos forms using the information the notebook provides. Lina also takes information from a chart with pockets and medical histories that is hung on the wall. The medical histories look complicated to me, and the work is slow. Lina tells me that the staff is of no help here, and they never help because they don't know how to fill out the Juntos forms.
>
> Lina and the other local managers can't find a few of the medical histories that they need. After forty-five minutes the nurse comes back and offers to help find the ones they are missing. She reads out the information from them and Lina fills in the form. Nothing is digitized, so it is a process of sifting through histories and personal health pamphlets, although with the nurse's help it is faster. In total, information is gathered for fewer than a dozen women over the course of an hour. Next we go into

a small room behind the front desk where all of the medical histories are kept, stacks and stacks of folders and pamphlets on metal shelves. Lina has to find the information on the children missed while she was verifying coresponsibilities over the past week. The histories are organized according to village and name, but they look through every folder in a given section because they are out of order. Lina says this is the process in all of the health posts, just looking through files. She spent all Saturday doing this as well. Lina goes to ask the nurse if there are any new pregnant mothers for March or April, and the nurse says yes but they don't have them in one file. The nurse looks for some, gives the names and dates of their last menstrual period, and Lina writes this down. We move on to look for information on the recent births.

Searching through files took two hours at the end of two consecutive long workdays monitoring conditions elsewhere, and Lina (as well as Felipe and Silvia) had to return the following day to finish the task (figure 14). This effort was expended on one clinic and, over the course of a month, was repeated at smaller clinics along the routes that the local managers each traveled.

Filling out the forms used to monitor women's compliance was time-consuming because it required local managers to find and transfer information. The local managers' direct supervisor explained to me that local managers received an email instructing them on how to fill out the education and health forms, and that this level of instruction was inadequate. Whereas the education forms were relatively straightforward, the health forms required local managers to gather and interpret technical medical information (figure 15). The majority of local managers were not trained as health professionals, and as a result, while some local managers reported that they picked up the terms and abbreviations quickly, it took others longer to develop a working knowledge. Medical histories with checkup dates, and vaccination and height and weight data, were often missing information, were illegible, and had bits of paper with supplementary data stapled to them. The local managers navigated these inconsistent paper trails, and they exercised discretion when they were provided with imperfect information. Local manager Paulino, who was a former public school teacher, explained how he and his colleagues relied on whatever help they could get from the health staff:

Paulino: The agreement that the Juntos program has with the Ministry of Health is that the personnel in the health posts will fill out the forms. But they don't do it. We have to do it ourselves. They do help us, because we don't have—we don't know the technical words that the health personnel use. More than anything, we just don't understand, so they help us and support us. . . . They use symbols, for example STP, which means a measles vaccine.

   TC: Ok, so you've learned a lot.

Paulino: Something, sure. Sure. Or sometimes there is a term about pregnancy that we don't know—"self-measurement," we don't know it; "perimeter" I think they call it—that we don't understand, so we ask and they tell us.

FIGURE 14. Local managers search for missing or misplaced medical histories. Photo by the author.

FIGURE 15. Local manager Lina reads a medical history to determine a mother's compliance. Photo by the author.

As local managers and their direct supervisor rightly insisted, it would be misguided to demonize local health staff, who worked under their own institutional constraints and were not trained by their own superiors to fill out the Juntos forms. Their supervisor, Ofelia, describes a conversation with a colleague from university who now works as a nurse. The two of them had been discussing Juntos and the work of monitoring women's compliance with program conditions:

> The [health personnel] don't collaborate in the work, no? Despite the fact that it is their responsibility, they don't see it like that—I'd imagine because of their workload. A [university] colleague of mine explained to me that it's terrible to fully complete a [child's growth and development controls], I think she said it takes up to an hour to do it well.[8] "And imagine it now!" she said to us, "when we have all this burden and then on top of it the Juntos program, [whose users] come and demand it of you—and really they demand it of you, because if not *they suspend them*." . . . Imagine that, on top of all this, they have to fill out the coresponsibilities form, that as you've seen is a "bedsheet," as we say [because of the color and size], because it is, you know?

The health and education staff I interviewed did not always agree with the way Juntos was implemented, a finding that corroborates survey data captured by MIDIS (MIDIS 2013a). The head nurse, Lisella, at the health post in Sonsonate had worked in the area for twenty years. She did not approve of the conditional aspect of the Juntos program, which she saw as overriding a more important focus on the actual health of the children:

> Yes, [the Juntos local manager comes to the clinic]. She comes but . . . once a month, or once every two months. The work—well to me it's *bad*. It's *really bad*. Because [the local manager] comes and she says, "Eh, let's see, I'm going to [verify coresponsibilities] for the beneficiaries." . . . She comes and takes the [medical] history and she looks over it. "Let's see, this boy," for example, "this boy Andreo, who doesn't have a [national identity document], is five months old, and came on such and such a date and had his checkup." And that's it. *That's* her work. She doesn't see if the boy is maybe malnourished, and if so, *why*. Nor does she try to say to [the mother], "*Look,* you are the beneficiary, they give you this money, they give it to you so that you *purchase* food for your *child*." She *doesn't see this.* She doesn't see this. . . . I think that as she is the program representative, she should do this follow-up. None of this telling the family, "Your child is malnourished, malnourished, malnourished," and then what? There isn't a *single* good result. *There aren't* results.

Health staff and frontline Juntos personnel, while often frustrated with one another, expressed similar concerns about a programmatic focus on compliance that overlooked more substantive impacts on health and education. While the nurse wasn't aware of the institutional dynamics shaping how local managers used their time, she accurately identified a programmatic prioritization of box checking.

When local managers expended over half of their time sifting through files and filling in forms, they had less contact with the households they managed. This was an (unfortunately missed) opportunity for the state to develop a more substantive understanding of the barriers and constraints women faced in caring for their families. Perhaps even more significantly, it meant local managers had less time for monitoring and reporting on the quality of services that program recipients were required to use. This was also an aspect of the local managers' job description, but one that I never observed being carried out. What the nurse did not articulate was the fact that this dynamic, rather than being a result of local managers' individual decisions, was a result of institutional choices that elided questions about quality and engagement in favor of recording a narrow set of metrics related to behavioral change. As a consequence, the relationship that the state had with rural mothers and their children via the local managers was largely about disciplining behavior and collecting data on how effectively this had been accomplished.

Once the local managers had collected all of the compliance data from the clinics and schools in their districts, they returned to Cajamarca city to input it into "the system," an online database that centralized and processed information for the purposes of determining which mothers would "collect" (*cobrar*) the cash payment and which would be suspended. Local managers had a tightly limited amount of time to accomplish this work. After the deadline imposed by the head office in Lima, the local managers were unable to emend information. The potential consequence of this for Juntos mothers was erroneous suspension. If the local manager did not finish entering all of the data into the system before the deadline, the mothers whose compliance information was left out of the system would be suspended.

In theory, local managers were meant to input the data using the computers at the regional head office. However, because the Cajamarca office was cramped and there were not enough computers to go around, several of the local managers brought their verification-of-coresponsibility forms to one of two Internet cafes and entered the information there. This was often done at their own expense, as local manager Elena explained to me: "Yes, we pay [for the Internet ourselves]. At first they gave us ten hours of [reimbursed] Internet [access], but these days I think that the budget—well, as there is no administrator,[9] eh, they haven't given it to us. We have to pay for it out of our own pocket. . . . But like I said, these days there's nothing. So if you don't finish your work in these ten hours, you have to pay out of your own pocket [in a café] wherever you want."

I observed Elena input data over a period of three days. In the crowded and noisy Internet café, she positioned the stack of completed forms below the keyboard on her lap and worked carefully to transfer the information correctly, double-checking her work before pressing "submit." It seemed to me that in spite of her diligence, there was a significant margin for error in this process owing to the distractions of the busy public café and the sheer size and detail of the forms. When deadlines were tight, local managers who had Internet access in their houses resorted to taking the forms home and soliciting family help. The local managers' direct supervisor, Ofelia, explained to me that the time-pressed task of entering data into the system also involved resources in addition to Internet access:

> I've always said this, and I also have evidence of it, that working for Juntos, Tara, is a family job. Because if you go to a local manager's house, in the field they collect a mountain of paperwork—birth certificate photocopies and things—because they have to update their work in the office too. So what happens? [She] is in her house with her boxes of paperwork, and her son knows how to do the titleholder change, and if her children are already in primary or secondary, they're *entering the system!* And her husband is filing [paperwork] in the folders, and the grandparents. I'm convinced that if you ask any family member of a Juntos worker, they know what a "titleholder change" is, they know what a "coresponsibility" is. They know because that's how a Juntos worker is, that's how their work is.[10]

This practice, which was not officially sanctioned by Juntos superiors, highlights the effort and cost of monitoring women's behavior and producing the data meant to demonstrate that imposing conditions is effective.

In addition to inputting compliance information every two months, local managers were responsible for keeping the system updated with other relevant information about the Juntos mothers' eligibility. For instance, when a baby was born to a Juntos mother, local managers were tasked with affiliating the baby to the program. Conversely, if a local manager discovered that a household was not meeting program conditions—for instance, if a youth had dropped out of school, or if a Juntos mother had migrated for work and was not residing in Juntos's area of intervention, the local manager was required to suspend the household through the online system. In order to do so, the local manager needed a functioning Internet connection. However in rural areas, Internet connectivity was limited to the district capitals, and even there it frequently failed. As a result, local managers often made unscheduled and time-consuming trips back to Cajamarca city when they needed to verify or update information regarding a Juntos user.

This was made very clear to me one day when I was observing the work of local manager Paulino in Labaconas District.

> During his rounds of the village, Paulino receives a call from Paula, the Juntos regional director. She asks him to come back to Cajamarca because there are twenty-five kids that have been missed in the system and, if they are not entered, then the mothers will not get their money on the upcoming payday. So we go to the municipal hall to try to "enter the system," but the Internet in the mayor's office is not working. The other local manager with whom he shares this district, Elena, is in Cajamarca but is not answering her phone, so Paulino says he will have to return to the city to do it. He tells me this is inconvenient, because it is expensive for him to return and come back to Labaconas again the next day. He decides to break for lunch and try again afterward.
>
> Later on, we return to the municipality to try the Internet in the office of the Glass of Milk Program director, who has offered Paulino the use of his computer. The Internet is very slow, but it works after the director resets the modem a few times. Paulino's new Juntos email account does not work, but he manages to get hold of Elena and she gives him the password to hers. In the email it turns out that there are seven children missing from the registry, not twenty-five. Paulino enters the children into the system. The Internet crashes several times, and he must start from the beginning each time. Because of the Internet problems, the whole process takes just under two hours. From what I can see, with a functioning Internet connection it should have taken fifteen minutes at most.

Because of the hours spent trying to access the Internet, Paulino was unable to attend to other tasks, including visiting a health post. On this particular day, he had no contact with Juntos mothers or their children, or local health or education staff. The only reason he did not have to make the long trip back to Cajamarca city to ensure that women's compliance was properly registered was because of the relationships he had formed with the municipal government, a member of which allowed him use of his imperfect Internet connection. Many of the Juntos staff that I spoke with who worked in the Cajamarca region told me that they believed Juntos's mission, to help people overcome poverty, was a good one. Yet situations like these were frustrating. Local managers felt that they spent too much time on activities that did not make a difference.

Despite the difficulties local managers encountered in meeting their professional responsibilities, I observed that, by and large, they "got the job done."
Imperative to doing so was the support of local actors who were not on Juntos's
payroll. Local managers built relationships with health, education, and other social
service personnel in the communities where Juntos intervened. These relationships
provided them with the resources that Juntos did not always provide: transportation, Internet access, a place to sleep. Local managers also relied on an additional
group of local-level actors who were not on the payroll of any government body at
all—Mother Leaders. The next section explores local managers' relationships with
other professionals and their relationships with Mother Leaders.

MOTHER LEADERS

One of the local managers' more significant resources for getting their work done
was a select group of Juntos recipients called Mother Leaders.[11] In the opening
paragraphs of this chapter I described an election for a new Mother Leader committee in Tinca village in Labaconas. That particular committee consisted of six
members, although my research revealed variation in the formation and presence of Mother Leader committees elsewhere. Some villages had a single Mother
Leader, while other, larger villages had a hierarchically organized committee of six
or eight members including a president, treasurer, secretary, and so on. Mother
Leader committees in the districts of this study ranged between two and eight
members. In 2010, there were a reported 687 Mother Leaders throughout Juntos's
area of intervention (Vargas Valente 2010), although a rough calculation based
on Juntos-hosted workshops with Mother Leaders in the same year suggests that
there might have been nearly twice that many. For perspective, this means that
Mother Leaders far outnumbered local managers.

Local managers in Labaconas and Santa Ana worked in close collaboration with
Mother Leaders, and for this reason, they developed preferences regarding the characteristics of the ideal Mother Leader. Most of the Mother Leaders in the fieldwork
sites of this study were literate. Before arriving at the meeting in Tinca, the local manager recounted that he and his colleague had decided that they would accept only
literate candidates who had at least a minimum of primary school education, remark-
ing, "If not, how are they going to serve their community?" According to another
local manager, "The Mother Leader has to be someone who at the very least knows
how to read. And who is dynamic, attentive. No? Who likes to participate, is someone who works on behalf of her companions." Some Mother Leaders had previous
experience as *promotoras comunales* (voluntary community workers) in other social
programs, and they tended to be the most outspoken Juntos recipients at community meetings. All of the Mother Leaders I interacted with owned mobile telephones,
which they used to communicate with local managers, although they often (understandably) complained that Juntos did not compensate them for the cost of airtime.

Local managers often explained to me that the Mother Leader was "the local manager in her community." This description pointed to the important role that these women played in program implementation. One of the few mentions of Mother Leaders that I could locate on the Juntos website was a press release that described the role of Mother Leaders as follows:

> In every community where Juntos intervenes, Mother Leaders help local managers guide and sensitize Juntos mothers so that they meet their coresponsibilities regarding health and education. Regarding health conditions, the Mother Leader helps identify pregnant women and promote the registration of all members of Juntos households for Public Health Insurance (SIS), attend health checkups, and through the local manager, inform Juntos if the household members are treated well in health establishments. Regarding education, the Mother Leader helps to identify all school-age minors in Juntos households, ensures that they are enrolled in and regularly attend an educational institution, and contributes to preventing tardiness, absences, and dropouts (UCI 2013).

My village-level observations confirmed that Mother Leaders performed many of these tasks, in addition to meeting the conditions that were imposed on Juntos recipients. Through these tasks, Mother Leaders helped local managers implement Juntos, and they also helped other mothers ensure that they received the cash incentive.

The press release above suggests that Mother Leaders would help Juntos understand how mothers were being treated in health establishments; my research shows that this point is highly questionable. As discussed in chapter 2, experts at Juntos and MIDIS were well aware of the poor quality of health services in rural Peru. Given what the experts perceived to be their inability to improve the services, they had narrowed the program focus to making sure that women and children used the services available, quality notwithstanding. Bearing this in mind, I'd like to further explore the contributions of Mother Leaders in the context of a narrow programmatic focus on achieving women's behavioral change. Put otherwise, how were Mother Leaders implicated in enforcing conditionality?

BEING THE STATE'S EYES AND EARS

Local managers relied on Mother Leaders to help them maintain a presence in Juntos communities when they could not be there themselves. When I interviewed head office staff from the Verification of Coresponsibilities Unit in Lima, which was charged with overseeing policy and practice related to conditionality, they described Mother Leaders as the local managers' primary point of contact in the field: "When the local manager returns [to the district], *their first point of contact* to learn about what has happened in these fifteen or twenty days in which *the local manager hasn't been there*, is the Mother Leader." This dynamic of Mother Leaders' work was given an embodied quality in a Juntos training guide:

REMEMBER! THE MOTHER LEADER is THE EYES and EARS of the Juntos Program in their community. We value the support they offer the Juntos Local Manager, by informing them of the needs of beneficiary mothers and of any change in the socio-economic situation, family composition, residency status, health problems, access or difficulties fulfilling coresponsibilities, new pregnancies, recent births, and changes to school enrollment that might come up in the households of their communities (Juntos 2011, original emphasis).[12]

Local managers relied upon the information that Mother Leaders provided them to ensure that the Juntos database was up to date, and that only those women who met the program requirements received the cash payment. In practice, acting as the Juntos program's eyes and ears meant monitoring the behaviors of their neighbors.

This eyes-and-ears dynamic was evident at a meeting in the district capital of Labaconas, when the Juntos regional coordinator asked a roomful of quietly seated Mother Leaders to inform their local managers about households that had "unregistered" children.[13] One of the local managers then read aloud the names of children whose identity document numbers were missing from the system, so that Mother Leaders could collect the required information. On this and other occasions, local managers relied on Mother Leaders to help them accomplish administrative tasks, as Paulino explained to me: "Another job [Mother Leaders] have is to collect documentation[,] . . . copies of national identity documents, copies of birth certificates, copies of proof of enrollment." The local managers' preference for literate Mother Leaders was understandable given that they were required to keep detailed records. According to local manager Elena, "The Mother Leader will have her notebook where she writes down the name of the program user, her children, their respective grades, the histories of each child; and if, for example, the mother is pregnant they write 'expectant mother,' and if the child has been born they go ahead and fill in the notebook." These administrative tasks helped mothers maintain updated records with the program, therefore avoiding suspension on account of missing or erroneous data. Their support also enabled local managers to get their work done.

Not all of the monitoring and informing work done by Mother Leaders had favorable consequences for other Juntos mothers. In addition to gathering data that proved women had met program conditions, Mother Leaders were asked to provide local managers with information that potentially had negative consequences for women, including suspension. Local manager Paulino explained this to me in an interview: "For example, [Mother Leaders] inform us that such and such child doesn't live in the community anymore, and so we process [the relevant] documents to disaffiliate these children. . . . They also tell us when mothers aren't living in the communities anymore—maybe for work they went to Lima, they went to Cajamarca city, so then we go ahead and disaffiliate these mothers." There were no institutional controls in place to ensure that local managers verified the authenticity of the third-party information they received. As a result, wrongful disaffiliations were always a possibility. If communities were always harmonious, this would not present an issue. However, tensions existed between some Mother Leaders and the Juntos recipients in their communities. Because Mother Leaders' committees were unregulated components of the program, there were no clear accountability mechanisms in place.

For Mother Leaders, being Juntos's eyes and ears sometimes entailed reporting on personal circumstances and choices that fell outside of the program's remit (which was to improve access to high-quality public health and education services). On several occasions I observed Mother Leaders—as well as a number of non-Juntos community members—inform local managers about CCT recipients whom they thought were spending the transfer on clothing or inappropriate food choices. As a matter of policy, Juntos did not officially direct women on how they should or should not spend the cash incentive. However, local managers had personal beliefs, and the way Juntos was organized gave rise to local managers' interest in certain issues, including consumption. One local manager explained in an interview how she had very few "problems" with mothers in her district insofar as their spending practices. Nevertheless, the Mother Leaders helped her to maintain an awareness of dynamics that could become "unsatisfactory": "[The program recipients] know that the Mother Leader is checking on them. We have a Mother Leader in every community, so, for example, they tell us: 'Miss, she is misspending the money,' no? So then, right away we go straight to this person. . . . [T]he Mother Leaders are who checks in; they support us, they know."

Understandably, a great deal of this was information that CCT recipients did not want to share. For instance, local managers frequently implored Mother Leaders to inform them when women in their communities became pregnant. Yet according to Lourdes, one of the Mother Leaders: "[The women] don't want to tell us." While attending prenatal exams was a requirement for pregnant women in order to receive the cash transfer, some women resisted releasing intimate information—such as the date of their last menstrual period—to Juntos staff. When Mother Leader Soledad urged a Juntos recipient to report her pregnancy to the local manager, the woman replied, "And Juntos, who are they? My husband?" The response of local managers to such resistance was to tell Mother Leaders that the women had to report their pregnancies whether they liked it or not; otherwise, "they'll be suspended."

Feminist scholars have suggested that the CCT program design positions poor mothers as "conduits" for a policy that seeks to improve the health and education of their children rather than the women themselves (Molyneux 2007). A focus on Mother Leaders showed this dynamic to be even more pernicious: as Mother Leaders were asked to participate in modifying other women's behavior, they were positioned as conduits for official policy and potentially whatever else local managers sought to improve or achieve.[14] Local managers frequently asked Mother Leaders to "guide" Juntos recipients in ways that diverged from official policy directives. In the meeting described at the opening of this chapter, the local manager encouraged women to make use of the municipal government's guinea pig initiative and to attend the reproductive-health training with their husbands, so as to interrupt the pattern in which women "continue having more and more babies." While Juntos did concern itself with children's nutrition insofar as it incentivized and tracked attendance at health checkups, local managers were not required to foster microentrepreneurship or monitor household consumption. Juntos incentivized pregnant women to attend prenatal checkups, and the local manager's job was to audit their attendance. Curbing (speculative) fertility rates was not part of the Juntos program's remit at all, and the number of children a woman reared was not the business of the local manager.

To be sure, educating parents on children's nutritional requirements or raising awareness about available reproductive services is not inherently wrong. My point is that Juntos created a situation in which poor women's personal choices became monitored and disciplined by their own neighbors. At the request of their local managers, Mother Leaders became entangled in the disciplining and surveillance of women's behavior that bled beyond what we might think of as "official" policy concerns.

It would be deeply misguided to locate the root of this unfavorable situation with the Mother Leaders. The World Bank suggests that Mother Leaders "can be useful in helping [CCT] clients understand the rules and verifying that complete and correct information is being used" (Grosh et al. 2008). The rules, however, were not transparent at the village level. They were no more transparent to the ordinary Juntos mothers than they were to the Mother Leaders. With local managers as their primary points of contact—or direct supervisors, really—Mother Leaders had very little access to alternative information. Whether the activities requested of a Mother Leader were officially sanctioned was not readily available information. Rather than viewing this practice as an aberration in an otherwise well-designed program, it is better understood as a reasonable outcome of imposing conditions and insisting on their measurement in a context of inadequate infrastructure and highly unequal power relations.

DEVELOPMENT THROUGH DISCIPLINE

Mother Leaders' work was guided by the same notion of "responsible motherhood" that disciplines women's compliance with program conditions in Juntos (and other CCT programs) more broadly (see Molyneux 2006). One morning I interviewed Mother Leader Eufemia in a new addition to the house she shared with her husband and children. They had received a grant from the national Techo Propio (My Own House) program for the construction. The room, which wasn't yet furnished, was a source of great pride to Eufemia—the house was now one of the nicer homes in the village. We sat on a shawl that Eufemia spread out on the cool concrete floor, and she spoke to me about what it took to be a Mother Leader:

> *TC:* What qualities do you look for in a Mother Leader? Why might you select one person over another?
>
> *Eufemia:* Well, above all she has to be responsible. Responsible.
>
> *TC:* Sure. And what does that mean?
>
> *Eufemia:* Well, for those who don't meet the conditions, the Mother Leader writes it down on a paper and gives it to the local manager. They do informing.
>
> *TC:* The Mother Leaders do informing?
>
> *Eufemia:* Yes, they inform the local manager. So then the local manager suspends those who don't meet their conditions.

At one community meeting, local manager Paulino told Mother Leaders that their role came with responsibilities: "As *leaders,* social agents in your communities, you have responsibility, authority." Unfortunately, much of the work Mother Leaders were asked to do related to disciplining the individual behaviors of poor women so that they met the requirements of the state. In this context, a job well done involved promoting the state's definition of responsible motherhood (i.e., meeting program conditions), monitoring others to make sure program goals were met, and helping local managers navigate both an expansive territory and the impossibility of knowing the intimate details of all of the households they were responsible for managing.

The state's reliance on these women leaders to discipline their neighbors and make them more responsible mothers has social costs that are worth considering. A 2009 study conducted by the think tank Instituto de Estudios Peruanos suggested that Mother Leaders presented an opportunity for Juntos to develop a closer relationship with its target population. In theory, the democratic election of a group of women intended to advocate on behalf of the oft-marginalized women of their community—in a spirit of solidarity and empowerment—seems like a hopeful and important advance for community-led development. Such an arrangement could lead to an increase in power not only for the elected women but also for the community as a whole. Imagine, for instance, the state equipping Mother Leaders with tools that would enable them to report on poor service quality and hold the state accountable.[15] The think tank's study, however, found that the opportunity was unrealized. Researchers discovered that Mother Leaders' committees frequently functioned as a mechanism for control of beneficiaries that "runs the risk of becoming oppressive" (IEP 2009). Among the concerns raised was the tendency for these committees to reproduce the hierarchical and authoritarian relationship between local managers and CCT recipients, which "emphasizes discipline over promotion of rights" (IEP 2009, 38).

I also observed the authority that Mother Leaders were granted run awry. Much like local managers, Mother Leaders could compel Juntos recipients to do things under threat of suspension that extended beyond what Juntos actually required. During informal conversations in one village, Juntos recipients told me that their Mother Leaders had called a meeting to request that they contribute part of their cash incentive toward a fellow Juntos recipient's medical costs; the woman's son had broken his leg. Upon further inquiry, Custodia, one of the Mother Leaders involved, said that she thought this was a reasonable request. In subsequent interviews, Juntos recipients reported that collaboration was obligatory. For instance, Juntos recipient Pepita said to me: "[The Mother Leaders] called a meeting and told us we have to contribute five soles, and if we don't contribute then they'll complain to the program that we didn't want to." I verified these Juntos mothers' reports in an informal discussion with the local manager later on. The local manager confirmed that she had given her support because she believed that it was the right thing for the mothers to do. Most Juntos mothers' accounts of the situation suggested they were unhappy about having to contribute, especially given news that the woman's son had been drunk. Despite this, the women had complied with what the Mother Leaders had asked and the local manager had sanctioned.

Rather than faulting individual Mother Leaders, it is worth considering how authority, the coercive power of an incentive, and a stretchy definition of responsible motherhood shaped this situation. Local managers called upon Mother Leaders to help them implement a set of ambiguous program conditions, and they did this by appealing to their sense of responsible motherhood. Mothers had already critiqued the irony of having to take children to short-staffed schools and unstocked clinics in order to be defined as "responsible mothers," and so being told to contribute to a broken-leg fund likely came as no surprise. What this scenario also illustrated was the distressing misuse of Mother Leaders' labor. Although development experts suggested that Mother Leaders could be empowering resources for CCT recipients—by, for instance, reporting on the quality of services—the potential for such an outcome is undercut by the very assumptions upon which CCTs are designed. CCTs are intended to change the behavior of individual mothers, not improve the rough conditions and paltry services with which they must contend. As a result, the tasks Mother Leaders were asked to perform had more to do with discipline than with group solidarity or empowerment. Instead of asking Mother Leaders to help state staff develop a deeper understanding of the barriers that rural women and their families faced, the state asked them to enforce a set of ironic conditions.

UNPAID LABOR AND MOTHER LEADERS

Mother Leaders did not appear on any organizational diagram, and they were not on Juntos's payroll. Yet by their own admission, local managers could not successfully implement Juntos without Mother Leaders' help, so it makes sense that staff would insist that Mother Leaders were "the local managers in their communities." Mother Leaders were, by all accounts, an institutionalized component of the program.

As much as the local managers confronted inadequate public transportation, so too did Mother Leaders, although they did not have access to institutional resources, like the municipal motorbike. Mother Leaders often commented to me that they spent a great deal of time walking in order to fulfill the tasks corresponding to their role. Acting as Juntos's eyes and ears required time and effort. At the meeting described at the opening of this chapter, the local manager acknowledged that Mother Leaders' work was "self-sacrificing," to which the mothers chorused in agreement. The substantial time commitment and lack of compensation that I observed in Cajamarca corroborated research with Mother Leaders elsewhere in Peru that noted an increase in women's time poverty (Vargas Valente 2010). Mother Leaders assisted local managers to ensure that women met their conditions and received the cash transfer. They helped Juntos achieve high rates of compliance and, as a result, fostered the circumstances in which Juntos was able to claim success in achieving an uptake of health and education service usage.

Despite their significant role in implementation, Mother Leaders were given very little recognition in official policy spaces. They were not featured in organizational diagrams and directories, even though they outnumbered local managers, and they had a marginal presence in external program reports and evaluations. The discrepancy between what I observed on the ground and how Mother Leaders featured in official accounts of implementation was deeply puzzling. When I asked for clarification from high-level experts at MIDIS and Juntos in Lima, they insisted that the relationship between Juntos and the Mother Leaders was informal:

TC: Are the Mother Leader committees a formal part of the program or not?

Expert: No. The Mother Leader is a figure that exists at the margin of Juntos. . . . [Mother Leaders'] activities are not a part of the Juntos program. We consider her a, a strategic ally of the community when we want to spread information, when we want to promote some activity, or if we want to listen—How is the service going? . . . But they are not part of the structure of Juntos.

TC: So there is no promotion of their activities?

Expert: Of the Mother Leaders, no. Nor are they paid. Absolutely nothing. It's a chore.

Experts claimed that while Mother Leaders were useful to Juntos from time to time, they were in effect outsiders to the program. This claim stood in stark contradiction to what I observed when shadowing local managers, who also emphasized the critical role that Mother Leaders played in program implementation. From this view, Mother Leaders were not "marginal" at all.

We might attribute the disconnect between how experts in Lima and local managers in Cajamarca talked about the role of Mother Leaders to a gap in experiential knowledge. Could it be that experts were unaware of the extent to which Juntos relied on the participation of Mother Leaders? To be sure, Juntos was administrated and implemented by two distinct sets of actors in geographically disparate areas. As a result, policy administrators in urban Lima were not regularly exposed to the everyday undertakings of implementation work. That said, in addition to the occasional policy document, there were other indications that experts in Lima were very much aware of the role Mother Leaders played in implementation. MIDIS and Juntos sponsored a number of workshops for Mother Leaders and released communications on the Juntos website detailing actions Mother Leaders had taken in conjunction with local managers. Staff at the Verification of Coresponsibilities Unit at Juntos headquarters in Lima shared with me their experiences organizing workshops with Mother Leaders in the southern Andean regions. All of the evidence suggested that Mother Leaders were not unknown to those in Lima.

Another explanation for why experts in Lima downplayed the role of Mother Leaders relates to gendered norms about women's "voluntary" labor. A common assumption all over the world is that the largely care-based activities that women perform in households and communities are not *work* and, therefore, that they are not entitled to compensation. Mother Leaders were referred to as volunteers by experts in Lima and in the few policy documents available, including one published by the World Bank (Grosh et al. 2008). Considering this possibility, what are the implications of the country's largest social program relying on an unpaid workforce of more than a thousand poor women?

Peru has a long history of relying on the unpaid labor of volunteers—mostly women—to fill holes in the social safety net and provide a variety of services where the state failed to do so. In response to this point, experts at MIDIS and Juntos suggested that Mother Leaders emerged from preexisting community networks such as water committees and savings committees that operate throughout the country. Some of these committees, like the community justice committees called *rondas,* were traditionally made up of men (Gitlitz and Rojas 1985). Many other committees took up traditionally maternal concerns and were composed only of women.

For instance, low-income rural and urban mothers in Peru have historically organized into committees that addressed their "practical and strategic interests" (Molyneux 1985). These committees were particularly important during the 1980s and 1990s, when the World Bank and International Monetary Fund imposed structural adjustment policies on Latin American countries. As state governments peeled back the few social supports that were in place, they simultaneously devolved responsibility for care of children, the sick, and the elderly to women in households and communities (Benería and Sen 1981; Feijoo and Jelin 1987; Rocha et al. 1989). In response, women formed neighborhood-based organizations, including communal kitchens, Mothers Clubs, and the Glass of Milk Program (Boesten 2010; Oliart 2003; Barrig 1991). These committees demonstrated "women's ability to establish informal networks of solidarity to help each other in their daily lives and with their family obligations" (Vargas 1991, 21). They helped women advance their practical interests as mothers and, at the same time, provided an opportunity for some women to advance their strategic interests through access to public spaces and power, at least at the local level.

Did Mother Leaders committees present an opportunity for women to build solidarity and help one another meet practical and strategic needs? My observations suggested this was unlikely. To be sure, Mother Leaders helped the women in their communities understand what Juntos required of them and, conversely, ensured that local managers had the information necessary to register a mother as eligible for Juntos. In these cases, women's practical needs were met because they received the cash payment. It is also true that Mother Leaders might have made individual gains. The women to whom the Mother Leader role was available were offered an opportunity to exercise individual rights and maintain an increased presence in the public sphere, at least at the community level (IEP 2009).[16]

These kinds of opportunities do contribute to increased self-confidence and self-esteem (Vargas Valente 2010). These benefits might explain why Mother Leaders were willing to do the work required, including monitoring and informing on their peers, in spite of the time-intensive and physical work.[17] Yet the thrust of Mother Leaders' work was not to empower poor women collectively, or even to support them in their caring tasks. Being Juntos's eyes and ears was intended to help the state enforce a set of conditions meant to benefit children; the specific sense in which the state benefited from this arrangement bears further interrogation.

When women and their labor have filled gaps in the social safety net, it typically isn't only children, the sick, and the elderly who benefit. Women's unpaid caring labor also subsidizes the state. Let's look at a historical example from Peru. One of Peru's largest social programs before Juntos was Glass of Milk, which tackled malnutrition in children and pregnant and breastfeeding women. The program was born out of a protest march in Lima in 1984, when an estimated twenty-five thousand mothers took to the streets to demand that all children had the right to one glass of milk a day (Copestake 2008). Glass of Milk, which is still active today, draws on federal-level funding that is allocated to municipalities to provide local women's committees with milk, cereals, and other foodstuffs. The committees then disburse these goods to mothers from registered low-income households. Like the Juntos Mother Leaders, Glass of Milk committees are composed of elected members who serve in specific roles, including director, treasurer, secretary, and so on. Without these unpaid committee members and the labor of thousands of other volunteers, the Glass of Milk program could not function. In fact, an evaluation conducted by the United Nations Development Fund for Women found that in one community, women's voluntary labor subsidized 23 percent of the $3 million budget (Razavi 2007a).

Comparison with the Glass of Milk program provokes an important set of reflections. If Juntos were unable to rely on a cadre of available, mobile women from local communities, the agency would be forced to contract a significant number of additional local managers, all of whom would expect a paycheck. Juntos's reliance on women's unpaid labor has at least two important implications. First, it undercuts the claim that CCT programs are efficient. Put more bluntly, perhaps conditional cash transfer programs are "cheap" only if a large portion of the labor used to monitor compliance is unpaid.

Second, it throws into sharp relief the absurdity of a social program that reinforces gendered drivers of poverty or, put more sharply, the absurdity of promoting children's well-being at the expense of their mothers. Women's poverty is a persistent feature of the social fabric in Peru and elsewhere, and it is persistent in large part because the majority of the caring work that women undertake in households and communities—whether disbursing fortified milk, nursing babies, or caring for the infirm—is not recognized as work worth compensating financially. Even if Mother Leaders committees offered women opportunities for collective empowerment, solidarity, or character growth, the state's failure to compensate these women for their labors functions as a ceiling to how much they are able to improve the living conditions of their families. Roughly half of the children in Juntos households will grow up to be women; these women are unlikely to look back and see Juntos as having had a sustained impact on their lives if society continues to insist that so much of their labor isn't worth compensating.

CONCLUSION

Mother Leaders' work exists in the shadows of the state; their labors aren't an "official" part of the policy, but they are necessary for it. The fact that Mother Leaders' work is substantial and unpaid undercuts the claim that conditionality has been implemented efficiently. Juntos was unviable without the availability of unpaid, literate, able-bodied, locally based laborers. Without them, the state would have been forced to invest much more money than it already did in human resources. The state relied on Mother Leaders to achieve high rates of compliance and avoid infiltration of the program by "undeserving" mothers. It just did not value Mother Leaders enough to pay them.

In a sense, Mother Leaders do exist at the margins of the program. The fact that they do essential implementation work and are not compensated for it illustrates how CCTs reproduce gendered drivers of poverty. While some individual gains might be had by some of the women, poor women on the whole lose out. To be sure, that women throughout Juntos do a great deal of extra—and inefficient—work at the behest of the state might be justified if we could count on the state to use its power over these women to achieve just ends, including for the women themselves. Juntos is by all accounts a well-intentioned social program, and the actors who design, administer, and implement it also have good intentions. But does state power flow through Juntos in ways that are consistently just? The next chapter tackles this question directly, examining what else happens in the shadows of conditional social policy.

6

_____

Shadow Conditions and the
Immeasurable Burden of Improvement

> *In Juntos, everything is a threat, that the program will be taken away. It's development done through fear.*
> CARLA, DIRECTOR OF A SMALL NONPROFIT FOR RURAL WOMEN AND
> GIRLS' EMPOWERMENT.

On a wet and muddy day in Santa Ana District, a Juntos local manager summoned all Juntos recipients from the villages of Sonsonate and Bellavista to a meeting. The local manager called the meeting on behalf of a community worker from the state-run day-care program called Cuna Más. The day-care program was part of a broader attempt by the Ministry of Development and Social Inclusion to improve early childhood development in poor and extremely poor communities throughout rural Peru. The day care offered free child-minding services, which were provided by unpaid women in the community, and nutritious snacks and lunch for children aged six months to three years. Cuna Más had been operating in the area for less than a year, and the community worker was having difficulty convincing women to use it.[1] Sonsonate and Bellavista each had a Cuna Más day care, as did some neighboring villages. In Sonsonate, it was set up in the newly constructed municipal hall, a clean but cold and windowless concrete building. The day care in Sonsonate had problems recruiting mothers to use the services, but it was the day care in Bellavista that was really a problem for the community worker. The state had set up the Bellavista day care in a small building beside the local cemetery, and the women refused to take their children there because they said it frightened them.

The Juntos local manager, rather than the Cuna Más community worker, had called the meeting to make sure the mothers attended. It was widely understood among frontline state and NGO workers in both districts where I carried out research that meetings called by Juntos were far better attended, because women thought they had to attend in order to earn the cash incentive. This particular meeting was held at ten in the morning in a simple, bright room adjoining the local health post. A few posters advising women about birth control decorated the concrete walls, which had been painted a powdery yellow. Most of the mothers arrived late, having waited until the rain let up before descending the muddy hills. By the end of the meeting, approximately eighty women, many of them winding wool on tall palitos, were seated on long wooden benches and spilling out of the doorway and onto the grassy front courtyard. A few silent husbands were scattered throughout the crowd. The Juntos local manager and the Cuna Más community worker, both of whom were women, sat facing the mothers. They had sunglasses tucked into their fair hair and the badges of their respective government programs embroidered on their official vests: bright red for Juntos and bubblegum pink for Cuna Más. The following vignette from my field notes describes what I observed at the meeting.

> The Cuna Más community worker stands at the front of the room and tells the Juntos recipients that they must leave their children under three years of age at the day care, regardless of whether or not the children cry. She says that perhaps the women might cry at first too, but afterward both mothers and children will become used to it. The crying, she says, is not an excuse. She tells the mothers that if they don't use the day care it will be taken away, and then maybe Juntos as well, because the ministry will think they obviously don't want social programs. Furthermore, after day care, children must go to kindergarten and then elementary school, and finally high school, whether they like it or not. The community worker tells the assembled mothers that they might as well accustom the children to being separated now, so that it is not hard for them to go to school. If not, it is only the mothers' fault if the children don't want to go to school. There is no one else to blame.
>
> The mothers have been seated the entire time, silently listening to the lecture; some of them are drifting into sleep or staring into the distance. Finally, the community worker asks the women if they have any questions or comments about the day care, because she knows that "things aren't always rosy" and tells them not to be afraid. This is again followed by silence, until one mother asks how old the baby must be to go to the day care. The community worker explains that women should begin taking their babies to the day care at six months of age, so long as the mother sends breast milk with the baby, and all children should attend until aged thirty months.
>
> Many of the women begin chatting among themselves, and the Juntos local manager instructs them sternly to leave their "gossip" at home, that meetings are not the place for it. A Mother Leader turns around from her position on a front bench and yells at the other women to be quiet. The local manager takes a turn speaking. She tells the mothers that as Juntos recipients they are obligated to take their children under three years of age to the day care. She reminds them of "the objectives of the Ministry of Development and Social Inclusion," which are "to create human capital" and "achieve the eradication of poverty and extreme poverty." She reminds them that they receive the two hundred soles not because "the government is really nice," that the cash is contingent upon fulfillment of the *coresponsibilities*— she stresses this word. She then enters into a lengthy lecture about education, health, and MIDIS. Many of the women are looking elsewhere; they appear bored. A mother seated near the door named Gloria says that she refuses to take her son to

the day care, because he cries too much. She is sorry, but she absolutely refuses. The local manager replies that she doesn't have a choice, she must leave her son there, and that all Juntos mothers must.

Both the Cuna Más community worker and the Juntos local manager told the mothers present at the meeting that their coresponsibilities as Juntos recipients included use of the day care. This was not true. The state did not require Juntos mothers to use the day care—at least not officially. Nevertheless, the Juntos local manager threw the weight of her authority behind the Cuna Más worker's fabricated assertion that MIDIS would take Juntos away if the mothers refused to use the day care. While the local manager did not have the institutional mandate to monitor women's compliance in using the day care, she did expect that following the meeting the mothers would amend their behavior and begin to use it.

In my observations I frequently saw local managers using their influence and threats of program suspension to get Juntos mothers to do things that were not officially mandated. This practice was not particular to Peru. Research in Mexico showed that mothers in the world's second-largest CCT program were required to do collective community work called *faenas* (González de la Rocha 2006, 129; Saucedo-Delgado 2011). This work included, among other activities, collecting rubbish, cleaning the school, and maintaining gardens. Development experts there suggested that the unpaid work was "voluntary," but mothers complained that the work was undignified and took them away from tasks they would rather be doing, including paid work (Rivero 2002, cited in Molyneux 2006, 435). To my knowledge, what follows is the most thorough and data-rich examination of what we should make of such events currently available in the peer-reviewed literature.

Ethnographers of development have suggested that policy is not made in the tidy offices of experts, but that it becomes what it is during implementation (Mosse 2005). Bearing this in mind, in the pages that follow I describe and analyze what happened when the implementation of Juntos collided with the needs, desires, and influence of a variety of actors within and outside of the program. Research on the impacts of CCTs that mentions these "additional" activities tends gloss over them, as though they were insignificant.[2] The unintended consequences of women's additional labor may not be apparent at all in evaluations that focus on the effectiveness of CCTs at achieving children's health and education uptake. When these activities are viewed from the women's perspective, however, they appear worthy of sustained and critical attention.

SHADOW CONDITIONS

When I asked Juntos mothers what they had to do to earn the cash incentive, they told me that they had to take their children to school and health appointments. They also told me that they had to do a whole bunch of other things. These included

FIGURE 16. Shadow condition 1: A painted Juntos flag signals that recipients of social assistance live here. Photo by the author.

a variable combination of the following: attending meetings; growing a garden (*biohuerta*); giving birth in a health clinic; keeping hygiene instruments (toothbrush, soap) organized; cooking for the school lunch program, Qali Warma; having a latrine; using the state day care, Cuna Más; participating in political parades and parades for local cultural events; painting the Juntos flag on the outside of their house (figure 16); contributing to the medical costs of a neighbor's broken leg; using a cocina mejorada (smokeless stove); attending hygiene trainings; participating in a regional cooking fair; attending a literacy workshop, and "doing whatever the [local manager] tells me to."[3]

In all of the interviews I conducted, women named at least two of these extra tasks; on average they named four or five. I also observed mothers in their roles as Juntos recipients participate in microproductive projects such as raising cuyes (guinea pigs) and producing handicrafts (figure 17). In Cajamarca city I once observed throngs of women, all wearing red hats, marching unenthusiastically through the streets behind banners advertising the incumbent regional governor's political party. A local NGO worker later told me the women were Juntos recipients that the governor's office had brought in on buses from rural villages.[4]

I refer to these additional tasks as shadow conditions (Cookson 2016).[5] I use the term *shadow* to evoke the idea that the activities were not present in the tangible spaces of policy. They were not featured on the Juntos website or in the manuals

FIGURE 17. Shadow condition 2: Producing handicrafts. Photo by the author.

used to train local managers. They were not listed on the verification-of-coresponsibility forms that Juntos used to monitor women's compliance with program conditions. From Lima, these activities were hard to see. Shadow conditions lurked behind and alongside those conditions that development experts insist are vital for the poor to meet in order to lift themselves out of poverty. While shadow conditions were shadowy by all official accounts, in the places where Juntos was implemented they were highly visible.

From the perspective of Juntos mothers, conditions were conditions. The conditions requiring women to take their children to school and health appointments were enforced and monitored by local managers, who often acted in coordination with school and health clinic staff. Shadow conditions were similar: local managers often worked in collaboration with other local authorities—including health and education staff, government bureaucrats and politicians, and employees from NGOs and other state social programs—to implement shadow conditions. Shadow conditions were thematically similar, too. Many of the activities were related to improving the health and education of children or sometimes the women themselves. Others benefited the household or local economies. Juntos's tagline was: "Working together so that our children live better than we do." And many of the shadow conditions fit under this banner. With the concept of shadow conditions in place, I'd like to elaborate on its meaning and significance with a few more practical examples.

Two commonly mentioned shadow conditions were having a latrine and keeping a tidy house. Several Juntos recipients had a handmade organizer in which they kept the family members' toothbrushes and soap (figure 18).[6] This was frequently hung on the wall of the outdoor sitting area, where families would receive visitors. Juntos mother Marisela told me, while we sat at a large wooden table that was covered in her children's homework, about having to meet conditions related to household hygiene. She had just finished telling me about the garden that Juntos required her to maintain, and I had asked if there was anything else she had to do.

> TC: And what else [in addition to keeping gardens] do you have to do to be in the [Juntos] program?
>
> Marisela: Well, for the program we also had to build a lavatory [baño].
>
> TC: A lavatory? What do you mean?
>
> Marisela: In the garden there is a latrine [rincón de aseo], and a place to keep the children's toothbrushes so they brush their teeth. And also we have to make sure that our children have their things, that they aren't missing any school supplies, and that they are nice and clean. That's what the local manager tells us.

Mothers frequently told me that the local managers entered their homes, uninvited, and "checked" to make sure that the house was "tidy." The women were unsure of

FIGURE 18. Shadow condition 3: Keeping hygiene instruments organized (note the Juntos flag). Photo by the author.

the schedule upon which the monitoring would occur. When I asked mothers what *tidy* meant, they usually said that it meant "not dirty," and that they housed their small animals outside of the sleeping quarters. This was not always a simple task, because many houses consisted of only one or two rooms. Women raised small animals like cuyes, chickens, and rabbits to feed their families or sell at the market. They were valuable and had to be protected against cold, loss, and theft.

Some of the conditions, like keeping a tidy house and maintaining lavatories and latrines, were to an extent aligned with Juntos's mission to improve children's health. Other shadow conditions, like participating in parades and fairs, seemed further removed from Juntos's stated aims.[7] Santos, a slight, gentle woman, had been receiving the Juntos payment for less than a year. She became a Juntos recipient shortly after taking over care of her five-year-old grandson. His mother's new partner had "problems" with the boy, and Santos had agreed to raise him. Santos and her husband had previously migrated seasonally to the coast to harvest corn and rice, poorly paid work that was extremely physically demanding. Now that her grandson was of school age, Santos and her husband could no longer migrate for work, and other work was scarce. So they moved to Sonsonate from Cajamarca city in order to meet Juntos's rural eligibility requirements. In Sonsonate they rented a small, humble home with packed-earth floors on someone else's plot of land. When I interviewed Santos, she explained what it was like when she first became a Juntos recipient. One of the things she talked about was participating in a year's-end celebration organized by the mayor. Juntos local managers asked the Juntos mothers to prepare local dishes and showcase the weaving they had done as part of an initiative implemented in conjunction with an NGO. This is what Santos said:

> *Santos:* The [local managers] also asked us to go to an activity the [Juntos] program organizes for the year's end. They wanted us all to be there, all wearing the same thing, a white blouse. I went to that too.
>
> *TC:* What was the activity for?
>
> *Santos:* They said it was a party. As I had just started in the program, I still didn't know much. They said we couldn't just go like this [*indicates current clothing*]; I had to wear [a white blouse].

On another occasion, at a Juntos meeting in the district of Labaconas, I observed a local manager implore a roomful of mostly reluctant mothers to march in the forthcoming carnival parade, which I later learned was sponsored by the district governor. The local manager capitalized on the enthusiasm of a few husbands present within the group to pressure the women into participating. By the end of the meeting the women had begrudgingly agreed. Once it was determined that the women would march, the mother seated next to me confided that the women didn't want to participate because there was likely to be excessive drinking, and if they went to the carnival, who would watch over the children?

All conditions, including shadow conditions, functioned via threat of suspension. Women complied with shadow conditions because they thought they could be suspended from the program if they did not. Threat of suspension was especially effective because what was actually required of Juntos mothers in order to receive the payment was not clear to them. I did not speak with a single Juntos recipient whose understanding of what she was supposed to do to earn the incentive matched what the state *actually* required her to do. Shadow conditions and official conditions blended seamlessly into one another, and none of them were activities that they were entitled to refuse. Suniva had been in the Juntos program for five years when I interviewed her and her sister, who was also a Juntos recipient. When I asked about program conditions, Suniva told me about the threats that women received from the local managers:

> *TC:* And what do you have to do to stay in the Juntos program?
>
> *Suniva:* Do what they tell us. Plant gardens, have vegetables, all this. Because if not, they say that they'll kick us out of the program. . . . They suspend us. Like that, they've said it to us.

The threats that local managers made were effective, but they did not always make sense to the mothers. Gardens were a good example of this. Yesenia, who had been in the Juntos program since it first arrived in Bellavista, voiced a common complaint among mothers. She said that Juntos made the mothers maintain gardens, but she, like the other mothers, didn't have access to "even one minute of irrigation a day." As a result, she was able to grow only certain plants such as eggplant and Andean tomato, and felt frustrated at what she perceived to be an unreasonable request. Juntos mother Marisela, too, was frustrated: "Sometimes we can't do [what the local manager asks], and she says things like: 'You all have to do this or I'll suspend you'—for example, with the gardens. But in this season there isn't any water; there's a drought, you see. There isn't any at all, so what are we going to water [the garden with], when there isn't even water to drink? Never mind [for the garden]."

Keeping gardens was not a reasonable request, given the infrastructure the mothers had at their disposal. The communities of Bellavista and Sonsonate, like others in the region, suffered from a water shortage and, as a result, did not have continuous access to irrigation. In order to equitably mange the insufficient water supply, members of both communities decided on a schedule for water use. As a result, women had a narrow, predetermined window of time when irrigation was available to them, and they made careful use of that schedule.[8] On many occasions I observed women staying home to await their turn to fill a water container or irrigate their small plot of land. To be sure, local managers did not live in the same communities as the mothers they managed, and so they did not experience the water shortages firsthand. Gardens might have seemed like an excellent idea, and one that was aligned with promoting children's good health. But these women had been contending with the water shortage long before Juntos arrived in their communities—which is to say that the local managers should have been aware of the mothers' particular constraints.

Access to resources and the intended benefits of the activities aside, shadow conditions like gardens, latrines, and participation in parades underscore the coercive potential of conditionality. The threats local managers used were effective. Shadow conditions, like the health and education conditions, were not couched in the language of volunteerism, choice, or self-improvement. Mothers understood that the cash incentive was attached to conditions, and the local manager would monitor whether those conditions were met.

THE COERCIVE POWER OF INCENTIVES

In chapter 3, I noted that there were at least two reasons why women complied with program conditions even when the quality of services was inadequate and when doing so generated costs for the mothers themselves. The first of these reasons was the material support that the cash transfer offered poor households. Juntos provided mothers who had few other reasonable economic opportunities with "a little bit of help" in meeting the material needs of their families. The second motivating factor behind women's compliance was the disciplining power of "responsible motherhood" narratives that circulated through policy language, through local managers' appeals for women's compliance, and through the language women used when describing one another's behavior. The need for material support and notions of responsible motherhood also disciplined women's compliance with an extensive list of shadow conditions. Yet given that shadow conditions imposed additional demands on their time and labor and compromised their dignity, it is worth revisiting the question of why women comply.

When I asked local managers why they thought women complied with shadow conditions, they told me the reason was simple: the mothers wanted the cash. For instance, "[Juntos mothers] think that 'if I miss a meeting they'll suspend me,' 'if I don't do this thing they'll suspend me.' And because they've become accustomed to their [two hundred soles every two months] . . . they are afraid that they'll be cut off, that they won't be paid." In one sense, we could say that mothers were materially accustomed to the CCT and so were willing to comply with extra tasks in order to earn the money. Yet this was not the full story. Shadow conditions illustrate another driver of women's compliance that has to do with women being socially accustomed, or disciplined. This was explained to me by the local managers' direct supervisor. In an interview, she emphasized the power of influence that local managers, as arbitrators of the incentive, had over the women they managed: "Unfortunately, because it gives out money, Juntos is very powerful. It has a lot of power because it gives out money. If a local manager says to the mothers, 'All of you must come down the hill tomorrow at ten at night,' all the mothers will come down the hill. They'll come down the hill because they know that they're conditioned [*están condicionadas*]."

To suggest that Juntos mothers "están condicionadas" could mean "mothers are required"—because the money was attached to conditions. Or, it could mean "the mothers are conditioned" in the sense that they were socially conditioned, or habituated, to respond in a particular way. It is worth examining the ambiguity of this phrasing. On one hand, women were required to engage in a set of activities in order to earn the cash payment. In a technical sense, that was how the incentive worked. On the other hand, figures of authority made a habit of using threats of suspension to discipline women's choices and behaviors, and this easily extended beyond the bounds of "official" policy. Whereas the cash itself provided a material impetus for running down the hill, the CCT also had a deeply coercive *social* element. To be clear, saying that women were habituated or disciplined was not to say that Juntos beneficiaries acted without agency. Rather, Juntos organized women's experiences in such a way that the *reasonable* thing to do was to run down the hill at ten o'clock.

The coercive power of Juntos—and its expansive quality—was illustrated in the weeks that followed the joint Juntos and Cuna Más meeting that opened this chapter. After the meeting, mothers spoke about having to take their young children to the day care despite not wanting to. At two focus groups with Juntos mothers, half of the group said they cried when they had to take their children to the day care. According to these women, it was not right that Juntos required them to do so, but they did it anyway. They said that using the day care took time away from other tasks because they had to go up the hill to get there. Some mothers who were afraid to leave their children at the day care chose to neglect their other tasks altogether and instead spent the day sitting outside the facility.[9] Juntos recipient Graciela said that she brought her baby to the day care only because Juntos obligated her to and she did not want to be suspended from the program, which was a fear her husband also shared.

Mothers' fear of suspension was sustained by the total fog surrounding what was and was not suspension-worthy, and by the power that local managers had to manipulate this fog. Local managers spent a great deal of time in a data collection exercise that was imprecise and required a good deal of discretionary decision-making. They were in a position to suspend a program user by error—if they had imperfect information—or by choice. When a local manager was unable to locate a medical history or encountered illegible information, they had the power to determine whether to register that particular Juntos mother as compliant or non-compliant, which determined whether that household would be suspended from the program or would continue receiving the cash transfer.

Such decisions were influenced by the personal relationships between the local manager and the mother. Like in CCT programs elsewhere, I observed that local managers made decisions that were colored by their perceptions of CCT beneficiaries' deservingness (Hossain 2010). On several occasions I watched that play out favorably for mothers. For instance, when Juntos mother Sunilda had not taken her daughter to all of the required health appointments (she missed the last one), she explained to her local manager that the nurse had told her not to bother coming. Instead of recording that Sunilda hadn't met the conditions, the local manager told Sunilda that she'd let it go this time. She did issue a warning—if her children did not attend checkups in future, she would be kicked out of the program.

On another occasion, I observed a local manager accept bags of freshly harvested corn from a Juntos family's plot after they asked her to overlook the fact that their seventeen-year-old son had migrated elsewhere to work, despite not having graduated high school. This would normally be cause for suspension, but in this instance the local manager agreed "to look into it." I also witnessed local managers castigate women whose behavior they deemed irresponsible. The same local manager who accepted the corn chastised a Juntos recipient later the same day for how she treated her elderly mother, saying that she had heard from other community members about the "disrespectful behavior." It was unclear to the mothers as well as to me how the local managers determined what was worthy of suspension.

Women's fears were not totally unfounded. During an interview, local manager Lina explained to me that local managers were responsible for filling out the verification-of-coresponsibility forms, and "[the forms] are money for the mothers."

Local managers ultimately determined whether a mother would receive the cash payment. This granted them a great deal of power over the women they managed. The local managers' direct supervisor told me in an interview that she believed the local managers should not have the opportunity to act "as judge and jury," granting or withholding the cash transfer according to personal discretion. She continued, saying, "*They can do this,* at the moment *it is* permissible to do it." The mothers were well aware of this dynamic and acted accordingly.

Narratives of responsible motherhood were at work in disciplining women's compliance with shadow conditions, too, and these converged with the lack of clarity and the threats of suspension that frightened mothers into complying. While half of the focus group I previously mentioned said that they cried when they had to take their children to the day care, the other half said that Cuna Más allowed them to participate in tasks other than child care, and that Cuna Más provided food. This was especially helpful because, according to the mothers, their children were "malnourished." Looking around at the plump babies, I found this a curious response. I also had become accustomed to hearing mothers repeat, verbatim, things that local managers often told them. Mostly these things related to the educational and health deficiencies of their children and to the merits of responsible motherhood. Women also heard these things from the many other social program workers and NGO employees who cycled through their villages, identifying deficiencies and lecturing women on how they could be improved. Women took up these narratives, referencing their self-improvement and identifying how they had previously been "irresponsible" in the ways they cared for their children and households.

I observed an illustrative example of this when local managers were monitoring women's conditions at a health clinic. Juntos mother Apollonia was being interrogated by her local manager about whether her children had attended their most recent health check. Apollonia's response, "Yes, miss, I don't neglect my children anymore," obviously indicated that she had been told previously that her behavior was neglectful. Juntos mother Ninón, who was chronically ill, told me about the ways local managers taught her to alter her domestic and hygiene habits: "[The local managers] teach us to keep ourselves a little tidier. You see, in the countryside we live all together with our small animals, and [the local managers] always tell us that we should live separately. To keep ourselves clean. It is nice to learn. In the campo we live how we live, and so they guide us. We learn. It's much better."

Women were constantly being "guided" by their local managers to mother more responsibly and to raise more professional children. When they did so, mothers commended one another's improvements. During a focus group, a very poor woman named Soledad, mother to two small girls, arrived late. As Soledad quietly took her seat, eyes averted, she was proudly introduced by a kindly Mother Leader, who said that Soledad had recently started taking her youngest daughter to the Cuna Más day care. According to the Mother Leader, Soledad wanted to take better care of her children, commenting that "before, they were dirty, as was she." Thankfully, Soledad had decided to "make a change." Narratives about good or responsible mother-hood were powerful; they disciplined women's behavior similarly to, if not more extensively than, other social programs (Molyneux 2006; Bradshaw 2008). Framing women's choices in terms of responsible motherhood "conditioned" women to walk and wait for poor-quality health services. These narratives extended well outside the bounds of "official" policy in the sense that local managers and other authorities often called upon mothers to meet shadow conditions in their roles "as mothers."

The only mother present at the focus group who did not use the day care was Eufemia. She had decided not to comply with the local manager's demand, because her husband told her that the program "is more trouble than it's worth." While Eufemia's decision to resist the local manager's pressure was not represen-tative of broader observations, it suggested the limits of Juntos's coercive power. Whether women complied—and on what terms—was shaped by women's agency, husbands' decision-making power, and analyses of the relative costs and benefits. Critical development studies scholars suggest that power is never only unidi-rectional, and even those at the margins have opportunities to resist (Scott 1985; Rankin 2001; Li 2007). This important point raises questions about what recourse CCT recipients had in the face of poor-quality services, abusive behavior, or unreasonable shadow conditions.

CONDITIONS FOR COMPLAINT

Juntos offered rural mothers the virtual equivalent of a complaint box. Unhappy women had the option of filing an official complaint online or by telephone. In the-ory, this system allowed Paloma, who was concerned about the teacher shortage, or Felisa, who couldn't access adequate health care at her nearest clinic, to register their concerns directly with Juntos's head office in Lima. In practice, this system was rife with absurdity. One consequence of historic underinvestment in educa-tion services in rural Peru is high female illiteracy. This enormous barrier, com-bined with the near total absence of Internet connection, made the option to file a complaint online almost laughable. The option to file a complaint by telephone was perhaps more reasonable but raised the question of how women were to locate the number for the hotline—I found it online. If the complaint in question concerned a local manager or health or education professional, it was highly improbably that the mother would seek to obtain the hotline number from any of them!

The third option available was to file a complaint in person at the Juntos regional office. However, for Paloma this would involve the time and financial cost of a two-hour journey by combi, and for Grimalda, up to six hours by foot and two or three combi rides, depending upon the availability of cars that day. This journey would have to be repeated on the way back, too. Another matter altogether was whether the complaint would actually make it to the relevant officials. On several occasions, I witnessed the security guard stationed outside the Juntos office in Cajamarca city refuse entry to campesinas who had traveled there.

Some researchers have suggested that CCTs open up new opportunities for citizens' engagement with the state, including the opportunity to complain about the poor quality of services (Hickey 2010; Hossain 2010). How effective these opportunities are is questionable. Juntos mothers' complaints, especially to one another and even sometimes to local managers, evidence low-income women's agency under constrained circumstances. However, the effectiveness of complaining is limited when you live isolated from the places where complaints can be effectively translated into meaningful improvements (Corbridge 2007, 197). The complaint system offered to rural mothers also raises the broader issue of transparency and accountability in program implementation. Women were unaware that institutional birth and participation in parades were not actual policy requirements—so why would they complain about them? Women's compliance was understandable when read against the combined factors presented here: intense social pressure to be a "responsible" mother, limited livelihood resources, and unclear information regarding what conditions Juntos recipients were actually required to meet.

INSTITUTIONAL BIRTH

While trying to maintain a garden might be futile and irritating, participation in a parade stigmatizing, and taking infants to day care emotionally stressful, the consequences of compliance with other shadow conditions had riskier consequences. The *parto institucional,* which meant "to give birth in a health center" (henceforth "institutional birth"), was one example of this. The subject of institutional birth came up frequently in my interviews and observations. The following vignette from my field notes describes a scene that took place at a Juntos meeting at the municipal hall in Labaconas.[10] The two local managers who worked in the district had summoned Mother Leaders and invited health staff and local government, so that everyone could be "on the same page" regarding what was required of the various actors in the forthcoming year insofar as Juntos was concerned. Whether Juntos recipients were required to have an institutional birth was one of the topics discussed.

> Quietly seated Juntos mothers have now been at the meeting forty-five minutes. In a raised voice, the female local manager insists that women give birth in a health facility, rather than at home: "Look—institutional births are obligatory! Let's be clear about this!" The mothers are being lectured like children who have misbehaved. A young female nurse begins to talk about why institutional birth is important. Contradicting the local manager, she says that she has received many complaints from women about the perceived requirement to have an institutional birth, and that "institutional births are not obligatory." However, she says, they "are better," and "what would happen if something went wrong at home?" The male local manager

interrupts to say that they will "sanction" and "suspend" those mothers who do not give birth at a health facility. He continues by saying that pregnant women must report when they are pregnant, and that Mother Leaders must ask the women and tell the local managers.

A mother named Janina from Comabamba village speaks out: "I am very sorry but I live very far away, so this is impossible—how would I ever be able to get there?" Other mothers voice their agreement. The young nurse responds saying they must try, as she has seen many maternal deaths. She says that she is frustrated by having to go to women's houses at nine, ten, eleven o'clock at night and not be allowed to attend a birth because the sister or mother-in-law is assisting. Near the point of yelling, she says that when she touches women giving birth "they protest, but not when the midwife does it! She can do whatever!"[11] She mimics women's wails and complaints as she imitates gently touching them, and then switches to the women's supposed silence when a midwife uses her knee along the lower back to assist the labor. Many of the mothers laugh, but the nurse does not. She replies angrily, "You don't let me work!" The female local manager interjects that the mothers should not do it for the two hundred soles [Juntos cash transfer] but for their "own well-being."

At the meeting, local managers told Juntos recipients that institutional birth was obligatory, threatened women with suspension, and enlisted the help of Mother Leaders in monitoring compliance. Other accounts I collected described women having been denied their newborns' birth certificates by health staff after home births unless they paid the health staff a fine. This particular abuse of power came up during informal discussions with Juntos women and was also reported by Maria, a nurse running a Cajamarca-based not-for-profit reproductive health clinic. She recounted that many Juntos mothers sought out her clinic for birth certificates after being refused at public institutions. Maria always provided the new mothers with the documents, free of charge.

At the Sonsonate clinic in Santa Ana District as well, the nurse told Juntos recipients that institutional birth was obligatory: "Regarding family planning, the Juntos program doesn't demand much of the mothers. But for the expectant mother, *yes.* They have to come for monthly checkups, and the birth has to be in a hospital. They have to give birth in a hospital or clinic. They can't give birth at home." She went on to relate that some women refused institutional birth, especially those whose prior births took place at home: "[The local managers] still haven't convinced 100 percent [of the women]. . . . [T]here are mothers that already have three, four, five children, and they *don't accept it,* that they have to give birth at the clinic. They still give birth in their houses."[12]

When I asked Juntos recipients if institutional birth was compulsory, their responses were mixed. Most of the time institutional birth was identified as a program condition; however, women whose children were older tended to respond that the institutional birth was optional, and others said they weren't sure.[13] The lack of clarity around the issue is understandable. Local managers often said one thing and then demanded another; and inconsistencies between local managers were rife. Health staff also operated with erroneous information about what Juntos actually required; this finding is consistent with evidence from studies in other regions where Juntos intervened (Díaz et al. 2008).[14]

Mothers offered a number of insights as to why some women "still [gave] birth in their houses," and these provided perspective on why the shadow condition requiring institutional birth was particularly insidious. In chapter 3, I discussed how rural women were frequently subject to discrimination and abuse when they interacted with the health and education systems on behalf of their children. Mothers also had unpleasant experiences when they accessed maternal care, which understandably shaped their preferences. Women described giving birth at home as more comfortable. Juntos mother Pepita explained to me that this was "because you have the help of your mother and husband"; at the clinic, the nurses are "brusque and you must lie down." Unlike many of the other clinics and health posts I visited, the public health facility in Sonsonate was very clean, which I associated with its university affiliation. The post was staffed by a technician, as well as a nurse who had worked there for many years. The nurse was organized and punctual, although some women in the community thought that she attended only "who she wanted, when she wanted" (Custodia, Juntos recipient).

While not all health staff treated women poorly, the generalized sense that women would not be treated fairly or with dignity if they went to the clinic spoke to deep-seated issues in the health system. In Peru, discrimination against campesinas and indigenous women is common and historically rooted in health policy and service delivery (Ewig 2010; Oliart 2003). Women, who are more likely than men to retain markers of ethnicity such as dress and language (de la Cadena 1992), commonly experience culturally insensitive and discriminatory treatment by urban white or mestizo health professionals (Ewig 2010).[15] Juntos mothers connected the poor treatment they received from health staff to the social position that poor campesinas occupied. Juntos mother Paloma explained to me that the poor treatment was because "we are humble people." Women's experiences of discrimination raise serious questions about whether incentives and conditions would be needed if the services were adequate and dignified.

The shadow condition requiring institutional birth was also harmful because of the underresourced environment in which it was implemented. As I discussed earlier, access to care was limited and unreliable. For an expectant woman, giving birth at a health clinic or post made sense if she lived within a short distance of it, had access to safe and reliable transportation, and was certain that when she arrived she would find it open and adequately staffed. This was not the reality for most of the women in my research. For many women in rural Peru, deciding to deliver a baby at a clinic entailed a journey of several hours on foot, and the very real risk that the clinic would not be open or would not be staffed by a qualified health professional.

I bore witness to how this scenario could play out on an otherwise quiet afternoon in February. I had accompanied a local manager in the district capital as he tracked down Juntos mothers who had recently given birth in order to collect their newborns' birth certificates. We had just returned from a failed attempt to speak with the nurse at a health facility in another village—the clinic had been closed, again. The furious local manager suggested that we would try again the following day, and so we returned to the district capital. We were chatting with a few municipal workers in the central plaza when a small commotion broke out. The social development director came running from the municipal hall speaking frantically into his mobile phone. Upon encountering a colleague, he related that a mother named Trinada was in labor in a village far away, and the district's one ambulance would not start. The two men surmised that the battery was dead and noted aloud that there wasn't a driver, anyway. Considering this, they tried to figure out how to get Trinada to the health facility. Despite the fact that the facility was located over an hour's walk away, the two men decided that she would have to make the descent. On our way to lunch, the local manager informed me that women often walked to the clinic to give birth, as there were few roads.

Upon further inquiry at the municipality, I discovered that the ambulance battery was routinely dead. In fact, the ambulance had not been functioning for the past year. Later that afternoon, another mother went into labor in a village located three hours away by foot. In her case, the social development director traveled on a municipal dirt bike to bring her down to the clinic. As illustrated earlier, if a mother decided to try to reach a clinic while in labor and were to find it open, she might have to confront discriminatory attitudes and practices exhibited by the health staff in the community meeting. In fact, she might have to receive care from the same health worker who had mocked women's labor pain at the meeting.

To be sure, many governments and global health and development experts have worked hard to successfully reduce the rates of maternal mortality by increasing the number of women who give birth in clinics and hospitals rather than at home. Yet pursuing institutional birth is safe only when facilities are sufficiently accessible, and it is reasonable only when women can expect to be attended in a dignified and caring manner. The fact that some women walk hours over rough terrain while in labor for fear that authorities will strip their families of social support is a grievous injustice.

SHADOW CONDITIONS: WELL-INTENTIONED DISTRACTIONS?

Juntos headquarters in Lima did not require or monitor women's participation in parades, where they stored their toothbrushes, or whether they maintained gardens full of leafy greens. Why did local managers? When Juntos was first implemented in 2006, activities like these were institutionally endorsed because experts in Lima viewed them as "complementary" to the program.[16] Local managers carried out a variety of activities in conjunction with regional government and civil society in the communities where they worked (Vargas Valente 2010, 28).[17] Mothers were expected to participate in the activities, but Lima did not require that their participation be monitored. In chapter 2, I discussed the institutional efforts to streamline Juntos's focus so that it enforced and monitored a narrow set of health and education conditions when Juntos was transferred to MIDIS. According to my interviews with experts in Lima, it was at that point that Juntos leadership decided that the program would no longer promote complementary activities.[18]

Yet time spent in the communities where Juntos was implemented revealed that many of these activities persist. For example, the gardens that mothers attempted to maintain formed part of a then-defunct initiative coordinated by Juntos and an NGO to improve household nutrition (Arroyo 2010). Juntos headquarters in Lima may no longer have supported the garden project, but women's accounts indicated that they believed tending the garden was yet another of the conditions they had to meet in order to receive the cash transfer.

Development experts at MIDIS and Juntos perceived shadow conditions as well-intentioned distractions from Juntos's mission. During interviews, I raised the issue of the extra tasks, expecting the revelation to come as a surprise. Policy makers and program administrators were, however, well aware of the practice. Some expressed the view that assigning women extra work was unfair, but they attributed shadow conditions to the good intentions of local managers, suggesting that a local manager's professional training determined the theme and endurance of the activities. For instance, one high-level expert told me that "if [the local manager] is a health worker they will be interested in health, that if it is someone specialized in agriculture they'll want to do projects in that." My observations indicated that while there may have been some correlation between a local manager's previous job and what she or he liked to see the mothers do, in fact shadow conditions extended well beyond professional interests. For instance, professional interests would not explain why a local manager trained as a teacher had women raising guinea pigs, participating in reproductive health training, marching in a carnival parade, and giving birth in hospitals.

Another high-level expert explained shadow conditions as follows, softly pounding her desk with her fist for emphasis: "Really great initiatives, all of these. But not a single one was part of the program; they all depended on the goodwill of the local manager. And they took time away from [the mother] fulfilling the program's objective [*pounds fist on desk*]." She continued: "The [Juntos] program has to report results to the country in terms of how many boys and girls have improved their health and have completed school attendance [*pounds fist on desk*]. . . . Juntos personnel have to dedicate themselves to what they are supposed to dedicate themselves, which is verifying that children are going to health and education services [*pounds fist on desk*]." While this perspective on shadow conditions may well have been valid in terms of what policy makers *intended* for Juntos, it missed a key point. Shadow conditions were not simply a series of distracting add-ons. Instead, shadow conditions were the direct result of making the cash transfer conditional.

THE MAKING OF SHADOW CONDITIONS

When power operates at a distance, people are not necessarily aware of how their conduct is being conducted or why, so the question of consent does not arise.
TANIA M. LI, *THE WILL TO IMPROVE*, 2007

In contrast with the view from Lima, the view from the villages beyond Cajamarca city revealed that shadow conditions were a durable feature of conditional aid. In fact, they are liable to arise as a consequence of giving bureaucrats impossibly difficult jobs and, at the same time, remarkable power over poor women. The previous chapters have illustrated how local managers relied on mothers to walk and wait, to manage up, and to act as their "eyes and ears" in order to successfully implement Juntos. In addition to depending on mothers, local managers also relied on other local authorities in order to get their work done. Local managers needed places to sleep when they were in the field; sometimes this meant renting a room in a boardinghouse, but in more isolated villages they relied on health staff to allow them to sleep in the clinic. The district governor in Labaconas granted the local manager use of the municipal dirt bike to move more quickly between communities and did so free of charge. These and other relationships, all of which helped local managers implement Juntos, contributed to the creation of shadow conditions.

I will illustrate this with an example. In response to the failed agreements with the health and education sectors, local managers dutifully assumed responsibility for filling out the verification-of-coresponsibility forms, which Juntos used to monitor women's compliance with health and education conditions. While local managers understood that filling out the forms was up to them, they still relied on health and education staff to cooperate. In practice this meant that the health posts and clinics had to be open—while unexpected closures were not a problem at schools, they were persistently frustrating for local managers monitoring conditions at isolated health clinics. Local managers also needed staff to allow them access to medical histories and attendance records. At clinics, local managers relied on staff to help them locate medical histories that were missing or filed under a different village (which happened frequently), to provide information about pregnant women's expected due dates, and to navigate technical medical terminology. When local authorities at clinics and schools resisted helping, frustrated local managers had to manage the relationships carefully. On several occasions I observed local managers grinning through their teeth while confronting reticent health or school staff. Local managers described the situation pragmatically: "Well, in order to get the job done and get along, we don't grumble or say anything." Frontline program workers become adept at maintaining the social and organizational relationships upon which their work depends (Ahmad 2002), and Juntos local managers were no exception.

Relationships, of course, go two ways. Local authorities viewed the influence local managers had on Juntos mothers as advantageous to themselves and their own work responsibilities. School and health staff, local and regional government employees, politicians, NGO workers, and employees of other state social programs also made requests of local managers. They solicited women's time in health and development interventions, fairs, and parades, and they solicited women's financial resources for school supplies, for documents that should have been free of charge, and for fiestas. Local managers yielded to many of these demands, but not all of them. There was an "I'll scratch your back if you'll scratch mine" dynamic, but local managers decided on a case-by-case basis whether they'd participate. A local manager who decided a request was reasonable, or who needed a favor in return, could inform the mothers in his or her charge that Juntos required them to participate in or contribute to whatever activity was in question. Conditionality, as malleable as it was, was an important work tool.

Sometimes shadow conditions were created when local managers did not have the power to refuse a solicitation, even if they had wanted to. This was the result of institutional practices and processes that shaped how local managers accomplished their work. For instance, if health staff asked Juntos to prompt women to give birth at the clinic, and the local manager needed the health staff's support in order to monitor conditions, how could the manager refuse? If the difficult work of monitoring conditions in places with no public transportation was facilitated by use of the government dirt bike, and then the governor requested mothers' participation in his carnival parade, would the local manager say no? I will illustrate with another example.

One bright day in the capital of Santa Ana District, I was accompanying a local manager and a new local-manager-trainee as they monitored conditions. Juntos headquarters in Lima had recently imposed a new rule requiring local managers to obtain a signature from a local authority—for instance, a school director, mayor, or doctor—in order to prove that the local manager had been at work.[19] The local manager and trainee decided to obtain the signature from the director of the elementary school. They had to visit the school anyway, because they needed the director to confirm that some children from Juntos households had graduated to the secondary school. My field notes from that day describe how a shadow condition developed in the interaction that ensued.

> The director's office is bright and enormous, with shiny wooden floors that look as though they had just been waxed. There is an enormous desk that the director sits at. Straightaway, the director tells Lina that he has been having some problems. The mothers are protesting that they don't want to cook for the Qali Warma lunch program, so he told them that they must all contribute two and a half soles each so that

they can hire a cook. The mothers are protesting this too, saying that they don't want to collaborate, and that the local manager told them they only have to "fulfill core-sponsibilities in health and education." This upsets the director, because Qali Warma is a state program and there should be some "agreement" on this point—but there isn't any. Furthermore, he says, there is "too much paternalism."

The local manager agrees with this, saying, "[The women] want everything from heaven." She is being very sweet to him, negating having previously told the women that they should fulfill only health and education coresponsibilities. The director says he wants to make an announcement that Juntos gives the mothers money for health and education, and that the lunch is vitamins and minerals so they must collaborate. The local manager concurs with this, noting that "now the children eat good food" at school, better than at home. So she agrees with his proposal, saying, "Of course, make the announcement." The director then signed the local manager's and trainee's proof-of-work papers, and we left the office.

At the school office, the local manager and the school director negotiated the creation of a shadow condition. The negotiation underscored how easily the coercive power of incentives could be perverted, and how the poor mothers who relied on Juntos bore the costs. The local manager needed the director's signature to both complete her monitoring work and help Juntos monitor her. The director, who was responsible for implementing the state-funded lunch program, wanted the local manager to coerce the Juntos mothers, who were resisting his wishes, to "volunteer" their culinary labor.

The director made this request of the local manager because he recognized the coercive power of the cash incentive. The local manager had the option to collaborate with the director or to refuse. On other occasions I witnessed the same local manager refuse teachers who proposed that she tell Juntos mothers that they were required to contribute money from the Juntos payment for school parties. Local managers did not agree to with every illicit proposal. Unfortunately in the instance above, if the local manager had refused to comply with the director's request, he in turn could have refused to sign her papers, which would have put the local manager's job at risk. And the director's power was not limited to that one instance; in future, he could have restricted the local manager's access to the school and attendance records. The local manager's ultimate decision to comply with the director's demands was not justified, but it was understandable. He had power over her.

Anthropologist David Mosse found that when development practitioners in Bangladesh set out to implement policy, local relationships were of primary importance. "Viewed from an individual's perspective, project implementation is not only (or primarily) about executing policy, or even putting schemes in place, but a matter of sustaining a set of relationships that secure a person's identity and status, and which are a precondition for action at every level. Effective relationships are necessary to win support, sanction the flow of resources, build reputations, trust and reliability; to fend off arbitrary judgment" (Mosse 2005, 130). The importance of building and sustaining effective local relationships for the frontline state workers in charge of implementing Juntos was obvious. Yet in this negotiation of policy and power, the actors who were already the most marginalized were those who ended up losing the most: poor mothers. While the subject of the negotiation was the women's labor, the women themselves were not given a say. The mothers in question were not present in the office, and although they had voiced their preferences to the director at a previous time, he decided to dismiss their concerns.

Local managers and other authorities justified shadow conditions through rationalizations that associated poor mothers with free labor, and social support with the requirement to prove deservingness. While Qali Warma, like Juntos, was designed to improve children's health, the two programs did not have an agreement by which mothers cooked lunches on account of their status as Juntos recipients. Nevertheless, the director rationalized his request on the basis of the nutritional benefits that Qali Warma provided to Juntos recipients' children. Cooking for the lunch program was the responsible thing for mothers to do. It was possible that the local manager rationalized the arrangement through a similar logic. When I interviewed her, she told me that she often spoke to mothers about what and how often they should feed their children. She believed that nutrition was central to a family's capacity to overcome their poverty.

By many accounts, Qali Warma was a good program—it provided students in rural Peru with nutritious meals that were often made with local ingredients, at no charge. Yet in order to do so, it relied on the unpaid labor of mothers. In this, Qali Warma was not unlike many other social programs throughout Peru's history that have provided goods and services through women's unpaid care work (Barrig 1991; Blondet and Trivelli 2004; Rousseau 2009). From the perspective of the director, why not use one social program to help another? And what was the problem with making sure that lazy, entitled women properly fed their children? When mothers in Santa Ana resisted the exploitation of their labor, the school director capitalized on the opportunity to use Juntos to bring them into line.

Shadow conditions draw our attention to the coercive power of incentives and the multiple possibilities for their perversion. On paper, conditional aid seems like a tidy technical mechanism for helping families improve their lives. In the real world of bodies, uneven development, and inequality, conditionality became a tool for more powerful groups to implement their own projects of improvement among less powerful groups. Authorities within and outside of Juntos used the program to discipline women's behavior, either for their own professional benefit or in order to achieve an end that they believed to be benevolent. If the governor believes that his political party's plan for regional development will help families overcome poverty, why not incentivize them to show support in the local parade? If the foreign volunteer corps believes that women need access to the market in order to overcome poverty, why not incentivize them to weave colored belts for sale in tourist centers? If the local manager believes that the women he manages must have fewer children in order to overcome poverty, why not incentivize them to use contraceptives?

Shadow conditions were not simply the well-intended distractions that experts in Lima supposed. Rather, shadow conditions were an integral feature of program implementation. Juntos was unviable unless local managers succeeded in getting school and health clinic authorities, among others, to assist them in tracking beneficiaries, filling out coresponsibility forms, and facilitating travel and accommodation. Local managers stretched the boundaries of what could and could not be made conditional in order to produce and obtain the data that Juntos required. The limits on this top-down power were unclear.

CONCLUSION

Global development experts claim that CCTs are important components of the global "safety net" (Fiszbein et al. 2009; World Bank 2017). Yet the experiences of Peruvian mothers who rely on conditional aid undercut this claim. Juntos mother Josepa captured this idea: "Well, it frightens me. I say to myself, 'Are they going to take [the transfer] away from me if I don't bring [my son] to the day care?'" With reason, a safety net feels less safe when rendered insecure by threats of local managers and other authorities.

Burdening poor women with microproductive projects while failing to address infrastructural barriers that complicate basic care work is unjust; conditioning poor women's access to social protection upon their ability to grow leafy greens is even more so. It would also be misguided to blame the local managers who used threats of suspension and shadow conditions to get their work done. While their abuses of power were undeniably wrong, these must be viewed within the broader context of uneven development, the difficulty of the tasks policy makers assigned them and their own precarious social position—only one or two rungs above the households they manage.

Technical interventions, of which the CCT is exemplary, can produce a host of unintended consequences when they fail to grapple with the messy social, economic, and political issues driving persistent inequities. Conditionality is a tidy arrangement curated and packaged in air-conditioned offices located far away from the impoverished communities, households, and bodies it is used to improve. Good intentions notwithstanding, Juntos mutated with ease. It quickly unraveled and became unruly in the real world, where economic policies, sexist assumptions, discriminatory attitudes, and uneven investments accord some people more power than others. As a result, poor rural mothers did not encounter a simple incentive program—they encountered shadow conditions and seemingly limitless demands on their time and labor. If the costs of conditionality remain in the shadows of the global policy landscape, they certainly were not hidden from these women.

7

Conclusion

Toward a Caring Society

Twenty years after the first large-scale conditional cash transfer programs were rolled out in Mexico and Brazil, imposing conditions is no longer the exclusive terrain of governments, and children's health and education are no longer the only targets for improvement. Thanks to the wonders of mobile money and the popularity of conditional aid among a growing range of nongovernmental organizations, social enterprises, research institutes, and philanthropists, you, too, can reform the misguided behaviors of a poor person. For instance, the award-winning social enterprise New Incentives offers you the opportunity to motivate a woman in rural Nigeria to give birth in a health clinic—which you can do from the comfort of your armchair. And you can trust that your incentive will have the desired effect, because New Incentives will disburse the cash only after they have verified with clinic staff that the mother gave birth as required.[1] Or, if sanitation strikes your fancy, you can incentivize a man in India to install a toilet. Reproductive health? A pilot program in Tanzania incentivizes youth to remain free of sexually transmitted infections. My hope is that, having read this book, you will think twice about the apparent simplicity of making aid conditional.

In undertaking the long and trying ethnographic work of comprehending conditional aid programs from the perspective of poor mothers, I have traveled from an interest in cash transfers, to the more skeptical stance of "thinking twice," and finally to the view that the contemporary practice of conditional aid is unjust. In the preceding chapters I have offered analytical contributions related to blind spots in our measurement of program impacts, the ironic conditions of clinics and schools, the unpaid work of walking and waiting, and the wild proliferation of shadow conditions. The broader arc of this book's argument is as much about speaking truth to power as it is as analytical; I have argued that these conditions are unjust.

To the development experts who boldly proclaim that CCTs "are a great thing to do," this book stands as a rebuke and a plea for humility. One of the appeals of conditional aid is its alleged efficiency, but in practice CCTs are efficient only if women's time and unpaid labor is worth nothing. When we account for all of the work that rural women are required to do to implement a CCT program, we inevitably uncover a number of hidden costs. CCTs are often rolled out in places where poor people have a difficult time accessing quality services. In Peru, rural mothers do a lot of walking and waiting. In the absence of safe and reliable transportation, and sometimes even roads, pregnant women walk to deliver their babies in clinics, and mothers walk to deliver their children to health appointments and school. They walk back and forth between home and the clinic until they encounter it open and staffed for service. They walk up and down the Andes mountains in the sun and the rain and the cold and the fog. Between journeys, women wait. They wait for attention from school staff, nurses, and bureaucrats in government offices. They wait for politicians to fulfill promises, and they wait for the state to deliver what wealthier, urban regions already have: teachers, doctors, water, jobs, and a sanitation system. They wait as long as the authorities ask them to wait, and in my observations, they wait patiently.

In the case of Juntos, women bore the cost of poor-quality services, and they also bore the cost of an inadequately staffed program. The state employed a cadre of hardworking frontline bureaucrats called local managers to enforce and monitor conditions, but they were responsible for an unrealistic number of households. The only way that local managers could meet their professional responsibilities was to rely on the help of the women they managed. Juntos mothers were required to "manage up." They attended meetings to save local managers travel time, and they walked and waited to make sure that Juntos maintained an updated database and an accurate list of who had complied with the program conditions. Managing up had a cost for women, who expended their time in service of Juntos rather than on any number of other productive, caring, or leisurely tasks.

In addition to the work of ordinary mothers required to manage up, local managers also relied on the organized labor of a group of "exemplary" Juntos recipients called Mother Leaders. Local managers referred to these women as "the local managers in their communities." The work of Mother Leaders bore a surprising resemblance to the job descriptions that program headquarters had written for local managers. The Mother Leaders, however, were not paid for their contributions. Here was yet another gendered cost, hidden between the line items of Juntos's administrative budget. If not for Mother Leaders, the state would have been required to hire many, many more local managers. The unpaid labor of these women subsidized the cost of implementing Peru's largest social program, which development experts hold up as a "model for the world."

On paper, conditionality seems like a simple technical arrangement. Yet in the real world of unequal resources and social hierarchies, a well-intended incentive can unravel into a coercive exercise of authority. Once Juntos arrived in the places it was meant to improve, conditionality became a tool for more authoritative groups to exercise power over subordinate groups. Experts in Lima intended for Juntos mothers to meet a strict schedule of health and education conditions, and they did. But they also complied with a host of additional directives put in place by Juntos's frontline staff and other local authorities. These "shadow conditions" were enforced through threats of suspension and accusations of irresponsible motherhood.

Although undoubtedly well-intentioned, Juntos was an example of development by *susto* (fear). Local managers yelled at mothers, telling them they had to take their children to school or the state would take Juntos away from them— and to an extent, this threat was based on official policy. But they also demanded that mothers use the state-run day care, keep tidier houses, participate in parades, and give birth in clinics. In theory, these were not things for which women could rightfully be suspended. In practice, there were no substantive checks on abuse of power. And so women bore the cost. They went running from one appointment to another, unsure of what was actually required of them. Shadow conditions were a manifestation of the coercive power of incentives; the limits of this power were unclear, its effects practically immeasurable. This is perhaps the most striking of the reasons that I call conditioning aid unjust.

Nearly a year after the fieldwork for this book took place, news broke that a group of local managers, in collusion with two cashiers from the National Bank, had stolen approximately one million soles from Juntos recipients' savings accounts.[2] This systematically organized heist took place over the course of two years and affected an unaccounted-for number of program beneficiaries. According to reports, local managers simply informed the mothers that they would not receive the cash transfer for a given period of time, and subsequently the bank cashiers siphoned the money from the agreed-upon accounts.

Media coverage of this scandal generally treated it as a rare and extreme event. However, I offer an alternative interpretation. The fact that local managers could withhold transfers from hundreds of Juntos women for months at a time with no explanation, knowing that these women had no recourse whatsoever, tells of a broader pattern. In the communities where I conducted fieldwork, the prevalence of shadow conditions stands as evidence that frontline workers seldom face repercussions when they use conditions for purposes that policy makers should be loath to condone. This theft surfaced unequal power dynamics that are widespread and routinely implicated in more ordinary and invisible forms of injustice. Imposing conditions on aid facilitates such abuses. Conditional incentives in the context of deep social and political inequities are not merely "powerful tools" but tools that give the more dominant groups unchecked power over subordinate groups.

Incentives *are* effective insofar as they change behaviors. Yet mothers' accounts of their everyday lives revealed that their children's poverty was less an issue of the women's misguided individual choices, and more an issue of the difficult conditions in which they cared for their families. Instead of focusing our good intentions and resources on motivating poor women to change their behavior, we might instead seek to change the persistent inequities that shape people's broader life conditions. By all accounts, this would require us to ask the challenging "political-economic questions" that simpler, technical fixes so often sideline (Li 2007). A nuanced and substantive way of refocusing on the broader conditions of people's lives is through a focus on care.

RECALCULATING THE COSTS OF CARE

Nearly four years after completing the fieldwork for this book, I returned to Yesenia's house in the village of Bellavista. On this visit, Yesenia looked happy and strong and as though she had been feeding herself well. I recalled how, on my last visit, Yesenia's young neighbor Judit had solemnly remarked that for women of humble means like them, breast cancer meant that you died or hoped that God would save you. Four years later, Yesenia had not died. The sky was dumping buckets on the hillside, and so Yesenia and I sat sipping hot water flavored with *hierba luisa* from the yard and caught up.[3] Yesenia recounted how she had traveled to Lima, where she underwent a mastectomy and several rounds of chemotherapy and radiation at the public hospital there. The hospital served low-income people who traveled there from all over Peru, people who did not have health insurance through formal employment, and who could not afford to pay for care at a private clinic. Despite the economic and geographical barriers, the grim prognosis of her neighbors, and her own fears, Yesenia survived the bout with breast cancer.

It was not only the benevolent support of the state's public care that got her through the illness. Survival required a steely amount of grit and determination on Yesenia's part. She endured multiple eighteen-hour bus rides from her home to Lima to obtain the surgery and for rounds of chemotherapy. Along with all of the other low-income people seeking affordable medical attention, Yesenia waited for care. She stood in line outside the hospital for hours, in the rain and the sun, while she patiently awaited her turn for attention. In no small part, Yesenia also owed her survival to the unpaid caring labor of her sister, who had migrated to Lima many years previously to look for work and continued to reside there. Yesenia's sister housed her, fed her, and nursed her throughout the course of her treatment.

Like women all over the country today and throughout history, Yesenia's sister stepped in where the state had retreated or, perhaps more accurately, had never really been present for people like them. While her sister's care work saved Yesenia the cost of lodging in a foreign city, she still had to pay for travel to and from Lima and within it, as well as for medication. Once she had completed the rounds of chemotherapy in Lima, she had to continue with oral treatment. The five-month course of medication that the doctor prescribed cost Yesenia eight hundred soles (approximately UD$245). For a household that falls below the poverty line, this was an enormous cost.

Development experts consider CCTs to be an important part of the social safety net, providing households with a cushion against unexpected shocks. Cancer is not an uncommon shock; and for women like Yesenia, the cost of the cure was substantial. The hundred soles that Juntos provided Yesenia every month helped her buy school supplies, mobile phone credit and chickens, and it surely softened her fall. Yet the absence of other vital social supports, including accessible and affordable health care, amounts to a barrier that for many is insurmountable. If Yesenia had not had the available caring labor of her sister in Lima, and her husband at home who cared for their children in Yesenia's absence, Yesenia would have been forced to "choose" not to access medical attention. Yesenia's neighbor Lydia had not faired as well. She had received a similar diagnosis and had not survived. The safety net available to Yesenia and her neighbors remains far too patchy.

Within the next two years, Yesenia will be disaffiliated from the Juntos program because her youngest daughter will graduate high school. During our conversation, I was reminded again what it meant to be a responsible mother in rural Peru. This time, I had walked up to Yesenia's house with Verónica, Judit's younger sister. Verónica was eleven years old and very studious. During our visit, Yesenia asked her all about her classes and which she preferred and why. When Verónica told us, gloomily, about a girl in her class that copied off Verónica's paper and ended up getting a very good score, Yesenia offered some advice. She recounted to Verónica a time when a student cheated by copying the work of her eldest daughter, Silvia. When this happened Silvia was very upset, but Yesenia told her that she had to keep studying, "because you cannot get ahead in life by cheating." She said to Silvia that she had to keep working on herself until she was the one receiving the top marks. Today, Yesenia told us, Silvia was studying to be an accountant at a technical college in the city. She had earned a scholarship on account of the many times she had won mathematics competitions—without cheating. Verónica sat listening, eyes glued to Yesenia.

On the walk home from Yesenia's house, Verónica listed the many kinds of books she liked to read, thoughtfully considering the idea that while mathematics was not her favorite, perhaps she could become a doctor or a nurse. I could not help but think that, once again, Yesenia had displayed precisely the kind of caring, responsible motherhood that governments, development experts, and the CCT programs they devise do too little to recognize or support.

Care work involves educating children and ensuring they have access to basic medical care. It also involves much more than this. Good care requires physical and emotional work, it requires significant expenditures of time, money, and effort. While the benefits of care work are disbursed broadly and benefit society as a whole, the costs of caring are disproportionately borne by women (Razavi 2007a, 12). We cannot reasonably expect women to "lift families out of poverty," as the popular adage goes, if we fail to account for the relationship between women's subordinate social status and the fact that care work is typically unpaid or poorly paid. All too often the way that we structure economic and social policy fails to recognize the value of care and the gendered costs of accomplishing it.

This is perhaps nowhere more stark than in common understandings of economic development. Care work is not recognized as "productive" labor in most aggregate measures of economic activity, such as the gross domestic product.[4] As a result, when we build policies to achieve economic growth, care and the majority of women who do it are omitted from the equation (Waring 1988). Some countries have taken steps to change this. In 1993, the System of National Accounts was revised to include undercounted (unpaid family work, home-based work, self-employment work, and informal-sector work) and uncounted (subsistence) work in GDP calculations. This was a considerable achievement, but it could go much farther. The System of National Accounts does not count important areas of unpaid care work, including homemaking; caring for children and sick, disabled, and elderly household members; and volunteer work. Some countries, including Canada, the United Kingdom, Switzerland, and Australia, decided to value these activities through use of "satellite accounts" (see Razavi 2007a, 5). These attempts to "count" care work recognize that the unpaid contributions of women like Yesenia are valuable.

In the context of international aid and development, we can use care as a touchstone to assess the substance and sustainability of agendas invoking women and their empowerment. As a Canadian and a feminist, I have tracked, celebrated, written letters about, and raised the occasional eyebrow at my current government's Feminist International Assistance Policy. It is still too early to tell what gains for women this self-proclaimed feminist agenda might deliver, but I'm optimistic. Having the courage to use the political term *feminist* already demonstrates a commitment to meaningful social change.

Something we might watch for is whether this new agenda positions women as a means to an end or as an end in themselves. There is little if anything feminist in the status quo approach to international development that views women and their labor as tools with which to benefit others, always others (the community, the economy, children, the nation). Investments in women and their empowerment are all too often crafted to achieve economic growth, better returns for philanthropic investors, bigger impacts for social entrepreneurs, and greater outcomes for foreign aid donors. Considering how often women's empowerment is evoked in relation to some other suffering group or ambitious cause, one could easily make the mistake of assuming that women already enjoy full social, political, and economic equality with men. But it was precisely by approaching women and their caring labor as free-of-charge resources that experts offering CCTs generated a host of gendered and unjust costs.

We might also assess the transformative potential of feminist international development assistance by how it recognizes and reduces women's unpaid-care burden. In addition to documenting the hidden costs of care, this will entail attending to the broader conditions of caring. Mothers in rural Peru still have to overcome a host of economic and geographical barriers that people in wealthier and better-serviced places do not. In the following paragraphs I offer a few reflections on the future of cash transfer programs and the prospects for a meaningful social safety net in places where development remains starkly uneven.

UNCONDITIONED CASH AND A STRONGER SAFETY NET

In the nearly four years I had been away, the village of Sonsonate had changed so dramatically that it was almost unrecognizable. The district government was finally fulfilling its promise to extend water and drainage pipes to all of the houses in the village. A grumbling excavator turned dirt roads and brushy pathways between houses into muddy canals, and long pipes lay waiting. Paloma, who had arrived in Sonsonate forty years previously, was happy about the forthcoming water services. She would no longer have to wait her weekly turn to irrigate the garden. As Paloma's three youngest children staged an impromptu photo shoot with my iPhone, we chatted about all of the other things that had changed in the village. Two new food-processing plants had set up shop, one on either end of the village, and the enormous white buildings stood in sharp contrast to the mostly concrete and adobe houses. One of the plants processed fruits and grains for export abroad. Paloma told me that it did not source the fruits and grains locally, however. Most people in Sonsonate were subsistence farmers, and their yields were too small to attract the plant's buyers. In any case, the plant paid very poorly for the produce and grains, much less than the going rate in the local market. Authorities had also promised the arrival of new jobs with the two plants, but neither of them appeared to be hiring locally.

It seemed that almost everyone that I talked to, whether in Cajamarca city or the villages outside, lamented what they perceived to be an increasing shortage of paid work. Paloma's kind husband, Edison, was among them. On both occasions that I got to visit with him on this return trip, he was dressed in a hard hat and safety vest and was covered in mud. Edison had gotten work helping install the village's new water and drainage system. The project was commissioned by the government, but it was a private contractor who hired him and a number of other able-bodied men from the community. Edison used to work as a day laborer in construction in Cajamarca city, but in the past three years the work had all but dried up. He told me that the work in the village was poorly paid, in large part because it was through a contractor, and contractors frequently paid wages well under what should have been the going rate. The job was temporary, expected to last for only three more weeks. While he was visibly disheartened, Edison took the work without complaint. What other choice, he asked, did he have?

It wasn't only people in the villages who lamented the downturn in local employment opportunities. It was also people in the urban middle class. I had lunch with Ofelia, who had worked for Juntos as the local managers' direct supervisor. Ofelia, like a score of other regional staff, had gone through several bouts of unemployment over the previous three years. She had left Juntos to work for another national social program that provided the elderly poor with unconditional cash transfers, called Pensión 65. Ofelia delighted in the work, which she thought was more about *accompanying* the poor than her previous role with Juntos. In large part this was because the unconditional nature of Pensión 65 meant no time spent monitoring conditions and plenty of time spent getting to know the elderly beneficiaries and what they needed. But the program underwent a series of administrative changes and Ofelia was let go. She looked for work, but to no avail. Ofelia explained to me that since Peru's growth rate had slowed in 2015 (largely owing to reduced activity in the extractive industries), the country's biggest social programs were cutting staff.[5] The job market was saturated with other people who, like her, had years of experience in public and private social programs and were now unable to find a job.[6]

Ofelia and her colleagues are members of Peru's "new middle class." Many of them came from the rural villages that they eventually managed as social-program frontline staff. Their parents were farmers or domestic workers who labored to overcome the barriers that rural people face and to provide their children with more opportunities than they had themselves. This was, of course, well before Juntos arrived in those very same villages. Ofelia, like others, had studied hard and won a place at the public university, where she eventually earned a master's degree. Since graduating, she had worked for a number of social programs and believed that it was possible to alleviate poverty. When Ofelia and I had lunch, she was in the first week of a new job. It was her fourth in four years, and it followed a stint of unemployment that had lasted just over six months. Ofelia was not sure how long she would be in this new post—would the economy pick up again? For members of Peru's new middle class, poverty was only a short fall away.

In the context of scarce employment opportunities, social safety nets play an important role, not only for the poorest, but also for members of the middle class whose world of work is precarious (World Bank 2017). While CCTs are frequently deployed to prompt improvements in children's health and education, they are also one of the many tools that policy makers use to weave a social safety net that prevents people from hitting rock bottom when they've endured a financial shock.

Following the robbery by employees at Juntos and the National Bank, some Peruvian legislators proposed suspending the Juntos program until all issues of "corruption" were resolved. The appropriately sharp response this proposal elicited from Carolina Trivelli, a rural economist and former minister of MIDIS (where Juntos is housed), serves as a reminder of the way that Juntos functions as a social safety net—by providing cash that helps buffer some of poverty's more acute effects on rural families. "Impossible, what are people going to do? Not eat, not buy their medicine, not pay their bills. The proposal does not make sense. These programs are crucial for the people who receive them to have minimum living conditions. There is no way to stop [the programs], it's not like these are people who have money to spare, they are people who need [the cash transfer] to survive" (*El Comercio* 2015). The Juntos recipients that I spent time with would likely concur with the former minister; when broader economic and political conditions make rural life difficult, every "little bit of help" is deeply important.

In this book I have argued that imposing conditions on cash is unjust. But what about providing cash *without* conditions? Policy makers, politicians, and activists in the global north and south are increasingly making a case for an expansion of the social safety net through cash transfers that do not come with conditions attached. In contexts where development experts perceive that the quality or accessibility of services is too low to require poor people to utilize them, many governments have already implemented unconditional cash transfer programs (UCTs). Today, 130 low-income countries are implementing at least one UCT program (Hagen-Zanker et.al 2016). Research shows that UCTs and CCTs can have comparable effects in terms of boosting household consumption and increasing service uptake (Gaarder 2012). UCTs are also an increasingly important component of humanitarian and natural-disaster response.[7] When governments give UCTs instead of food rations, this allows recipients to purchase food, mobile phone credit, or other basic supplies *as they see fit*. Because UCTs are frequently implemented in places where public services are poor, they do not eliminate the requirement that people walk and wait for the things they need. But because they do not impose conditions, they greatly reduce the administrative burden of monitoring compliance and the abuses of power that result in shadow conditions and the exploitation of women's time.

It is not only low- and middle-income countries that are experimenting with UCTs, either. In Canada, the province of Ontario is piloting a "basic income" for four thousand citizens between the ages of eighteen and sixty-four who are either unemployed or earning a low salary (less than thirty-four thousand Canadian dollars, or twenty-seven thousand US dollars annually). The government "tops up" the beneficiary's annual income by up to nearly seventeen thousand Canadian dollars (nearly fourteen thousand US dollars), with an additional monthly allowance for people living with a disability. The pilot launched in 2017 and will continue for three years. During this time, researchers will assess the UCT's effects on a number of factors, including beneficiaries' labor market participation, levels of stress and anxiety, use of health care services, and housing stability (Government of Ontario, 2017).

Unconditional cash transfers are still highly targeted, in that they direct cash to specific socially and economically marginalized groups. However, the way that development experts think about targeting is changing, and target groups might eventually include middle-class women like Ofelia. In South Africa and Namibia, there is a movement to expand UCTs into a universal basic income (UBI) grant that would be given to everyone, regardless of income bracket, in an attempt to reduce poverty and soften the effects of mass unemployment. Advocates of the UBI suggest that providing cash grants to everyone could form the basis of a more just way of organizing social, political, and economic life in low-, middle-, and high-income countries alike (Standing 2002; Ferguson 2015).[8]

One high-income country experimenting with the UBI is Finland. The Finnish government currently provides two thousand people between the ages of twenty-five and fifty-eight with a monthly payment of 560 euros (607 US dollars), independent of other income sources or status of employment. The experiment, which began in January 2017, will last two years. At the end of the pilot study, researchers will assess the impact of the UBI on the employment rate. They will also determine whether the UBI met another objective: reduction of bureaucracy and simplification of an otherwise complex social security system (Kela 2017).

For some, the UBI is a practical response to automation and an economy that no longer guarantees the majority of people decent, dependable, formal work. It has the potential to be a form of social support that offers a little bit of help consistently, without relying on women's unpaid labor or disciplining their motherly choices. Advocates suggest that the UBI would reduce the potential for abuses of bureaucratic authority, because recipients would not be required to demonstrate to a middleman that they have "earned" it. Universally provisioned cash would modestly reduce income inequality, and it would also reduce the stigma associated with welfare because everyone would receive it. The grant would not be a significant benefit for middle- and upper-class households, but it also wouldn't be a waste; better-off families and individuals would simply invest it back into the economy, probably through leisure activities like going to the movies or dining out.

Anthropologist James Ferguson optimistically suggests that a universal basic income could form the basis of a "new distributive politics." He asks, "What if a poor person could receive a distributive payment neither as a reciprocal exchange for labour (wages) or good conduct (the premise of conditional cash transfers) nor as an unreciprocated gift (assistance, charity, a helping hand) but instead as a share, a rightful allocation due to a rightful owner?" (Ferguson 2015, 178). A universal cash payment based on the notion of a rightful share has compelling implications, especially if we consider it in relation to unpaid care. Ferguson suggests that instead of thinking narrowly about livelihoods in terms of productive labor and wages, a distributive politics could recognize the necessary relationship between care work and a productive society. He writes, "Since childhood (and before that infancy) always precedes adulthood, the slogan of a distributive radical politics might be this: before a man can produce, he must be nursed—that is, the receipt of unconditional and unearned distribution and care must always precede any productive labour" (45). Ferguson's proposal could have profound implications for gender equality, reframing how we think about care work and the value of the women who do it.

Could a universal basic income provide the basis for a more caring society? Maybe, and it is certainly a worthwhile experiment. If a new distributive politics such as this is to have substance, it will require material efforts that extend beyond optimism and a new vocabulary. Ferguson suggests that, instead of being a handout, the cash could be conceived of as a rightful share. Language is powerful, but as I have shown in this book, talking about inclusion, rights, or a *share* is not enough. Development is full of "fuzzwords," terms like *empowerment* and *participation*, which make people feel good but easily are invoked by projects that have little substance (Cornwall and Eade 2010). Development experts sold Juntos as a mechanism for rights and inclusion and were still able to claim success even after the intervention had been evacuated of its more substantive aims (Cookson 2016). Using feel-good language can dull the imperative to do the more difficult and uncomfortable work of tackling deeply rooted legal, political, economic, and social arrangements through which some people become rich and others stay poor.

For a distributive politics to be meaningful to women, it would first have to advance a narrative about care as essential work and work of value—and then it would have to put substance behind those words. While a cash stipend helps buffer the financial costs of caring at the household level, good care requires a mix of support from individuals and institutions, and it requires emotional labor, skills, and infrastructure. As women's accounts in this book have illustrated, caring requires more than cash. A caring society is also one that provides accessible, affordable, and high-quality health care and education. A caring society supports and adequately compensates people who care professionally: teachers, nurses, doctors, care aides, nannies, and domestic workers, among others. Cash transfers, even if distributed more justly, would still be just the beginning.

CHECKING THE BLIND SPOTS

Finally, as we consider the transition from imposing conditions to cultivating conditions for caring and living well, I offer reflections on how we may know whether we are making progress. In this book, I demonstrate how a narrow focus on a handful of quantitative metrics created a blind spot that hid the gendered costs of imposing conditions on aid in rural places. Such blind spots abound in global development. Rates of monetary poverty continue to fall, in part owing to governments' implementation of cash transfer programs, and many development experts now celebrate places like Peru for having become middle-income countries. Yet most of the world still lives on less than ten dollars a day, and income inequality continues to grow (OECD 2015). The drivers of this dilemma are impossible to comprehend if we attend to the wrong metrics.

In order to overcome persistent inequality, the world has lined up behind a new set of United Nations Sustainable Development Goals. These goals have a unifying aim: leave no one behind. The goals come with more indicators than any previous global development agenda, and countries are actively encouraged by development banks and private funders to measure their progress. Many of these metrics have their merits, yet if we don't want this agenda to leave anyone behind, we still need to check our blind spots. One current, major gap in our understanding of inequality is produced by a lack of census data that can tell us about women's lives. For this reason, philanthropic leaders like Melinda Gates and the Clinton Foundation have partnered with international organizations like UN Women to collect "gender data" on a previously unheard-of scale.

This push for gender data shows real promise and, if successful, will lead to policies and programs that effectively address the drivers of gender inequality. Yet many women's rights activists and development practitioners take the recent buzz with a hearty dose of reservation. This is because "gender data" is often equated with sex-disaggregated statistics, and calls for gender data collection tend to exclude the kinds of qualitative evidence that women's rights organizations routinely use to guide their work. As a result, many view the "measurement imperative" as an externally imposed, impractical, and burdensome distraction from the political work to be done—and funded. They wonder whether the aim of the "gender data revolution" is merely to "count women." Their concerns are not unfounded. After all, one of the most striking lessons from the implementation of CCTs is that numbers tell a partial story. For the gender data movement to transform the unjust conditions of our world, it must go beyond technical indicators and ask uncomfortable questions about identity, power, wealth, and justice. Gender data must include women's accounts of their own lives.

If we are to leave no one behind, we need to do slow research to complement the fast gains of quantitative evaluations. Slow research is no silver bullet, but when done well it can reveal depth and nuances in the conditions of people's everyday lives. To be sure, in this approach to data collection the answers do not come quickly. Yet the tendency of slow research to instill a level of humility in those who seek to improve this world is also its biggest promise. By looking slowly, by patiently learning which questions to ask, and by taking the time to listen with care, we can begin to see those things that otherwise remain in the shadows. The messy features of social life, the pernicious economic and political arrangements that harm so many—these unjust conditions are available for investigation. And it is not just the more wicked aspects of our world that we can come to understand. Through slow research, we may identify the openings, levers, and possibilities for crafting a more just and caring society.

NOTES

1 INTRODUCTION: MAKING AID CONDITIONAL

"World Bank to Name and Shame Countries That Fail to Prevent Stunting in Children," *The Guardian*, September 30, 2016, www.theguardian.com/global-development/2016/sep/30/world-bank-name-and-shame-countries-fail-stunted-children?utm_source=esp&utm_medium=Email&utm_campaign=Poverty+Matters+2016&utm_term=193350&subid=5454778&CMP=EMCGBLEML1625.

1. As far as I am aware, there is no direct English translation for *la garúa*. Occurring generally during the winter months, it is a rain so light, yet so dense, that it appears as fog.

2. In Latin America, this "inclusive" shift has led many to argue that we are witnessing a shift toward a "post-neoliberal" model of governance (Grugel and Riggirozzi 2009; Macdonald and Ruckert 2009). That said, the general consensus in much of the literature is that there is no singular, coherent post-neoliberal paradigm (Cortes 2009; Andolina et al. 2009; Yates and K. Bakker 2014).

3. See Rachel Glennerster and Michael Kremer, "Small Changes, Big Results: Behavioral Economics at Work in Poor Countries," *Boston Review* (March–April 2011), http://bostonreview.net/archives/BR36.2/glennerster_kremer_behavioral_economics_global_development.php.

4. "Local manager" is a direct translation from the Spanish *gestor local*. Before 2012, local managers were called *promotores*, which could be translated as "community workers."

5. Across Peru the payment was disbursed every two months, and so Josepa would receive two hundred soles six times a year.

6. For a history of the concept of uneven development and its usage in various political, economic, and geographical schools of thought, see Smith 2010. For an analysis of uneven geographies of intentional development interventions in Peru, see Bebbington 2004. For an analysis of uneven development in a high-income country (United Kingdom), see Massey 1995.

7. A great number of communities in Andean Peru are located at or above this level.

8. In Peru, mestizo is an ethnic/racial category indicating mixed race, usually Spanish and indigenous.

9. I define *class* as a socioeconomic marker of difference that indicates positioning in relation to gendered modes of production and reproduction (Armstrong and Connelly 1989). In order to emphasize inequality that is also cultural, I use the term *ethnicity* to signify regional, racial, and physical constructions of social difference (for a comprehensive account of ethnicity in Peru, see Thorp and Paredes 2010). In Cajamarca, *campesino/campesina* is the ethnic identifier used by regional inhabitants; it translates roughly to "peasant." Other scholars prefer the term *race* to describe unequal social relations between Peruvian indigenous, mixed-race, and European-descendant peoples (de la Cadena 2000; Ewig 2010).

10. Maternal mortality has decreased significantly in Peru: a 64.9 percent decrease from the period 1990–1996 (265 out of 100,000 live births) to the period 2004–2010 (93 out of 100,000 live births; INEI 2014a).

11. The census was created in 2004 by the Peruvian Ministry of Finance as a mechanism by which to promote efficient targeting of state social programs. It collects household socioeconomic information in the General Household Registry. In 2012, the census was transferred to MIDIS.

12. Program conditions have undergone some changes over the years. Shortly before my fieldwork, Juntos changed the education condition; previously, children had to remain in school until fourteen years of age, and once all children in a household had turned fourteen, the family was removed from the program. Mothers reported that changes such as these were confusing, and they often had little understanding of what the age requirements actually were.

13. Smith refers to institutional ethnography as a "sociology for people," suggesting that even when research begins with the standpoint of women, it must work for both men and women (2005, 1).

14. Smith draws on Sandra Harding's thinking on standpoints. See Harding 1986.

15. Institutional ethnography (IE) might be considered unorthodox in that it does not require a rigorously identified "sample" of informants. Rather, it seeks a careful analysis of how an often broad assembly of differently situated actors are tied together through institutional processes. According to DeVault and McCoy, "Clearly, the selection of informants is more open-ended in IE investigations than it is in more conventional positivist studies, but the process is not haphazard. Rather, fieldwork and interviewing are driven by faithfulness to the actual work processes that connect individuals and activities in the various parts of an institutional complex. Rigor comes not from technique—such as sampling or thematic analysis—but from the corrigibility of the developing map of social relations" (DeVault and McCoy 2002, 764).

16. Other factors include cultural practices and laws that limit women's access to land, political power, and economic resources.

17. Two important bodies of thought informing the scholarly literature on the care economy are generated from feminist economics and gender and social policy. See Razavi 2007a for a comprehensive account.

18. In international development, gender and development scholars and practitioners have been saying at least since the 1970s that development interventions did not adequately

(or in many cases, did not at all) account for women's unpaid-work burden (particularly in terms of subsistence production). Economist Ester Boserup's *Women's Role in Economic Development* (1970) made visible women's significant unpaid contributions to the agricultural economy in sub-Saharan Africa. Her research formed the basis for the Women in Development approach, which challenged the dominant view in development that women were limited to the roles of mothers and wives. Women in Development advocates contested mainstream definitions of *work* and spurred changes to data collection methods for generating national statistics. For instance, the System of National Accounts was revised in 1993 to include undercounted (unpaid family work, home-based work, self-employment work, and informal-sector work) and uncounted (subsistence) work in calculations of gross domestic product. However, core areas of unpaid *care* work were omitted, including domestic tasks related to keeping a house; care of children, sick, disabled, and elderly household members; and volunteer work. Some countries, including Canada, the UK, Switzerland, and Australia, did come to value these activities through use of "satellite accounts" (see Razavi 2007a, 5).

19. Analyses of care have in large part been generated from scholarship focusing on developed capitalist economies. Nevertheless, they offer useful insights for low- and middle-income-country contexts like the one presented in this book, particularly given that development is largely driven by ideas, policies, and priorities generated by developed capitalist economies.

20. Unpaid care must not be idealized. Such a view "ignores the compulsory side of 'altruism' in unpaid caring, or the social pressures on women to provide unpaid care, as well as the risks of self-exploitation and economic insecurity to which unpaid carers are frequently exposed. As Elson (2005, 2) put it, the fact that much 'unpaid care work is done for love, does not mean that we always love doing it'" (Razavi 2007a, 16).

21. To speak of costs, however, is not to deny that unpaid care work can also generate physical, social, and emotional benefits, including stronger relationships, intimacy, and higher-quality services for care-receivers (Folbre 2006).

22. *Social reproduction* is another term used in feminist scholarship to emphasize the centrality of women's unpaid work in reproducing whole societies (Benería 1979; Picchio 1992). Reproductive labor, which includes all of the activities necessary for the reproduction and maintenance of society and care of the environment, is a core element of care economics. A key benefit of the term *social reproduction* is that it draws attention to the artificial boundaries between productive and reproductive labor and thus works well to challenge capitalism. The term *social reproduction* was especially popular in the 1970s and 1980s. "Care" is a critical element of social reproduction (Folbre 2014), as well as a more popular term contemporaneously, in large part because of its attention to human relations and emotion (Anttonen 2005).

23. Nancy Folbre (2006) argues for a move beyond the term *unpaid care* to a more disaggregated analysis that distinguishes among forms of care work, in order that it might better be accounted for. This analysis would account for the work's relationship to the market, characteristics, and types of beneficiaries. For the purposes of this book, I retain a simplified understanding of unpaid care work.

24. See the article by Javier Lizarzaburu, "Forced Sterilisation Haunts Peruvian Women Decades On," December 2, 2015, *BBC News*, www.bbc.com/news/world-latin-america-34855804.

25. When this happens, the intervention and its aims may be reconfigured or reframed and another attempt made. See Ferguson 1990; Li 2007; Keshavjee 2014.

26. Li draws on anthropologist James Ferguson's description of planned development as an "anti-politics machine" that "insistently repos[es] political questions of land, resources, jobs, or wages as technical 'problems' responsive to the technical 'development' intervention" (Ferguson 1994, 270, as cited in Li 2007, 7).

2 SETTING THE CONDITIONS

G. A. Fine and D. Shulman, "Lies from the Field: Ethical Issues in Organizational Ethnography," in *Organizational Ethnography: Studying the Complexity of Everyday Life*, ed. Sierk Ybema et al. (London: Sage, 2009).

1. The event sponsors included the World Bank, the Inter-American Development Bank, USAID, the Ministry of Women, and the gender-focused NGO Care (MIDIS 2012d).

2. MIDIS 2012d. Subsequently, in 2013, the annual, weeklong event was dedicated to early childhood development, with the slogan "Childhood First": in 2014, the slogan "Results That You Feel" highlighted the impacts of the ministry's social programs.

3. Over the course of seven days, a series of conferences, panels, and project launches were organized around themes including social and financial inclusion, economic empowerment, and experiences of social entrepreneurship, with a closing award ceremony for the Rural Women Entrepreneur Contest.

4. Ministerio de Desarrollo e Inclusión Social, "Quiénes Sómos?" www.midis.gob.pe/index.php/es/nuestra-institucion/sobre-midis/quienes-somos, accessed January 27, 2018.

5. MIDIS's definition reflects that of the World Bank, which defines *social inclusion* as "the process of improving the ability, opportunity and dignity of people, disadvantaged on the basis of their identity, to take part in society" (Bordia Das 2013, 4).

6. Many of these communities located in the Andes had also experienced violence at the hands of the state: during the internal conflict between the Maoist political group Shining Path and the national government (Taylor 2006); and as a result of the forced-sterilization campaign of the late 1990s (Boesten 2010).

7. Juntos was situated in the Presidential Council of Ministers, and functioned under the guidance of the Juntos Directive Council, until 2012, when it was shifted to the newly formed Ministry of Development and Social Inclusion. The council consisted of an executive director and one representative member for each of the following: the president of the republic; the Ministry of Education; the Ministry of Health; the Ministry of Women and Social Development, which became the Ministry of Women and Vulnerable Populations in 2012; the Ministry of Economy and Finance; Caritás Peru, the national branch of the social service, relief, and development arm of the Catholic Church; the National Confederate of Private Business, a nongovernmental organization that represents the interests of Peruvian private enterprise; the National Association of Centres for Investigation, Social Promotion and Development; the National Conference on Social Development; and Peru's largest union, the General Confederation of Peruvian Workers (PCM 2005). The directive council met monthly and was responsible for appointing the executive director, approving strategic plans, and evaluating and monitoring the quality and impact of the program.

8. Jamie Peck and Nik Theodore also found that policy makers spoke about the Brazilian CCT program in terms of citizenship rights. See Peck and Theodore 2015b.

9. In Latin America, some scholarship has characterized this shift toward increased state participation in social issues as "post-neoliberal" (Grugel and Riggirozzi 2009; Macdonald and Ruckert 2009) or as social neoliberalism (Andolina et al. 2009).

10. This contention was not unfounded. Health and education policy in Peru is historically informed by discriminatory attitudes that produce and reproduce a host of gender, ethnic, and geographical inequalities (Thorp and Paredes 2010; Boesten 2010; Ewig 2010; Oliart 2003). For instance, the deep disparities that exist in education in rural and urban regions are the result of discriminatory public policies that inequitably allocate resources. In a particularly insidious case, the Fujimori government rolled out the "reproductive health" campaign, mentioned in chapter 1, that specifically targeted thousands of rural indigenous women and some men for coercive sterilization (Boesten 2010).

11. This argument is commonly made in the context of cash transfers in sub-Saharan Africa.

12. The discussion in the media was overwhelmingly "anti-Juntos." Other MIDIS social programs were also under constant scrutiny, to the extent that I developed a strong feeling of sympathy for the minister for MIDIS, who at some point seemed to issue almost weekly statements defending the ministry's work.

13. The speaker here used the word *paternalism* to imply a parental relationship between the state and its citizens, in which citizens rely on the state for care.

14. The schedule of growth and nutrition checkups is referred to as the Control de Crecimiento y Desarrollo.

15. Latin: *Ne sutor ultra crepidam.* This proverb suggests that people should concern themselves only with things they know about.

16. Mainstream development interventions often peddle women's empowerment as yielding widespread returns for children, households, communities, business, the economy, and so on. The view that women's empowerment is an efficient and effective route through which to achieve broader development aims is often touted as "smart economics." This approach informs a number of interventions, including microfinance. On one hand, women are provided with capital that they themselves control; on the other, the microenterprises they start stimulate local economies and increase household consumption. Policy makers suggest that giving the money to women instead of men is a prudent move because women are more likely to invest the money in their households and communities. In contrast, men are more likely to spend it on antisocial behavior such as the consumption of alcohol. Benefits and rationalities aside, feminist researchers have questioned the underlying motives and long-term impacts of such an approach, pointing out that smart economics is mostly about efficiency "with elements of empowerment bolted on the side" (Chant and Sweetman 2012, 523).

17. Raising the issue of women's empowerment ruffled the feathers of high-level policy administrators at Juntos and MIDIS. When women's empowerment was referenced, the narratives mostly hinged on economic empowerment (reflective of MIDIS's Social Inclusion Week). For instance, a development expert at MIDIS explained to me during an interview that "the thing that is most connected with empowering women in Juntos is financial inclusion." (See also Schwittay 2011; Meltzer 2013.) The version of citizenship that MIDIS

offers Juntos mothers is reduced, fiscal, and contingent upon fulfilling program conditions. An occasional comment associated the CCT with a reduction in domestic violence. Radcliffe found that domestic violence is often used as an index of rural, racialized women's empowerment in Ecuador (see Radcliffe and Webb 2015).

18. To be sure, not all practitioners who identify their work with venture philanthropy or impact investing are so narrowly focused on a handful of quantitative metrics that they miss the particularities of the myriad situations that the data are said to measure. For example, Kevin Starr has urged philanthropists to "get out of the office" and do nuanced qualitative fieldwork to gauge social programs (Starr 2014).

3 THE IRONIC CONDITIONS OF CLINICS AND SCHOOLS

1. The parents' association is called Asociación de Padres de Familia.

2. While Paloma requested my services as a native English speaker, I am also a certified instructor of English as a second language.

3. Few systematic studies address the issue of teacher absenteeism in schools. The most recent example of quantitative evidence from Peru reports that in the poorest and most remote areas of the country, absenteeism is as high as 16 and 21 percent, respectively (Alcázar et al. 2017).

4. Nationally, 19.8 percent of students registered an "initial" level of literacy, meaning that they fell somewhere between illiterate and able to read words and simple sentences; 49.3 percent of students were registered as "in process," having the ability to identify information in a brief and simple text. In Cajamarca, 31.2 percent registered an initial level of literacy, and 51.8 percent were "in process."

5. Other indicators of empowerment have not been evidenced; a recent study on the Peruvian program showed that in Juntos, participation had no direct impact on women's agency, such as freedom of movement, or on their relations with their male partners (Alcázar et al. 2016).

6. To be sure, my social standing as a white, Anglophone foreigner, in addition to having offered my services free of charge, very likely influenced the director's decision to accept Paola's proposition.

7. Maxine Molyneux and Marylin Thomson (2011) found that CCT programs in Peru, Bolivia, and Ecuador had mixed effects on women's self-esteem. For instance, mothers felt that receiving the cash allowed them to leave the home and to access public spaces such as banks, and that this had a positive effect on their self-esteem. At the same time, however, they were treated badly by authorities in these spaces. At the bank, women were told that they smelled, they were asked to wash their feet before entering, and they were refused service on the basis of being unable to sign their names.

8. It wasn't until I requested the keys to unlock the gate myself that the secretary produced them.

9. In her research among women CCT recipients in Colombia, Maria Elisa Balen found similar dynamics regarding compliance. Although they were subject to poor-quality services and abuse from authorities, mothers relied on the cash transfer to help them overcome structural barriers to the good health and prosperity of their families, including forced displacement and lack of access to the formal economy. In a context of high vulnerability, mothers used the cash transfer to buy food and pay for medical bills and transportation. See Balen, forthcoming.

10. For an account of resistance by CCT recipients in Brazil, see Garmany 2017.

11. *Globalization and the Changes in Cultures of Care and Survival: Local and Global Dimensions* (Accra: Institute of African Studies, University of Ghana, 2012).

12. While I did not observe a specific example of a local manager exercising discretion in favor of an ill mother, I did observe the regional Juntos manager mention to Juntos staff that local managers were no longer permitted to make "exceptions" for households that did not meet all of the program conditions. This suggests that local managers had been breaking program rules to accommodate particular cases.

13. In the years following my fieldwork for this book, health care expenditure increased annually. In 2014, it was at a record high, at 3.319 percent of GDP. This does not indicate what proportion of the expenditure was dedicated to rural areas or capture the magnitude of improvements required to achieve an adequate level of service quality. For data, see World Bank, "Health Expenditure, Public (% of GDP)," 1995–2014, http://data.worldbank.org/indicator/SH.XPD.PUBL.ZS?end=2014andlocations=PEandstart=1995andview=chart.

4 RURAL WOMEN WALKING AND WAITING

1. Combis are generally old, privately owned Nissan or Toyota minivans that serve as public transit. They are notorious for being operated in an unsafe manner with overcrowding of passengers and intoxicated drivers. They are frequently involved in fatal accidents. Low-income Peruvians often do not have alternative transit options.

2. See chapter 2 for a discussion of policy makers' mostly ambivalent positions on the impacts of Juntos on women's empowerment.

3. Queues of women have become emblematic of CCT programs across Latin America. Maria Elisa Balen (forthcoming) refers to the extended periods of waiting required of CCT recipients in Colombia as "queuing under the sun" because of the women's prolonged exposure to high temperatures on paydays.

4. Rates of illiteracy among middle-age rural women in Peru is high, owing to scarce and poor-quality education and to patriarchal attitudes that historically prioritized men's education over women's.

5. In order to preserve the anonymity of the two districts, I have assigned them numbers of users from different but similar districts.

6. Meetings also afforded women access to public spaces and socialization that they may not otherwise have had. One of the mothers I interviewed told me that because of Juntos she spent more time outside of her home, and that she enjoyed this.

7. I have argued elsewhere that requiring women to walk and wait for poor-quality services creates "new moments for exclusion" (Cookson 2016). *Inclusion* and *exclusion* are contemporary development buzzwords, and I continue to see value in shedding light on their lack of substance. However, I am grateful for the comments of one of my reviewers, who encouraged me to point out that exclusion is in fact subordination.

5 PAID AND UNPAID LABOR ON THE FRONTLINE STATE

1. The World Bank document referred to *promotoras comunales,* a term commonly used to reference mostly unpaid women who provide community-based support work to a variety of NGOs and public programs, particularly related to health.

2. I learned very quickly to call the local managers the night before a scheduled observation, and then again very early in the morning, to make sure that we were still set to meet. On more than one occasion I traveled a great distance only to find that they had been called back to Cajamarca or that the planned event had been rescheduled.

3. While I did not have a large sample size of sex-disaggregated data on the local managers, it was my perception that there were no stark differences between the number of male and female local managers at any one time. An interesting question for further research concerns gendered rates of turnover. Owing to the extensive time away from home that was required of them, female local managers often remarked that once a woman becomes pregnant and has children, the job is no longer appropriate.

4. See Rolando Franco, Martín Hopenhayn, and Arturo León, "The Growing and Changing Middle Class in Latin America: An Update," *Cepal Review* 103 (April 2011). http://repositorio.cepal.org/bitstream/handle/11362/11468/103007025I_en.pdf?sequence=1.

5. The local managers' working conditions and related opportunities for social mobility provide a provocative view of the new "precarious middle class" in Latin America. I do not venture a deeper analysis of their situation here, as my intent with this book is to maintain focus on the experiences of Juntos mothers. However, I hope that the view I do provide here sparks interest in further research on the oft-precariously positioned implementers of social inclusion policy and the availability of sustainable routes out of poverty.

6. I received multiple reports of high staff turnover among local managers from regional Juntos staff, although I did not have the data to confirm these.

7. See Lipsky 1980 for an analysis of bureaucrats' work in welfare in the US and the mass processing of clients it requires.

8. These are referred to as *control de crecimiento y desarrollo*, or CRED.

9. The office had been without an administrative officer for several months at this time.

10. While none of the local managers themselves admitted to me that they recruited family members (unsurprising, given that this practice was not officially sanctioned), they did reference entering the system from home.

11. In refining this analysis of Mother Leaders, I compared several data sources: policy documents, ethnographic observations of Mother Leaders' meetings, and conversations with Mother Leaders, other Juntos recipients, and local managers. This data shows clearly that Mother Leaders do unpaid work that is hidden in routine program evaluations. I believe this point adds another layer of support for one of the broader arguments of this book: CCT programs are not efficient when viewed from the perspective of poor, rural women. That said, featuring a wide range of perspectives is both a strength and a limitation of many institutional ethnographies; I am aware that my treatment of the Mother Leader role is cursory. There are many important questions about Mother Leaders and their experiences that this chapter does not ask or answer, but which future ethnographic research certainly should.

12. I found this guide on the Juntos website. While I did not observe the guide being used, the working relationship between Mother Leaders and local managers was consistent with the procedures outlined in the guide.

13. All children must be registered with Juntos and meet program conditions pertaining to attendance at health and education institutions until eighteen years of age or secondary

school graduation. If one child fails to meet the conditions, the entire family is suspended from the program.

14. Of course, Mother Leaders were able to choose to communicate some messages and not others, or participate or not in activities local managers requested. Rather than denying them agency, my point here regards what was asked of them.

15. An increasing number of interventions equip community leaders and ordinary citizens with digital tools to promote good governance of public services. Many of these are mobile-phone applications that leverage high rates of phone ownership, including in low-income communities. For a review of these interventions, their potential, and their limitations, see I. Holeman, T. P. Cookson, and C. Pagliari, "Digital Technology for Health Sector Governance in Low and Middle Income Countries: A Scoping Review," *Journal of Global Health* 6, no. 2 (2016).

16. In Colombia, Mother Leaders sometimes leverage their social status to help CCT recipients skip long queues at the bank—for a fee. See Balen, forthcoming.

17. Mother Leaders' motivations are beyond the scope of this chapter; this is an important area for further research.

6 SHADOW CONDITIONS AND THE IMMEASURABLE BURDEN OF IMPROVEMENT

1. Along with Juntos and the school lunch program Qali Warma, Cuna Más is one of MIDIS's five social programs and also forms part of its national Incluir para Crecer (Include to Grow) strategy. Cuna Más and Juntos share the same target population, and many Juntos mothers would be eligible to use the day care. Cuna Más uses frontline program workers similar to the Juntos local managers, referred to as "community workers" (promotoras comunales), who are responsible for overseeing the running of the day-care centers and for encouraging women to use the service, which is not obligatory. Other than being based in MIDIS, sharing a target population, and seeking to develop children's human capital, Juntos and Cuna Más are administratively unrelated programs.

2. A notable exception is Odra Angélica Saucedo-Delgado's doctoral thesis. See Saucedo-Delgado 2011, chap. 7.

3. I narrowly escaped being implicated in the creation of a shadow condition myself. At a Mother Leaders meeting the local manager introduced me very formally to the women in attendance, saying that I would be working with Juntos and that I wanted to know how the program "is progressing" and "how they are fulfilling their coresponsibilities." He hoped that everyone would "collaborate with me," and he told them we would be coming by their houses and through the communities. This is, of course, not what I had said to him. A number of introductions such as this contributed to my decision to conduct research in two distinct research sites and not to interview women users in this particular district.

4. Several rumors circulated about actors external to Juntos getting women to do or not do things on the basis of their status as program users. In some regions of Cajamarca where mining is a particularly contentious issue, several reports surfaced of local authorities threatening Juntos women with suspension if they participated in protests against the extractive activities of Canadian, US, French, and Peruvian firms.

5. I first developed the notion of shadow conditions in my doctoral dissertation and later used the concept in a journal article published in *Antipode* while I was turning the dissertation into this book. I am indebted to early conversations with Sarah Radcliffe, who suggested the term *shadow conditionalities* when I described the dynamics I had observed in the field. Mulling over "shadows" in the subsequent years has encouraged the more mature analysis of shadow conditions that I present here.

6. Many indigenous and campesina women in Peru and elsewhere have historically experienced the state as a series of racist and discriminatory projects intended to improve and modernize their hygiene practices (see Larson 2005; Oliart 2003).

7. I was aware of four such parades or festivals during the period of my research. These included a carnival parade and a festival celebrating local produce, both of which were sponsored by Labaconas's district government; a village celebration for year's end in Santa Ana, sponsored by the mayor; and a parade in support of the governor's reelection, in Cajamarca city.

8. It is worth noting that approximately forty miles away, the Peruvian state, in collaboration with the World Bank, grants national and foreign firms a steady supply of water in order to operate the world's second-largest gold mine (Vela-Almeida et al. 2016; see also F. Li 2015).

9. Typically, rural women multitask, wrapping babies to their backs so that they can complete their household and agricultural tasks. For many mothers, the idea of the day care was culturally foreign.

10. I discussed other parts of this meeting in chapter 3.

11. In this context *midwife* might have referred to a female family member or an informal health practitioner operating outside of Peru's formal health system.

12. In 2013, 69.8 percent of births in rural Peru occurred in a health establishment, compared to 59 percent in 2009 (INEI 2014a). A 10 percent increase over six years is significant. My observations indicate that a fruitful line of inquiry would investigate a possible connection between the increase in institutional births and Juntos's implementation, which began in 2006 and was ramped up significantly at the turn of the decade.

13. I was also told by local managers and other Juntos staff that Juntos monitored program conditions more closely after it was transferred to MIDIS in 2012. Women's whose children were older may have given birth when Juntos was not strictly enforcing conditionality, or had their children before Juntos had been implemented in their communities.

14. In one week I observed a local manager tell a roomful of Mother Leaders that the regional Juntos office had received a complaint about local managers threatening women with suspension or fines if they didn't attend meetings. He then proceeded to tell them that attendance at meetings *wasn't* obligatory. However, only days before, the same local manager had told me that if local managers don't threaten the women to attend the meetings, the latter do not show up.

15. Markers of ethnicity for rural and indigenous women in Peru include traditional forms of dress such as full skirts and shawls and the use of nondominant languages such as Quechua and Aymara.

16. As part of the national economic growth strategy Crecer, activities included installation of latrines, the cocinas mejoradas (smokeless stoves) program, literacy classes for mothers, and the Vivienda Saludable (healthy housing) program.

17. With the new guidelines and elimination of this component of the program, connections with the NGOs have been severed. I observed that this was a point of contention for local NGO workers when I attended a meeting of representatives from local government and civil society organizations whose mandate it is to alleviate poverty or promote some other aspect of social welfare. One representative from an NGO that had operated in the region for many years, including before Juntos was instituted, said she believed that work in poor communities should involve more than "giving out two hundred soles." She expressed frustration that Juntos doesn't consult NGO workers as people "who really work in the communities" and know what the local problems are. Indeed, some regionally positioned Juntos staff also hold these views.

18. The only remaining exception is Proyecto Capital, a savings account program that is implemented alongside Juntos in some communities (Meltzer 2013). Proyecto Capital was not implemented in Cajamarca and so is not discussed in this book.

19. Juntos faced a supposed problem with staff absenteeism: local managers reportedly hid in their houses instead of visiting communities. Local managers and their direct field managers told me that in the few instances where this did indeed happen, the local managers were tired from a work burden that involved managing a larger number of households, and a greater spatial area, than is possible and from being consistently away from their families.

7 CONCLUSION: TOWARD A CARING SOCIETY

1. New Incentives originally incentivized pregnant women who were HIV positive, or who met other criteria associated with risky pregnancies, to give birth in specific health clinics. Shortly before publication of this book, the nonprofit organization changed its model and now incentivizes mothers to vaccinate their children. See https://blog.ycombinator.com/new-incentives/.

2. One million soles was equivalent to approximately US$386,000 in April 2013. This amount equated to approximately ten thousand stolen cash transfer payments.

3. Hierba luisa is a lemon-flavored herb common in the Andes.

4. Nancy Folbre (2006) argues for a move beyond the term *unpaid care* to a more disaggregated analysis that distinguishes among forms of care work so that it might better be accounted for. This analysis would account for the work's characteristics, types of beneficiaries, and relationship to the market. For the purposes of this book, I retain a simplified definition of unpaid care work.

5. I was unable to verify this claim with government records. However, talk of Peru's slowed growth rate was widespread among the middle class. Whether or not economists would agree, middle-class citizens described their insecure economic situation in relation to the country's "recession."

6. I also spoke with former employees of the Yanacocha gold mine who had been laid off and remained unemployed as the mine reduced its operations, as well as former taxi drivers and restaurant owners, whose industries were unsustainably yoked to local and national economies of extraction.

7. Important work in the humanitarian and natural disaster response sector is being carried out by the Cash Learning Partnership. This organization brings together over 150

organizations and five thousand individuals to conduct research, share knowledge, and co-ordinate action related to the appropriate use of cash transfer programming for humanitarian aid. For case studies and analysis, see their inaugural 2018 report, *The State of the World's Cash Report: Cash Transfer Programming in Humanitarian Aid.*

8. The increasingly lively conversation around the UBI is not limited to low- and middle-income-country contexts. In 2016, the motion to implement a UBI in Switzerland made it to a national vote. While the motion failed to pass, the debate caught the attention of the world.

REFERENCES

Afshar, H., and C. Dennis. 1992. *Women and Adjustment Policies in the Third World*. Basingstoke, UK: Macmillan.

Aguirre, L., B. González Harbour, L. Almodóvar, and Á. De la Rúa. 2012. "La ayuda debe ir a los más pobres, no a países con ingresos medios como Perú." *El País*. http://sociedad. elpais.com/sociedad/2012/02/22/actualidad/1329913536_647673.html.

Ahmad, M. M. 2002. "Who Cares? The Personal and Professional Problems of NGO Fieldworkers in Bangladesh." *Development in Practice* 12 (2): 177–191.

Alcázar, L., M. Balarin, and K. Espinoza. 2016. *Impacts of the Peruvian Conditional Cash Transfer Program on Women Empowerment: A Quantitative and Qualitative Approach*. Lima: Partnership for Economic Policy. www.pep-net.org/sites/pep-net.org/files/typo3doc/pdf/ files_events/2016_Manila_conference/final_report/PERU_LORENA_ALCAZAR_ PEP_PARTNER_LED_RESEARCH_GRANT.pdf.

Alcázar, L., F. H. Rogers, N. Chaudhury, J. Hammer, M. Kremer, and K. Muralidharan. 2017. "Why Are Teachers Absent? Probing Service Delivery in Peruvian Primary Schools." *International Journal of Educational Research* 45 (3): 117–136.

Andersen, C. T., S. A. Reynolds, J. R. Behrman, B. T. Crookston, K. A. Dearden, J. Escobal, S. Mani, A. Sánchez, A. D. Stein and L. C. Fernald. 2015. "Participation in the Juntos Conditional Cash Transfer Program in Peru Is Associated with Changes in Child Anthropometric Status but Not Language Development or School Achievement." *Journal of Nutrition* 145 (10): 2396–2405. http://jn.nutrition.org/content/early/2015/08/12/ jn.115.213546.abstract.

Andolina, R., N. Laurie, and S. A. Radcliffe. 2009. *Indigenous Development in the Andes: Culture, Power, and Transnationalism*. Durham, NC: Duke University Press.

Angelucci, M., and O. Attanasio. 2009. "Oportunidades: Program Effect on Consumption, Low Participation, and Methodological Issues." *Economic Development and Cultural Change* 57 (3): 479–506.

Antonopoulos, R., and I. Hirway, eds. 2010. *Unpaid Work and the Economy: Gender, Time Use and Poverty in Developing Countries.* Houndmills, UK: Palgrave Macmillan.

Anttonen, A. 2005. "Empowering Social Policy: The Role of Social Care Services in Modern Welfare States." In *Social Policy and Economic Development in the Nordic Countries,* edited by O. Kangas and J. Palme. London: Palgrave Macmillan.

Armstrong, P., and M. P. Connelly. 1989. "Feminist Political Economy: An Introduction." *Studies in Political Economy* 30:5–12.

Arroyo, J. L. 2010. *Estudio cualitativo de los efectos del Programa Juntos en los cambios de comportamiento de los hogares beneficiarios en el distrito de Chuschi: Avances y evidencias.* Lima: Programa Juntos.

Attanasio, O., et al. 2005. *The Short-Term Impact of a Conditional Cash Subsidy on Child Health and Nutrition in Colombia.* London: Institute of Fiscal Studies.

———. 2010. "Children's Schooling and Work in the Presence of a Conditional Cash Transfer Program in Rural Colombia." *Economic Development and Cultural Change* 58 (2): 181–210.

Auyero, J. 2012. *Patients of the State: The Politics of Waiting in Argentina.* Durham, NC: Duke University Press.

Bakker, I., and S. Gill. 2008. "New Constitutionalism and Social Reproduction." In *Beyond States and Markets: The Challenges of Social Reproduction,* edited by I. Bakker and R. Silvey, 19–33. New York: Routledge.

Ballard, R. 2013. "Geographies of Development II: Cash Transfers and the Reinvention of Development for the Poor." *Progress in Human Geography* 37 (6): 811–821.

Bando, R., L. F. López-Calva, and H. A. Patrinos. 2005. "Child Labor, School Attendance, and Indigenous Households: Evidence from Mexico." Understanding Children's Work Project, Working Paper Series no. 3487, World Bank, Washington, DC.

Barham, T. 2005. *The Impact of the Mexican Conditional Cash Transfer on Immunization Rates.* Berkeley, CA: Department of Agriculture and Resource Economics, University of California, Berkeley.

———. 2011. "A Healthier Start: The Effect of Conditional Cash Transfers on Neonatal and Infant Mortality in Rural Mexico." *Journal of Development Economics* 94 (1): 74–85.

Barham, T., and J. A. Maluccio. 2009. "Eradicating Diseases: The Effect of Conditional Cash Transfers on Vaccination Coverage in Rural Nicaragua." *Journal of Health Economics* 28 (3): 611–621.

Barrientos, A., J. Gideon, and M. Molyneux. 2008. "New Developments in Latin America's Social Policy." *Development and Change* 39 (5): 759–774.

Barrientos, A., and C. Santibáñez. 2009. "New Forms of Social Assistance and the Evolution of Social Protection in Latin America." *Journal of Latin American Studies* 41:1–26.

Barrig, M. 1991. "Women and Development in Peru: Old Models, New Actors." *Environment and Urbanization* 3 (2): 66–70.

Bebbington, A. 2004. "NGOs and Uneven Development: Geographies of Development Intervention." *Progress in Human Geography* 28 (6): 725–745.

Behrman, J. R., S. W. Parker, and P. E. Todd. 2005. "Long-Term Impacts of the Oportunidades Conditional Cash Transfer Program on Rural Youth in Mexico." Ibero-America Institute for Economic Research (IAI) Discussion Papers, no. 122, Ibero-America Institute for Economic Research.

Balen, M. E. Forthcoming. "Queuing in the Sun: The Salience of Implementation Practices in Recipients' Experience of a CCT." In *Cash Transfers in Context: An Anthropological Perspective,* edited by J. Olivier de Sardan and E. Piccoli. London: Berghahn Books.

Beltrán, A. B., and J. Seinfeld. 2013. *La trampa educativa en el Perú: Cuando la educación llega a muchos pero sirve a pocos.* Lima: Universidad del Pacífico. http://hdl.handle. net/11354/1419.

Benería, L. 1979. "Reproduction, Production and the Sexual Division of Labour." *Cambridge Journal of Economics* 3 (3): 203–225.

———. 1999. "Structural Adjustment Policies." In *The Elgar Companion to Feminist Economics,* edited by J. Peterson and M. Lewis, 687–695. Cheltenham, UK: Edward Elgar.

Benería, L., and G. Sen. 1981. "Accumulation, Reproduction, and 'Women's Role in Economic Development': Boserup Revisited." *Signs* 7 (2): 279–298.

Best, J. 2013. "Redefining Poverty as Risk and Vulnerability: Shifting Strategies of Liberal Economic Governance." *Third World Quarterly* 34 (1): 109–129.

Blondet, C., and C. Trivelli. 2004. "Cucharas en alto, del asistencialismo al desarrollo local: Fortaleciendo la participación de las mujeres." Institute for Peruvian Studies working paper no. 135, IEP, Lima. http://repositorio.iep.org.pe/handle/IEP/351.

Boesten, J. 2010. *Intersecting Inequalities: Women and Social Policy in Peru, 1990–2000.* University Park: Pennsylvania State University Press.

Bordia Das, M. 2013. *Inclusion Matters: The Foundation for Shared Prosperity.* Washington, DC: World Bank. https://openknowledge.worldbank.org/handle/10986/16195.

Bradshaw, S. 2008. "From Structural Adjustment to Social Adjustment." *Global Social Policy* 8 (2): 188–207.

Bradshaw, S., and A. Q. Víquez. 2008. "Women Beneficiaries or Women Bearing the Cost? A Gendered Analysis of the Red de Protección Social in Nicaragua." *Development and Change* 39 (5): 823–844.

Buss, D. 2015. "Measurement Imperatives and Gender Politics: An Introduction." *Social Politics: International Studies in Gender, State and Society* 22 (3): 381–389.

Cardoso, E., and A. P. Souza. 2003. "The Impact of Cash Transfers on Child Labor and School Attendance in Brazil." Working paper, Department of Economics, Vanderbilt University. http://hdl.handle.net/1803/20.

Cash Learning Partnership. 2018. *The State of the World's Cash Report: Cash Transfer Programming in Humanitarian Aid.* www.cashlearning.org/downloads/calp-sowc-report-web.pdf.

Cecchini, S., and A. Madariaga. 2011. *Conditional Cash Transfer Programmes: The Recent Experience in Latin America and the Caribbean.* United Nations Economic Commission for Latin America and the Caribbean. Cuadernos de la CEPAL no. 95. New York: United Nations.

Cecchini, S., and F. V. Soares. 2015. "Conditional Cash Transfers and Health in Latin America." *The Lancet* 385 (9975): e32–e34.

Chant, S. 2008. "The 'Feminisation of Poverty' and the 'Feminisation' of Anti-poverty Programmes: Room for Revision?" *Journal of Development Studies* 44 (2): 165–197.

Chant, S., and C. Sweetman. 2012. "Fixing Women or Fixing the World? 'Smart Economics,' Efficiency Approaches, and Gender Equality in Development." *Gender and Development* 20 (3): 517–529.

Chaudhury, N., et al. 2006. "Missing in Action: Teacher and Health Worker Absence in Developing Countries." *Journal of Economic Perspectives* 2:91–116.

Cookson, T. P. 2016. "Working for Inclusion? Conditional Cash Transfers, Rural Women, and the Reproduction of Inequality." *Antipode* 48 (5): 1187–1205.

Copestake, J. 2008. "Multiple Dimensions of Social Assistance: The Case of Peru's 'Glass of Milk' Programme." *Journal of Development Studies* 44 (4): 545–561.

Corboz, J. 2013. "Third-Way Neoliberalism and Conditional Cash Transfers: The Paradoxes of Empowerment, Participation and Self-Help among Poor Uruguayan Women." *Australian Journal of Anthropology* 24 (1): 64–80.

Corbridge, S. 2007. "The (Im)possibility of Development Studies." *Economy and Society* 36 (2): 179–211.

Cornwall, A., and D. Eade, eds. 2010. *Deconstructing Development Discourse: Buzzwords and Fuzzwords*. Warwickshire, UK: Practical Action Publishing, in association with Oxfam GB.

Correa Aste, N., and T. Roopnaraine. 2014. *Pueblos indígenas y transferencias condicionadas: Estudio etnográfico sobre la implementación y los efectos socioculturales del Programa Juntos en seis comunidades Andinas y Amazónicas de Perú*. Washington, DC: International Food Policy Research Institute, Pontificia Universidad Católica del Perú, Banco Interamericano de Desarrollo.

Cortes, R. 2009. "Social Policy in Latin America in the Post-neoliberal Era." In *Governance after Neoliberalism in Latin America*, edited by J. Grugel and R. Pia, 49–66. New York: Palgrave Macmillan.

Cruzado, R. 2013. "Padres de familia se quejan de ausencia de profesores." *La Panorama*. May 14. https://issuu.com/panoramacajamarquino.com/docs/diario-16-05-2013.

Currie-Alder, B. 2016. "The State of Development Studies: Origins, Evolution and Prospects." *Canadian Journal of Development Studies/Revue canadienne d'études du développement* 37 (1): 5–26.

Dammert, A. C. 2009. "Heterogeneous Impacts of Conditional Cash Transfers: Evidence from Nicaragua." *Economic Development and Cultural Change* 58 (1): 53–83.

de Brauw, A., and J. Hoddinott. 2011. "Must Conditional Cash Transfer Programs Be Conditioned to Be Effective? The Impact of Conditioning Transfers on School Enrollment in Mexico." *Journal of Development Economics* 96 (2): 359–370.

Deere, C. D. 1990. *Household and Class Relations: Peasants and Landlords in Northern Peru*. Berkeley: University of California Press.

———. 2005. *The Feminization of Agriculture?: Economic Restructuring in Rural Latin America*. Geneva: UNRISD.

de la Cadena, M. 1992. "Las mujeres son más indias." *Espejos y travesías* (16).

———. 2000. *Indigenous Mestizos: The Politics of Race and Culture in Cuzco, Peru, 1919–1991*. Latin America Otherwise series. Durham, NC: Duke University Press.

DeVault, M. L., and L. McCoy. 2002. "Institutional Ethnography: Using Interviews to Investigate Ruling Relations." In *Handbook of Interview Research*, edited by J. Gubrium and J. Holstein, 751–776. Thousand Oaks, CA: Sage.

Devereux, S., et al. 2013. "Evaluating Outside the Box: An Alternative Framework for Analysing Social Protection Programmes." Institute of Development Studies Working Paper, vol. 2012, no. 431. http://onlinelibrary.wiley.com/doi/10.1111/j.2040-0209.2013.00431.x/epdf.

Díaz, R., et al. 2008. *Análisis de la implementación del Programa JUNTOS en Apurímac, Huancavelica y Huánuco: Informe de consultoría.* Edited by Institute for Peruvian Studies. Lima: IEP.

Dyck, I. 2005. "Feminist Geography, the 'Everyday,' and Local-Global Relations: Hidden Spaces of Place-Making." *Canadian Geographer / Geographe Canadien* 49 (3): 233–243.

ECLAC (Economic Commission for Latin America and the Caribbean). 2014. *Social Panorama of Latin America 2014.* Santiago, Chile: United Nations. http://repositorio.cepal.org/bitstream/handle/11362/37627/4/S1420728_en.pdf.

———. 2018. Non-contributory Social Protection Programmes in Latin America and the Caribbean Database. United Nations Economic Commission for Latin America and the Caribbean. http://dds.cepal.org/bpsnc/.

El Comercio. 2013a. "Editorial: Alas para volar." http://elcomercio.pe/politica/opinion/editorial-alas-volar-noticia-1531022.

———. 2013b. "Editorial: Cambiando el chip." http://elcomercio.pe/politica/opinion/editorial-cambiando-chip-noticia-1574646.

———. 2013c. "El gobierno dará S/.446 millones para los colegios."

———. 2015. "Carolina Trivelli se opone a paralizar programas sociales." http://elcomercio.pe/politica/gobierno/carolina-trivelli-opone-paralizar-programas-sociales-369373.

El Panorama. 2013. "Cajamarca necesita 24 milliones para contratar a docentes."

Elson, D. 1991. "Male Bias in Macro-economics: The Case of Structural Adjustment." In *Male Bias in the Development Process,* 164–190.

———. 1995. *Male Bias in the Development Process.* 2nd ed. Manchester, UK: Manchester University Press.

———. 2005. "Unpaid Work, the Millennium Development Goals, and Capital Accumulation." Paper presented at the conference "Unpaid Work and the Economy: Gender, Poverty and the Millennium Development Goals," United Nations Development Programme and Levy Economics Institute of Bard College, Annandale-on-Hudson, New York, October 1–3.

Elwood, S., V. Lawson, and E. Sheppard. 2016. "Geographical Relational Poverty Studies." *Progress in Human Geography* 41 (6): 745–765.

England, K. 2006. "Producing Feminist Geographies: Theory, Methodologies and Research Strategies." In *Approaches to Human Geography: Philosophies, Theories, People and Practices,* edited by S. Aitken and G. Valentine, 286–297. London: Sage.

Englund, H. 2006. *Prisoners of Freedom: Human Rights and the African Poor.* Berkeley: University of California Press.

Ewig, C. 2010. *Second-Wave Neoliberalism: Gender, Race, and Health Sector Reform in Peru.* University Park: Pennsylvania State University Press.

Farmer, P. 2003. *Pathologies of Power: Health, Human Rights, and the New War on the Poor.* Berkeley: University of California Press.

———. 2015. "Failure to Collide: Ebola and Modern Medicine." UNDP Kapuscinski Development Lecture. King's College, London, April 20.

Feijoo, M. D. C., and E. Jelin. 1987. "Women from Low Income Sectors: Economic Recession and Democratization of Politics in Argentina." In *The Invisible Adjustment: Poor Women and the Economic Crisis,* 2nd ed., edited by UNICEF, the Americas and the Caribbean Regional Office: Regional Programme Women in Development, 137–166. Santiago: UNICEF.

Ferguson, J. 1990. *The Anti-politics Machine: "Development," Depoliticization, and Bureaucratic Power in Lesotho.* Cambridge: Cambridge University Press.

——. 2015. "Give a Man a Fish: From Patriarchal Productionism to the Politics of Distribution in Southern Africa and Beyond." Audrey Richards Annual Lecture, University of Cambridge, Centre of African Studies, March 26.

Fernald, L. C., P. J. Gertler, and L. M. Neufeld. 2008. "Role of Cash in Conditional Cash Transfer Programmes for Child Health, Growth, and Development: An Analysis of Mexico's Oportunidades." *The Lancet* 371 (9615): 828–837.

——. 2010. "10-Year Effect of Oportunidades, Mexico's Conditional Cash Transfer Programme, on Child Growth, Cognition, Language, and Behaviour: A Longitudinal Follow-Up Study." *The Lancet* 374 (9706): 1997–2005.

Fernando, J. L. 1997. "Nongovernmental Organizations, Micro-credit, and Empowerment of Women." *Annals of the American Academy of Political and Social Science* 554 (1): 150–177.

Figueroa, A., R. Thorp, and M. Paredes. 2010. "Persistent Inequalities in Education." In *Ethnicity and the Persistence of Inequality*, 70–88. London: Palgrave Macmillan.

Fiszbein, A., N. R. Schady, and F. H. G. Ferreira. 2009. *Conditional Cash Transfers: Reducing Present and Future Poverty.* Washington, DC: World Bank.

Folbre, N. 2006. "Measuring Care: Gender, Empowerment, and the Care Economy." *Journal of Human Development* 7 (2): 183–199.

——. 2014. "The Care Economy in Africa: Subsistence Production and Unpaid Care." *Journal of African Economies* 23 (S1): i128–i156.

Foucault, M. 1977. *Discipline and Punish: The Birth of the Prison.* London: Allen Lane.

——. 1982. "The Subject and Power." *Critical Inquiry* 8 (4): 777–795.

Foucault, M., et al. 1991. *The Foucault Effect: Studies in Governmentality.* Chicago: University of Chicago Press.

Gaarder, M. 2012. "Conditional versus Unconditional Cash: A Commentary." *Journal of Development Effectiveness* 4 (1): 130–133.

Gaarder, M., A. Glassman, and J. E. Todd. 2010. "Conditional Cash Transfers and Health: Unpacking the Causal Chain." *Journal of Development Effectiveness* 2 (1): 6–50.

Galasso, A. 2011. "Alleviating Extreme Poverty in Chile: The Short-Term Effects of Chile Solidario." *Estudios Economicos* 38:101–127.

Gammage, S. 2011. "Conditional Cash Transfers and Time Poverty: An Example from Guatemala." In *Cuadragésima sexta reunión de la Mesa Directiva de la Conferencia Regional sobre la Mujer de América Latina y el Caribe.* Santiago: Economic Commission for Latin America and the Caribbean. www.cepal.org/mujer/noticias/noticias/1/43711/GAMMAGE_Conditiona_Cash_Transfers_and_Time-Poverty_03102011.pdf.

Garmany, J. 2016. "Neoliberalism, Governance, and the Geographies of Conditional Cash Transfers." *Political Geography* 50:61–70.

——. 2017. "Strategies of Conditional Cash Transfers and the Tactics of Resistance." *Environment and Planning A* 49 (2): 372–388.

Geertz, C. 1973. *Thick Description: Towards an Interpretive Theory of Culture.* New York: Basic Books.

Gertler, P. 2000. *Final Report: The Impact of PROGRESA on Health.* Washington, DC: International Food Policy Research Institute.

———. 2004. "Do Conditional Cash Transfers Improve Child Health? Evidence from PRO-GRESA's Control Randomized Experiment." *American Economic Review* 94 (2): 336–341.

Gitlitz, J. S., and T. Rojas. 1985. "Las rondas campesinas en Cajamarca-Perú." *Apuntes: Revista de Ciencias Sociales* (16): 115–141.

Glassman, A., et al. 2013. "Impact of Conditional Cash Transfers on Maternal and Newborn Health." *Journal of Health, Population, and Nutrition* 31 (4, S2): S48–S66.

Goetz, A. M. 1997. "Managing Organisational Change: The Gendered Organisation of Space and Time." *Gender and Development* 5 (1): 17–27.

———. 2001. *Women Development Workers: Implementing Rural Credit Programmes in Bangladesh.* London: Sage.

González de la Rocha, M. 2006. Los hogares en las evaluaciones cualitativas: Cinco años de investigaciones." In *Procesos domesticos y vulnerabilidad: Perspectivas antropologicas de los hogares con oportunidades,* edited by M. González de la Rocha, 87–172. DF, Mexico: CIESAS. www.oportunidades.gob.mx:8010/en/docs/docs2006.php.

Government of Ontario. 2017. *Ontario's Basic Income Pilot: Studying the Impact of a Basic Income.* Ministry of Community and Social Services. https://files.ontario.ca/170508_bi_brochure_eng_pg_by_pg_proof.pdf.

Grosh, M., et al. 2008. *For Protection and Promotion: The Design and Implementation of Effective Safety Nets.* Washington, DC: World Bank. http://siteresources.worldbank.org/SAFETYNETSANDTRANSFERS/Resources/For_Protection_and_Promotion_complete.pdf.

Grugel, J., and P. Riggirozzi. 2009. *Governance after Neoliberalism in Latin America.* Basingstoke, UK: Palgrave Macmillan.

Gupta, A. 2012. *Red Tape: Bureaucracy, Structural Violence, and Poverty in India.* New Delhi: Orient BlackSwan.

Handa, S., et al. 2009. "Opening Up Pandora's Box: The Effect of Gender Targeting and Conditionality on Household Spending Behavior in Mexico's Progresa Program." *World Development* 37 (6): 1129–1142.

Hagen-Zanker, J., F. Bastagli, L. Harman, V. Barca, G. Sturge, and T. Schmidt. 2016. "Understanding the Impact of Cash Transfers: The Evidence." ODI Briefing. Overseas Development Institute (London). www.odi.org/sites/odi.org.uk/files/resource-documents/10748.pdf.

Harding, S. G. 1986. *The Science Question in Feminism.* Ithaca, NY: Cornell University Press.

Hickey, S. 2010. "The Government of Chronic Poverty: From Exclusion to Citizenship?" *Journal of Development Studies* 46 (7): 1139–1155.

Hickey, S., and S. King. 2016. "Understanding Social Accountability: Politics, Power and Building New Social Contracts." *Journal of Development Studies* 52 (8): 1225–1240.

Himmelweit, S. 2005. "Can We Afford (Not) to Care: Prospects and Policy?" GeNet Working Paper no. 11. Gender Equality Network, Economic and Social Research Council, Cambridge, UK.

Hoddinott, J., and E. Skoufias. 2004. "The Impact of Progresa on Food Consumption." *Economic Development and Cultural Change* 53 (1): 37–61.

Holeman, I., T. P. Cookson, and C. Pagliari. 2016. "Digital Technology for Health Sector Governance in Low and Middle Income Countries: A Scoping Review." *Journal of Global Health* 6 (2).

Hossain, N. 2010. "School Exclusion as Social Exclusion: The Practices and Effects of a Conditional Cash Transfer Programme for the Poor in Bangladesh." *Journal of Development Studies* 46 (7): 1264–1282.

Huicho, L., et al. 2016. "Child Health and Nutrition in Peru within an Antipoverty Political Agenda: A Countdown to 2015 Country Case Study." *Lancet Global Health* 4 (6): e414–e426.

IDB (Inter-American Development Bank). 2009. *Review of the Need for a General Capital Increase of the Ordinary Capital and Replenishment of the Fund for Special Operations: Progress and Next Steps.* Washington, DC: Inter-American Development Bank. https://publications.iadb.org/handle/11319/2533?locale-attribute=en.

IEP (Institute for Peruvian Studies). 2009. *Estudio de percepción sobre cambios de comportamiento de los beneficiarios y accesibilidad al Programa Juntos en el Distrito de San Jerónimo (Andahuaylas—Apuerímac).* Lima: Instituto de Estudios Peruanos. www.juntos.gob.pe/modulos/mod_legal/archivos/Estudio-de-percepci%C3%B3n-cambios-de-comportamiento-en-San-Jer%C3%B3nimo-%E2%80%93-IEP-Feb-2009.pdf.

INEI (Instituto Nacional de Estadística e Informática). 2014a. *Perú: Encuesta demográfica y de salud familiar 2013.* Lima: INEI. www.inei.gob.pe/media/MenuRecursivo/publicaciones_digitales/Est/Lib1151/index.html.

———. 2014b. *Perú: Perfil de la pobreza por dominios geográphicos, 2004–2013.* Lima: Instituto Nacional de Estadística e Informática.

ISSC (International Social Science Council), IDS (Institute of Development Studies), and UNESCO. 2016. *World Social Science Report 2016, Challenging Inequalities: Pathways to a Just World.* Paris: UNESCO. http://unesdoc.unesco.org/images/0024/002458/245825e.pdf.

Jones, N., R. Vargas, and E. Villar. 2008. "Cash Transfers to Tackle Childhood Poverty and Vulnerability: An Analysis of Peru's Juntos Programme." *Environment and Urbanization* 20 (1): 255–273.

Juntos. 2011. *Guía de orientación no. 1: Conociendo Juntos para las representates de los hogares-madres líderes.* Lima: MIDIS. www.juntos.gob.pe/modulos/mod_legal/archivos/GUIA-PARA-LAS-MADRES-LIDERES.pdf.

———. 2012. *Informe de evaluación del plan operativo institucional.* Lima: Unidad Gerencial Planeamiento, Presupuesto y Evaluación. www.juntos.gob.pe/docs/planificacion/Eval-POI-I-Trimestre-2012.pdf.

———. 2015a. "Misión y visión." www.juntos.gob.pe/index.php/quienes-somos/vision-y-mision.

———. 2015b. "Quienes son los usuarios." www.juntos.gob.pe/index.php/usuarios/quienes.

Kabeer, N., and H. Waddington. 2015. "Economic Impacts of Conditional Cash Transfer Programmes: A Systematic Review and Meta-analysis." *Journal of Development Effectiveness* 7 (3): 290–303.

Kandpal, E., et al. 2016. "A Conditional Cash Transfer Program in the Philippines Reduces Severe Stunting." *Journal of Nutrition* 146 (9): 1793–1800.

Karlan, D., and J. Appel. 2011. *More Than Good Intentions: How a New Economics Is Helping to Solve Global Poverty.* New York: Dutton.

Kela (Social Insurance Institute of Finland). 2017. *Basic Income Experiment at Halfway Point.* Social Insurance Institute of Finland. http://blogi.kansanelakelaitos.fi/arkisto/4352.

Keshavjee, S. 2014. *Blind Spot: How Neoliberalism Infiltrated Global Health*. Oakland: University of California Press.

Lagarde, M., A. Haines, and N. Palmer. 2007. "Conditional Cash Transfers for Improving Uptake of Health Interventions in Low- and Middle-Income Countries." *Journal of the America Medical Association* 298 (16): 1900.

La Republica. 2013. "De 2,125 maestros que dieron examen sólo 25 aprobaron."

Larson, B. 2005. "Capturing Indian Bodies, Hearths, and Minds: The Gendered Politics of Rural School Reform in Bolivia, 1920s–1940s." In *Natives Making Nation: Gender, Indigeneity and the State in the Andes,* edited by A. Canessa, 32–59. Tucson: University of Arizona Press.

Latapí, A. E., and M. G. de la Rocha. 2008. "Girls, Mothers and Poverty Reduction in Mexico: Evaluating Progresa-Oportunidades." In *The Gendered Impacts of Liberalization: Towards Embedded Liberalism?* edited by S. Razavi, 435–468. New York: Routledge/UNRISD.

Lavigne, M. 2013. *Social Protection Systems in Latin America and the Caribbean: Peru,* edited by S. Cecchini. Santiago, Chile: Economic Commission for Latin America and the Caribbean. http://archivo.cepal.org/pdfs/2013/S2013059.pdf.

Lavinas, L. 2013. "21st Century Welfare." *New Left Review* 84 (November–December): 5–40.

Leroy, J. L., M. Ruel, and E. Verhofstadt. 2009. "The Impact of Conditional Cash Transfer Programmes on Child Nutrition: A Review of Evidence Using a Programme Theory Framework." *Journal of Development Effectiveness* 1 (2): 103–129.

Levy, D., and J. Ohls. 2007. *Evaluation of Jamaica's PATH Program: Final Report*. Washington, DC: Mathematica Policy Research.

Li, F. 2015. *Unearthing Conflict: Corporate Mining, Activism, and Expertise in Peru*. Durham, NC: Duke University Press.

Li, T. 2007. *The Will to Improve: Governmentality, Development, and the Practice of Politics*. Durham, NC: Duke University Press.

———. 2010. "Revisiting *the Will to Improve*." *Annals of the Association of American Geographers* 100 (1): 233–235.

Liebowitz, D. J., and S. Zwingel. 2014. "Gender Equality Oversimplified: Using CEDAW to Counter the Measurement Obsession." *International Studies Review* 16 (3): 362–389.

Lim, S. S., et al. 2010. "India's Janani Suraksha Yojana, a Conditional Cash Transfer Programme to Increase Births in Health Facilities: An Impact Evaluation." *The Lancet* 375 (9730): 2009–2023.

Lindert, K., and V. Vincensini. 2010. *Social Policy, Perceptions and the Press: An Analysis of the Media's Treatment of Conditional Cash Transfers in Brazil*. World Bank. http://siteresources.worldbank.org/SOCIALPROTECTION/Resources/SP-Discussion-papers/Safety-Nets-DP/1008.pdf.

Lipsky, M. 1980. *Street-Level Bureaucracy: Dilemmas of the Individual in Public Services*. New York: Russell Sage Foundation.

Lister, R. 2004. *Poverty*. Cambridge, UK: Polity.

Luccisano, L. 2006. "The Mexican Opportunidades Program: Questioning the Linking of Security to Conditional Social Investments for Mothers and Children." *Canadian Journal of Latin American and Caribbean Studies* 31 (62): 53–85.

Macdonald, L., and A. Ruckert. 2009. *Post-neoliberalism in the Americas*. Basingstoke, UK: Palgrave Macmillan.

Mahon, R., and F. Robinson. 2011. Introduction to *Feminist Ethics and Social Policy: Towards a New Global Political Economy of Care,* edited by R. Mahon and F. Robinson, 1–20. Vancouver: University of British Columbia Press.

Maluccio, J. A., and R. Flores. 2005. *Impact Evaluation of a Conditional Cash Transfer Program: The Nicaraguan Red de Protección Social.* Washington, DC: International Food Policy Research Institute. www.ifpri.org/sites/default/files/pubs/pubs/abstract/141/rr141.pdf.

Massey, D. 1994. *Place, Space and Gender.* Minneapolis: University of Minnesota Press.

———. 1995. *Spatial Divisions of Labor: Social Structures and the Geography of Production.* 2nd ed. New York: Routledge.

Mayer, E. 2009. *Ugly Stories of the Peruvian Agrarian Reform.* Durham, NC: Duke University Press.

Medlin, C., and D. de Walque. 2008. "Potential Applications of Conditional Cash Transfers for Prevention of Sexually Transmitted Infections and HIV in Sub-Saharan Africa." World Bank Policy Research Working Paper Series, no. 4673.

MEF (Ministerio de Economía y Finanzas). 2008. *Presupuesto por resultados: Conceptos y líneas de acción.* Lima: Ministerio de Economía y Finanzas. https://mef.gob.pe/contenidos/presu_publ/ppr/conceptos_lineas_accion.pdf.

Meltzer, J. 2013. "'Good Citizenship' and the Promotion of Personal Savings Accounts in Peru." *Citizenship Studies* 17 (5): 641–652.

Merry, S. E. 2011. "Measuring the World." *Current Anthropology* 52 (S3): S83–S95.

MIDIS (Ministry for Development and Social Inclusion). 2012a. "Convenio de apoyo presupuestario al Programa Nacional de Apoyo Directo a los más Pobres 'JUNTOS,' entre el Ministerio de Economía y Finanzas y el Ministerio de Desarrollo e Inclusión Social, MIDIS." https://www.mef.gob.pe/contenidos/presu_publ/ppr/europan/convenio_MEF_MIDIS.pdf.

———. 2012b. *Manual de operaciones del Programa Nacional de Apoyo Directo a los Mas Pobres, Juntos.* Lima: Ministerio de Desarrollo e Inclusión Social. http://spij.minjus.gob.pe/Graficos/Peru/2012/Octubre/13/RM-176-2012-MIDIS.pdf.

———. 2012c. *A Policy for Development and Social Inclusion in Peru.* Ministry of Development and Social Inclusion. Lima: Ministerio de Desarrollo e Inclusión Social. www.midis.gob.pe/files/doc/midis_politicas_desarrollo_en.pdf.

———. 2012d. "Semana de la inclusión social: Programación del 15–19 October." Advertisement for Social Inclusion Week, in the possession of the author.

———. 2013a. *El rol de los convenios de gestión Juntos—gobiernos regionales.* Lima: Ministerio de Desarrollo e Inclusión Social. www.midis.gob.pe/dgsye/evaluacion/documentos/sintesis1_convenios_gestion_juntos.pdf.

———. 2013b. *Verificación del cumplimiento de coresponsabilidades.* Lima: Ministerio de Desarrollo e Inclusión Social. www.juntos.gob.pe/docs/n_origen/vcc.pdf.

MINEDU (Ministerio de Educación). 2009. "Convenio marco de cooperación interinstitucional entre el Ministerio de Educación y el Programa Nacional de Apoyo Directo a los más Pobres—'Juntos.'" Programa Juntos. www.juntos.gob.pe/docs/convenios/CONVENIO%20MINEDU.pdf.

———. 2013. *Evaluación Censal de Estudiantes 2012.* Lima: Ministerio de Educación. www2.minedu.gob.pe/umc/ece2012/informes_ECE2012/Difusion/Encartes_regionales/INFORME_ECE2012_Nacional.pdf.

MINSA (Ministerio de Salud). 2006. "Convenio de Cooperación Interinstitucional entre el Programa Nacional de Apoyo Directo a los más Pobres—'Juntos' y el Ministerio de Salud, Programa Juntos." www.juntos.gob.pe/docs/convenios/CONVENIO%20MINSA.pdf.

Molyneux, M. 1985. "Mobilization without Emancipation? Women's Interests, the State, and Revolution in Nicaragua." *Feminist Studies* 11 (2): 227–254.

———. 2006. "Mothers at the Service of the New Poverty Agenda: Progresa/Oportunidades, Mexico's Conditional Transfer Programme." *Social Policy and Administration* 40 (4): 425–449.

———. 2007. *Change and Continuity in Social Protection in Latin America: Mothers at the Service at the State?* Geneva: UNRISD.

Molyneux, M., N. Jones, and F. Samuels. 2016. "Can Cash Transfer Programmes Have 'Transformative' Effects?" *Journal of Development Studies* 52:1087–1098. http://dx.doi.org/10.1080/00220388.2015.1134781.

Molyneux, M., and M. Thomson. 2011. *CCT Programmes and Women's Empowerment in Peru, Bolivia and Ecuador.* CARE International Policy Paper. London: CARE International.

Montgomery, R. 1996. "Disciplining or Protecting the Poor? Avoiding the Social Costs of Peer Pressure in Micro-credit Schemes." *Journal of International Development* 8 (2): 289–305.

Morris, S. S., R. Flores, P. Olinto, and J. M. Medina. 2004. "Monetary Incentives in Primary Health Care and Effects on Use and Coverage of Preventive Health Care Interventions in Rural Honduras: Cluster Randomised Trial." *The Lancet* 364 (9450): 2030–2037.

Mosse, D. 2005. *Cultivating Development: An Ethnography of Aid Policy and Practice.* London: Pluto Press.

———. 2010. "A Relational Approach to Durable Poverty, Inequality and Power." *Journal of Development Studies* 46 (7): 1156–1178.

Murray, S. F., B. M. Hunter, R. Bisht, T. Ensor, and D. Bick. 2014. "Effects of Demand-Side Financing on Utilisation, Experiences and Outcomes of Maternity Care in Low- and Middle-Income Countries: A Systematic Review." *BMC Pregnancy and Childbirth* 14 (1): 30.

Nagels, N. 2014. "The Social Investment Perspective, Gender and the Conditional Cash Transfer Programs in Peru and Bolivia." In *Analyzing Public Policies in Latin America: A Cognitive Approach,* edited by M. Rocha Lukic and C. Tomazini, 1–24. Newcastle-upon-Tyne, UK: Cambridge Scholars Publishing.

OECD (Organization for Economic Cooperation and Development). 2015. *In It Together: Why Less Inequality Benefits All.* Paris: OECD Publishing.

———. 2016. *PISA 2015 Results.* Vol. 1: *Excellence and Equity in Education.* Paris: OECD Publishing.

Oliart, P. 2003. *El estado Peruano y las politicas sociales dirigidas a los pueblos Indígenas en la década de los 90.* Austin: University of Texas, Centre for Latin American Social Policies.

Paredes, M., and R. Thorp. 2015. "The Persistence of Horizontal Inequalities and the Role of Policy: The Case of Peru." *Oxford Development Studies* 43 (1): 1–19.

Parmar, A. 2003. "Micro-credit, Empowerment, and Agency: Re-evaluating the Discourse." *Canadian Journal of Development Studies / Revue canadienne d'études du développement* 24 (3): 461–476.

PCM (Presidencia del Consejo de Ministros). 2005. *Decreto Supremo No. 032-2005-PCM.* Lima: Presidencia del Consejo de Ministros. www.juntos.gob.pe/docs/n_origen/DS-032-2005-PCM.pdf.

Peck, J., and N. Theodore. 2015a. *Fast Policy: Experimental Statecraft at the Thresholds of Neoliberalism*. Minneapolis: University of Minnesota Press.

———. 2015b. "Paying for Good Behavior: Cash Transfer Policies in the Wild." In *Territories of Poverty: Rethinking North and South*, edited by A. Roy and E. Shaw Crane, 103–125. Athens: University of Georgia Press.

Perova, E., and R. Vakis. 2009. *Welfare Impacts of the "Juntos" Program in Peru: Evidence from a Non-experimental Evaluation*. Washington, DC: World Bank.

Picchio, A. 1992. *Social Reproduction: The Political Economy of the Labour Market*. Cambridge, UK: Cambridge University Press.

Radcliffe, S. A. 2015. "Development Alternatives." *Development and Change* 46 (4): 855–874.

Radcliffe, S. A., and A. J. Webb. 2015. "Subaltern Bureaucrats and Postcolonial Rule: Indigenous Professional Registers of Engagement with the Chilean State." *Comparative Studies in Society and History* 57:248–273.

Rahman, A. 1999. "Micro-credit Initiatives for Equitable and Sustainable Development: Who Pays?" *World Development* 27 (1): 67–82.

Ranganathan, M., and M. Lagarde. 2012. "Promoting Healthy Behaviours and Improving Health Outcomes in Low- and Middle-Income Countries: A Review of the Impact of Conditional Cash Transfer Programmes." *Incentives and Health* 55 (S2): S95–S105.

Rankin, K. N. 2001. "Governing Development: Neoliberalism, Microcredit, and Rational Economic Woman." *Economy and Society* 30 (1): 18–37.

———. 2002. "Social Capital, Microfinance, and the Politics of Development." *Feminist Economics* 8 (1): 1–24.

Rasella, D., R. Aquino, C. A. T. Santos, R. Paes-Sousa, and M. L. Bareto. 2013. "Effect of a Conditional Cash Transfer Programme on Childhood Mortality: A Nationwide Analysis of Brazilian Municipalities." *The Lancet* 382 (9886): 57–64.

Rawlings, L. B., and G. M. Rubio. 2005. "Evaluating the Impact of Conditional Cash Transfer Programs." *World Bank Research Observer* 20 (1): 29–55.

Razavi, S. 2007a. "The Political and Social Economy of Care in a Development Context: Conceptual Issues, Research Questions and Policy Options." Gender and Development Programme Paper no. 3. Geneva: United Nations Research Institute for Social Development.

———. 2007b. "The Return to Social Policy and the Persistent Neglect of Unpaid Care." *Development and Change* 38 (3): 377–400.

Resende, A. C. C., and A. M. H. C. de Oliveira. 2008. "Avaliando Resultados de um Programa de Transferencia de Renda: O Impacto do Bolsa-Escola sobre os Gastos das Famillias Brasileiras." *Estudos Economicos* (Sao Paulo), 38 (2): 235–265.

Rist, G. 2010. "Development as Buzzword." In *Deconstructing Development Discourse: Buzzwords and Fuzzwords*, edited by A. Cornwall and D. Eade, 19–28. Oxford: Practical Action Publishing, in association with Oxfam GB.

Rocha, L., et al. 1989. *Women, Economic Crisis and Adjustment Policies: Interpretation and Initial Assessment*. Santiago: UNICEF Regional Office for Latin America and the Caribbean.

Rousseau, S. 2009. *Women's Citizenship in Peru: The Paradoxes of Neopopulism in Latin America*. New York: Palgrave Macmillan.

Roy, A. 2010. *Poverty Capital: Microfinance and the Making of Development*. London: Routledge.

Ruckert, A. 2010. "The Forgotten Dimension of Social Reproduction: The World Bank and the Poverty Reduction Strategy Paradigm." *Review of International Political Economy* 17 (5): 816–839.

Ruiz Muller, M. 2006. *Farmers' Rights in Peru: A Case Study*. Lysaker, Norway: Fridtjof Nansen Institute. www.fni.no/docandpdf/FNI-R0506.pdf.

Sadoulet, E., F. Finan, A. de Janvry, and R. Vakis. 2004. "Can Conditional Cash Transfer Programs Improve Social Risk Management? Lessons for Education and Child Labor Outcomes." Social Protection Discussion Paper no. 0420, World Bank, Washington, DC.

Saucedo-Delgado, O. A. 2011. *Moral Discourse in Social Policy Interfaces: A Mexican Case*. Norwich, UK: University of East Anglia School of International Development. https://ueaeprints.uea.ac.uk/34309/1/2011Saucedo-DelgadoOAPhD.pdf.

Schultz, P. T. 2004. "School Subsidies for the Poor: Evaluating the Mexican Progresa Poverty Program." *Journal of Development Economics* 74 (1): 199–250.

Schwittay, A. F. 2011. "The Financial Inclusion Assemblage: Subjects, Technics, Rationalities." *Critique of Anthropology* 31 (4): 381–401.

Scott, J. C. 1985. *Weapons of the Weak : Everyday Forms of Peasant Resistance*. New Haven, CT: Yale University Press.

Serrano, C. 2005. "Familia como unidad de intervención de políticas sociales: Notas sobre el Programa Puente-Chile Solidario." In *CEPAL: Políticas hacia las Familias, Protección e Inclusión Sociales*. Santiago: Economic Commission for Latin America and the Caribbean. www.cepal.org/dds/noticias/paginas/2/21682/Claudia_Serrano.pdf.

Skoufias, E., et al. 2001. "Conditional Cash Transfers and Their Impact on Child Work and Schooling: Evidence from the PROGRESA Program in Mexico." *Economía* 2 (1): 45–96. The article includes comments.

Smith, D. E. 2005. *Institutional Ethnography: A Sociology for People*. Walnut Creek, CA: Rowman Altamira.

Smith, N. 2010. *Uneven Development: Nature, Capital, and the Production of Space*. Athens: University of Georgia Press.

Sparr, P. 1994. *Mortgaging Women's Lives: Feminist Critiques of Structural Adjustment*. Chicago: Zed Books.

Spicker, P., et al. 2007. *Poverty, an International Glossary*. London: Zed Books.

Stampini, M., and L. Tornarolli. 2012. *The Growth of Conditional Cash Transfers in Latin America and the Caribbean: Did They Go Too Far?* Washington, DC: Inter-American Development Bank. https://publications.iadb.org/bitstream/handle/11319/1448/The%20growth%20of%20conditional%20cash%20transfers%20in%20Latin%20America%20and%20the%20Caribbean%3a%20did%20they%20go%20too%20far%3f.pdf?sequence=1andisAllowed=y.

Standing, G. 2002. *Beyond the New Paternalism: Basic Security as Equality*. London: Verso.

Starr, K. 2014. "Get Out of the Office." *Stanford Social Innovation Review*. https://ssir.org/articles/entry/get_out_of_the_office.

Stiglitz, J. E. 1998. *More Instruments and Broader Goals: Moving toward the Post-Washington Consensus*. Helsinki: United Nations University World Institute for Development Economics Research.

Tabbush, C. 2009. "Is Latin America Sacrificing Poor Women in the Name of Social Integration?" *Global Social Policy* 9 (1): 29–33.

———. 2011. "Gender, Citizenship and New Approaches to Poverty Relief: Conditional Cash Transfer Programmes in Argentina." In *The Gendered Impacts of Liberalizations: Towards "Embedded Liberalism"?* edited by S. Razavi. Geneva: UNRISD.

Taylor, L. 2006. *Shining Path: Guerrilla War in Peru's Northern Highlands, 1980–1997*. Liverpool, UK: Liverpool University Press.

Thaler, R. H., and C. R. Sunstein. 2008. *Nudge: Improving Decisions about Wealth, Health and Happiness*. New Haven: CT: Yale University Press.

Thorp, R., and M. Paredes. 2010. *Ethnicity and the Persistence of Inequality*. London: Palgrave Macmillan.

Tronto, J. 1993. *Moral Boundaries: A Political Argument for an Ethic of Care*. Chicago: Psychology Press.

UCI (Unidad de Comunicación e Imagen). 2013. *Madres Lideresas del Programa Juntos orientan a usuarias sobre el cumplimiento de coresponsibilidades*. Lima: Juntos. www.juntos.gob.pe/index.php/notas-de-prensa/189-madres-lideresas-del-programa-juntos-orientan-a-usuarias-sobre-el-cumplimiento-de-corresponsabilidades.

UN. 2015. *The World's Women 2015: Trends and Statistics*. New York: United Nations Department of Economic and Social Affairs. https://unstats.un.org/unsd/gender/worldswomen.html.

UNDP (United Nations Development Programme). 2003. *Human Development Report 2003*. New York: Oxford University Press.

———. 2006. *Apreciación sustantiva del Programa Nacional de Apoyo Directo a los más Pobres "Juntos."* Lima: Programa de las Naciones Unidas para el Desarrollo: Peru.

UNICEF. 2014. *UNICEF Annual Report 2013—Peru*. www.unicef.org/about/annualreport/files/Peru_COAR_2013.pdf.

Vargas, V. 1991. "The Women's Movement in Peru: Streams, Spaces and Knots." *Revista Europea de Estudios Latinoamericanos y del Caribe / European Review of Latin American and Caribbean Studies*, no. 50:7–50.

Vargas Valente, R. 2010. *Gendered Risks, Poverty and Vulnerability in Peru: A Case Study of the Juntos Programme*. London: Overseas Development Institute.

Vela-Almeida, D., et al. 2016. "Lessons from Yanacocha: Assessing Mining Impacts on Hydrological Systems and Water Distribution in the Cajamarca Region, Peru." *Water International* 41 (3): 426–446. www.tandfonline.com/doi/full/10.1080/02508060.2016.1159077.

Waring, M. 1988. *If Women Counted: A New Feminist Economics*. New York: Harper and Row.

Watkins-Hayes, C. 2009. *New Welfare Bureaucrats: Entanglements of Race, Class, and Policy Reform*. Chicago: University of Chicago Press.

Willis, K. 2006. "Interviewing." In *Doing Development Research*, edited by V. Desai and R. B. Potter, 144–152. London: Sage.

World Bank. 2017. *Closing the Gap: The State of Social Safety Nets, 2017*. Washington, DC: World Bank Group. http://documents.worldbank.org/curated/en/811281494500586712/Closing-the-gap-the-state-of-social-safety-nets-2017.

Yates, J. S., and K. Bakker. 2014. "Debating the 'Post-neoliberal Turn' in Latin America." *Progress in Human Geography* 38 (1): 62–90.

INDEX

fig. after a page number indicates an illustration
map after a page number indicates a map